Power, Change, and Gender
Relations in Rural Java

This series of publications on Africa, Latin America, Southeast Asia, and Global and Comparative Studies is designed to present significant research, translation, and opinion to area specialists and to a wide community of persons interested in world affairs. The editor seeks manuscripts of quality on any subject and can usually make a decision regarding publication within three months of receipt of the original work. Production methods generally permit a work to appear within one year of acceptance. The editor works closely with authors to produce a high-quality book. The series appears in a paperback format and is distributed worldwide. For more information, contact the executive editor at Ohio University Press, 19 Circle Drive, The Ridges, Athens, Ohio 45701.

Executive editor: Gillian Berchowitz
AREA CONSULTANTS
Africa: Diane M. Ciekawy
Latin America: Brad Jokisch, Patrick Barr-Melej, and Rafael Obregon
Southeast Asia: William H. Frederick

The Ohio University Research in International Studies series is published for the Center for International Studies by Ohio University Press. The views expressed in individual volumes are those of the authors and should not be considered to represent the policies or beliefs of the Center for International Studies, Ohio University Press, or Ohio University.

Power, Change, and Gender Relations in Rural Java

A Tale of Two Villages

Ann R. Tickamyer
Pennsylvania State University
and
Siti Kusujiarti
Warren Wilson College

Ohio University Research in International Studies
Southeast Asia Series No. 125
Ohio University Press
Athens

Library of Congress Cataloging-in-Publication Data

Tickamyer, Ann R.
Power, change, and gender relations in rural Java : a tale of two
villages / Ann R. Tickamyer and Siti Kusujiarti.
    p. cm. — (Ohio University research in international studies,
Southeast Asia series ; no. 125)
  ISBN 978-0-89680-284-1 (pb : alk. paper) — ISBN 978-0-89680-480-7
(electronic)
1. Women, Javanese—Social conditions—Case studies. 2. Rural
  women—Indonesia—Java—Social conditions—Case studies. 3. Sex
  role—Indonesia—Java—Case studies. I. Kusujiarti, Siti. II. Title.
HQ1754.J39T53 2011
305.409598'2—dc23   2011036225

*Siti would like to dedicate this book
to her late parents;
Ann to her mother and late father.*

Contents

Illustrations

Photos

Following page 92

Acknowledgments

This book has been more than fifteen years in the making. When we began the research, we had no idea how long it would take, how many people it would involve, how much we would learn, or how dramatically our lives would change in the duration. The numbers of people involved in this project and who have assisted us literally span the globe and are so numerous that it would take a separate volume to list them all. As a start, we are grateful to our families, friends, colleagues, students, and many informants and contacts in the United States and in Indonesia. Numerous students and research assistants have contributed to this volume. Nona Norris at Ohio University helped with translation and transcription of interviews. Barby Badayos-Javer at Penn State provided important assistance in the final stages of manuscript preparation and index construction. The book has benefited from the close reading of formal and informal reviewers, especially Rachel Rinaldo and Carolyn Sachs, Elizabeth Collins, and anonymous readers. The advice and patience of senior editor Gillian Berchowitz of the Ohio University Press is much appreciated. The support of the National Science Foundation, the Toyota Foundation, and grants and fellowships from our respective universities made this research possible.

Ann is indebted to funding and support for this work from three universities: University of Kentucky, Ohio University, and in the last phase, Penn State University. At both UK and OU, she benefited from the help and advice of friends, colleagues, students, and the patient instruction of two Bahasa Indonesia teachers: Bu Popon at UK and Bu Harni at OU. The OU Center for International Studies, International Development Studies, Southeast Asian Studies, and the Department of Sociology and Anthropology faculty, staff, and students were invariably stimulating and motivating. Elizabeth Collins, Joani Kraynanski, and members of the gender and development learning community were key sources of input and moral support while working on this project. Ann Bennett was always a rock. Bambang Suwarno and the warmth and generosity of his delightful family must receive credit for stimulating the interests that led to this book. In both the U.S. and Indonesia, Siti's family has been especially helpful through their assistance, hospitality, friendship, and information. The welcome and assistance of Imam and Gita Prosodjo and family and the large numbers of "OU mafia" contributed generously to Ann's education and travels in Indonesia. As always, Ann's family has been a major source of support and welcome distraction.

Siti is grateful for the opportunities, funding, and support provided by the universities and college that she has been affiliated with or has connection to: University of Bengkulu, Gadjah Mada University, University of Kentucky, Ohio University, Western Carolina University, and Warren Wilson College. The Center for Women's Studies at Gadjah Mada University, through its two chairs, Prof. Dr. Mary Astuti and Prof. Dr. Nurhayati, enabled Siti to obtain research permits for the fieldwork; the Department of Sociology at the university, especially Prof. Dr. Sunyoto Usman, Prof. Dr. Nasikun, and Dr. Partini, facilitated finding research assistants and provided advice for the research. Siti also would like to thank her family, especially her husband, daughter, parents, brother and sister, sister-in-law, and brother-in-law, who have provided enormous support during the fieldwork and writing process.

We also want to express our gratitude to numerous people from Sleman and Bantul including the district heads, village heads, and especially those from the two villages: Bapak and Ibu Zaenal, Pak and Ibu Bagio, Pak and Ibu Seco, Pak and Ibu Rahmat Hartono,

Ibu Raharjo, and Ibu Trahwati. They have shared their lives and perspectives, providing inspiration, and without them we would not have been able to write this book. Finally, the resilience, openness, and interest of the women and men in the two villages have supplied the material and motivation for this effort, and it is to them that the credit is due.

Abbreviations and Glossary

ani-ani. A single-bladed knife used by women to manually harvest rice.

arisan. A rotating credit association where members pay a fixed amount of money or goods every meeting (usually every month or thirty-five days) and draw a name or names as the winner for the sum of money or goods collected by the group. It also serves as a social safety net; if there is an emergency need, a member can request to be the recipient. In most cases, an *arisan* is combined with a savings group.

ayam kampung. Free-range chicken. This chicken is a local breed and is not treated with hormones.

bahasa. Language. The national language is called Bahasa Indonesia or Indonesian language.

bapak. Or *pak*. Literally means "father," but the term is usually used to show respect and politeness when addressing a married or middle-aged man. *Pak* or *bapak* is also used before the name as a title of respect, for example, Pak Mahmud.

bawon. A rice-harvesting system where agricultural laborers receive a share of the output instead of monetary compensation.

becak. A three-wheeled rickshaw, or pedicab, where the driver rides at the back and the passenger seat is located in the front part of the vehicle.

bengkok. Agricultural land provided as a form of payment to local officeholders.

Bina Keluarga Balita (BKB).	An assistance program for families with children under five years of age.
bu.	See *ibu.*
bupati.	The head of a *kabupaten*, or district.
dalang.	A puppet master in the *wayang* or the shadow puppet theater.
desa.	A village (also called *kelurahan*). This is a governmental structure below the subdistrict level. The head of a *desa*, or *kelurahan*, is called a *kepala desa (kades)* or *lurah*. These terms were used nationwide during the New Order government, but since Reformasi, *lurah* and *kelurahan* are used mainly in Java; different terms are used in other areas depending on local custom.
Dewan Perwakilan Daerah (DPD).	An assembly for the regional representatives, who are chosen through general election. The DPD is a national-level institution.
Dewan Perwakilan Rakyat (DPR).	People's Representative Assembly. The members of the DPR are chosen through a general election. DPR is the national level of the assembly or legislature body.
Dewan Perwakilan Rakyat Daerah (DPRD).	Regional People's Representative Assembly. DPRD is located both at the provincial level (DPRD Provinsi or DPRD Tingkat I or DPRD level I) and at the district, or *kabupaten*, level (DPRD Kabupaten or DPRD Tingkat II or DPRD level II).
Dharma Pertiwi.	An organization of the wives of military officers.
Dharma Wanita.	An organization of the wives of government employees or civil servants.
DPD.	See *Dewan Perwakilan Daerah.*
DPR.	See *Dewan Perwakilan Rakyat.*
DPRD.	See *Dewan Perwakilan Rakyat Daerah.*
dukun.	A subvillage head, also known as *kepala dusun* (see *dusun*).
dusun.	A subvillage (also called *pedukuhan*). This is a governmental level below regular village level.

The head of a *dusun*, or *pedukuhan*, is a *kepala dusun*, or *dukuh*. The New Order government used the terms *dusun* and *kepala dusun* nationwide; since Reformasi, *pedukuhan* and *dukuh* are the terms used in Java.

Gerakan Indonesia Raya (GERINDRA). The Great Indonesian Movement Party.

GERWANI—Gerakan Wanita Indonesia. The women's organization of the Indonesian Communist Party (PKI, or Partai Komunis Indonesia); the party and GERWANI were disbanded after the failed coup in 1965.

Golkar Party— Golongan Karya. Literally means "functional groups" or "the party of functional groups." It was the ruling political party during the New Order era and still remains an active political party.

gotong royong. Reciprocity or mutual help. It is a social institution commonly found in Java where a group of people help one another in community tasks or projects.

ibu. Also *bu.* Literally means "mother," but it is usually used to show respect and politeness in addressing a married or middle-aged woman. *Bu* or *ibu* is also used before the names, for example, *Bu* Tini, as a title of respect.

Idul Fitri. A Muslim holiday that marks the end of Ramadan, the Islamic holy month of fasting. This is one of the most important holidays for most Indonesians and a time when people visit friends and family members to seek forgiveness for their past deeds.

Institut Keguruan dan Ilmu Pendidikan (IKIP). An institute of teaching and educational sciences. These higher-education institutions focus on educating teachers and educators. There were several IKIPs in Indonesia; institutes of this type have been renamed Universitas Negeri, or State University. However, unlike the others, IKIP Bandung is now called Universitas Pendidikan Indonesia (UPI).

Insus—Intensifikasi Khusus.	"Special intensification" is a method of agriculture (mostly rice) introduced by the New Order government. One of the main goals was to increase yield and productivity by implementing new techniques such as the use of high-yielding seed or plant varieties, pesticide, better water or irrigation management, and fertilizer, as well as increasing the roles of farmers' groups in the production, harvesting, and even marketing processes.
jilbab.	The scarf or headcovering worn by Muslim women in Indonesia to signify adherence to Islamic law and practice.
JUKLAK.	Also *Petunjuk Pelaksanaan*. Instructions for program implementation.
kabupaten.	A district that is the governmental structure just below province level, this jurisdiction became most prominent in the decentralization that accompanied the restructuring of politics after the end of the New Order government. The head of a *kabupaten* is a *bupati*.
kampong.	An urban, working-class neighborhood.
Karang Taruna.	A youth organization. Even though it was supposed to be a politically neutral organization, during the New Order government it was used as a vehicle to control and monitor youth social and political activities and was closely associated with Golkar, the government-backed party.
kecamatan.	A subdistrict. This governmental structure is below the district or *kabupaten* level. The head of a *kecamatan* is a *camat*.
kekeluargaan.	A sense or principle of family togetherness that includes a responsibility to treat others who are nonrelatives as if they are family members.
Kelompok Kerja Lembaga Ketahanan Masyarakat Desa (KKLKMD).	The working group for the Village Resilience Organization (LKMD).
kelurahan.	See *desa*.

kerja bakti.	Community work that is usually conducted by a group of people in a village or a subvillage to maintain, refurbish, or build public facilities such as roads, ditches, or irrigation systems.
kodrat.	A Javanese concept of predestined rights, obligations, and characteristics often connected to cultural conceptions and religious prescriptions for gender.
kotamadya.	An urbanized district or municipality that is equivalent to a *kabupaten*, except the *kotamadya* is located in an urban center. The head of a *kotamadya* is a *walikota*.
Kongres Wanita Indonesia (KOWANI).	The Indonesian Women's Congress, an umbrella organization for Indonesian women's organizations.
krismon—krisis moneter.	Monetary crisis. This is the Indonesian term used to describe the Asian economic crisis of 1997.
kyai.	A traditional Islamic religious teacher.
Lembaga Ketahanan Masyarakat Desa (LKMD).	Village Resilience Organization. This primarily village-level institution was used to coordinate village social organizations during the New Order government.
lurah.	A village head, formerly called a *kepala desa* or *kades* (see *desa*).
Menteri Pemberdayaan Perempuan.	Ministry for the Empowerment of Women renamed after the end of the New Order government and then later amended to *Menteri Pemberdayaan Perempuan dan Anak*, Ministry for the Empowerment of Women and Children.
munaslub.	A special session of a national meeting; the *munaslub* was initiated by the PKK in 2000.
musyawarah.	A consensus-based decision-making process.
Nahdlatul Ulama (NU).	The biggest formal Islamic group or organization in Indonesia led by the assembly of *ulama*. It is usually perceived as the traditional group compared to Muhammadiyah. NU organizes many *pesantren*, or Islamic boarding schools, throughout Indonesia.

Nasakom—Nasionalis, Agama, Komunis.	Nationalism, religion, and communism. A term coined by Sukarno, Indonesia's first president, in his attempt to unite different significant ideologies in Indonesia.
NU.	See *Nahdlatul Ulama.*
pak.	See *bapak.*
pamomong.	Also called *pamong.* Leaders, elders, or those who take care of their subordinated groups. It is usually used in the context of government officials, especially during the colonial period, but it was also used during the New Order government.
PAN.	See *Partai Amanat Nasional.*
Panca Dharma Wanita.	Women's five responsibilities: (1) loyal partner and supporter of her husband; (2) caretaker of the household; (3) producer of the nation's future generations; (4) secondary income earner; and (5) Indonesian citizen.
Pancasila.	Literally means "five principles." *Pancasila* is an official philosophical foundation of the Indonesian state consisting of: (1) belief in the one and only God; (2) a just and civilized humanity; (3) the unity of Indonesia; (4) democracy guided by the inner wisdom in the unanimity arising out of deliberations among representatives; and (5) social justice for the whole of the people of Indonesia.
Partai Amanat Nasional (PAN).	National Mandate Party.
Partai Demokrasi Indonesia Perjuangan (PDIP).	Indonesian Democratic Party of Struggle.
Partai Karya Peduli Bangsa (PKPB).	Party for the National Concern.
Partai Keadilan Sejahtera (PKS).	Prosperous Justice Party.
Partai Komunis Indonesia (PKI).	Indonesian Communist Party.

PAUD.	See *Pendidikan Anak Usia Dini*.
PDIP.	See *Partai Demokrasi Indonesia Perjuangan*.
Pedoman Pengahayatan Pengamalan Pancasila (P4).	One of the New Order's programs to institutionalize the teaching of its national ideology of *Pancasila*.
pedukuhan.	See *dusun*.
pembinaan.	Guidance. This is a term used by the New Order government to describe the roles of government institutions or officials that provide guidance to the people.
Pembinaan Kesejahteraan Keluarga (PKK).	Family Welfare Program. After the reformation it became the *Pemberdayaan dan Kesejahteraan Keluarga* or the Family Welfare and Empowerment Program.
Pendidikan Anak Usia Dini (PAUD).	Education for young children.
Pendidikan Kesejahteraan Keluarga.	Family welfare education.
Pendidikan Masyarakat (PENMAS).	Nonformal educational programs to eradicate illiteracy or provide or improve practical skills.
penebas.	Agricultural laborers that harvest the fields.
pengajian.	An Islamic religious gathering held periodically, usually once a month or every thirty-five days (a month in the Javanese calendar). During the *pengajian*, a speaker usually gives a sermon, and in some *pengajians*, the attendees also recite the Qur'an. These meetings are usually held in a mosque, but some are held in private homes or public places.
Peningkatan Peranan Wanita Menuju Keluarga Sehat dan Sejahtera (P2WKSS).	Program to Improve Women's Roles in Healthy and Prosperous Families. A program coordinated by the Ministry of Women's Affairs/ Empowerment.
PENMAS.	See *Pendidikan Masyarakat*.
pesantren.	Also called *pondok pesantren*. An Indonesian Islamic boarding school.

petugas, penyuluh lapangan (PPL).	Agricultural extension workers.
Petunjuk Pelaksanaan.	See *JUKLAK.*
P4.	See *Pedoman Pengahayatan Pengamalan Pancasila.*
PKI.	See *Partai Komunis Indonesia.*
PKK.	See *Pembinaan Kesejahteraan Keluarga.*
PKPB.	See *Partai Karya Peduli Bangsa.*
PKS.	See *Partai Keadilan Sejahtera.*
pondok pesantren.	See *pesantren.*
posyandu—pos pelayanan terpadu.	An integrated health clinic usually located in a subvillage or village.
PPL.	See *petugas, penyuluh lapangan.*
priyayi.	The aristocracy, but now expanded to include all high-status individuals.
provinsi.	Province. The highest governmental level under the central government. The head of a province is the governor.
P2WKSS.	See *Peningkatan Peranan Wanita Menuju Keluarga Sehat dan Sejahtera.*
raskin.	A government program of subsidized rice targeted for the poor after the Asian economic crisis.
Reformasi.	Reformation. A social and political movement demanding Suharto's resignation and advocating social and political change in Indonesia that took place after the 1997 economic crisis. It resulted in the fall of Suharto's New Order and a movement to democratize and decentralize the Indonesian state.
REPELITA II.	Second Five-Year Development Plan, 1974–1979.
RT.	See *rukun tetangga.*
rukun.	A sense of harmony and efforts to avoid conflict.
rukun tetangga (RT).	A neighborhood association that commonly consists of two to five neighborhood blocks within a subvillage.

rupiah.	The Indonesian currency.
satay.	Also called *sate.* A dish consisting of diced or sliced chicken, goat, mutton, or beef grilled or barbecued over a wood or charcoal fire, then served with various spicy seasonings. The more authentic version uses skewers from the midrib of the coconut leaf, although bamboo skewers are often used.
syari'ah.	The body of Islamic religious law that deals with many aspects of day-to-day life, including politics, economics, banking, business, contracts, family, sexuality, hygiene, and social issues.
tebasan.	A harvesting process in which farmers sell standing crops to a middle person who hires a group of harvesters with sickles at a fixed-wage rate.
Usaha Peningkatan Gizi Keluarga (UPGK).	Family Nutrition Improvement Program.
wayang.	Indonesian shadow puppet theater.

Power, Change, and Gender
Relations in Rural Java

Introduction

A CONUNDRUM AND
TWO RESEARCHERS

IN THE SPRING OF 2010, a woman was elected the *bupati* of Bantul, the head of a sprawling and diverse district (*kabupaten*) adjoining the city of Yogyakarta, Indonesia. *Ibu* Midiwati is the first woman bupati in the special province of Yogyarta and one of the few in the entire Republic of Indonesia. Her election appears to be another step in the formal empowerment of women in a nation where recent transformation of the political system has promised to offer new opportunities for democratic politics and where conflicting perceptions and interpretations of women's real power and status have been the subject of controversy for years. The appearance of progress is somewhat belied by deeper knowledge of the circumstances surrounding Bu Midiwati's election, which in many ways reflects very old patterns. She was convinced to run by the political supporters of her husband, the previous bupati, when he reached his limit of two terms in that office. As the former bupati's wife, her political education and administrative experience come from being the formal head of the PKK and Dharma Wanita, women's auxiliary organizations whose membership and leadership were automatically conferred upon the wives of government officials during the previous political regime.

Bu Midiwati herself is the first and "official" wife of the former bupati, who has been the subject of rumor and gossip about possible additional wives, a practice that previously was a rarity in Indonesia and met with ambivalence at best by women in the society, but is becoming increasingly common among those who can afford it. She has experienced condemnation from some religious leaders who believe women are religiously prohibited and spiritually unfit for political office. As if to validate these doubts, she openly acknowledges that she has appointed a special consultant to help her in her new duties—her husband, the previous bupati. Like her more famous compatriot, the former president of Indonesia, Megawati Sukarnoputri, the sources of her power and authority appear to lie in her relationship to a powerful male political figure, and her own identification with and execution of her position involve numerous ambiguities and contradictions. Does Bu Midiwati's election represent increasing power and public space for women in a society that already has a strong record of according women relatively high status and power, or is it an example of a "deceptive distinction" (Epstein 1988) that masks deep culturally sanctioned limits to their power?

The status of women in rural Java appears contradictory to observers from both inside and outside the culture. On the one hand, past studies indicate that women have high status and power in Javanese society, with substantial access to resources inside the household and in the larger society, especially in comparison to women from other Asian societies and Islamic cultures. Other, more recent accounts create doubt about this assessment, suggesting that Javanese women are neither as powerful nor as autonomous as previous studies have described. These two contrasting approaches view Javanese gender relations from two different perspectives, focusing on different aspects of women's lives. Javanese women have major responsibilities in supporting their families, often as the primary income earners in their households. They typically control household finances, and they own and manage property in their own names. Increasingly, their presence is evident in public office. Yet these symbols and potential sources of independence and influence are tightly circumscribed by a culturally prescribed, state-reinforced, patriarchal gender ideology that limits women's autonomy and mobilizes their labor for particular political ends. The contradiction pervades gender relations and is reflected both in Javanese women's lives and in the studies that attempt to explain them.

Contradictions in gender roles and practices are not unique to rural Java or Indonesia and have been broadly identified and analyzed in numerous social and political settings. Yet these contradictions remain deeply puzzling to gender analysts, all the more so when they appear as starkly evident as in modern Indonesia, a society that has long stood at the crossroads of cultures and development trajectories. Thus, it is not surprising that unraveling the conundrum of Javanese gender relations would come to preoccupy the intellectual energies of two feminist scholars from opposite ends of the world, each of whom brought to the research both general interest in gender relations and specific interest in Indonesia.

Ann Tickamyer is an American-born sociologist who first visited Indonesia in 1986. Siti Kusujiarti is an Indonesian-born sociologist who first came to the United States two years later. As our worlds and interests intersected, we found ourselves increasingly preoccupied by the seeming contradictions that envelop Indonesian women's lives and livelihoods. This book represents the efforts of two sociologists who share an interest in gender roles and development to understand the status of women in rural Javanese villages in Yogyakarta, Indonesia. As an Indonesian from Yogyakarta, steeped in Javanese culture and tradition; and as an American veteran of second-wave academic feminism, we brought very different backgrounds and perspectives to this study, but we were united in our perplexity at understanding the "true" status of women in Indonesian society. As we studied and discussed past research, popular culture, and our own experiences and impressions, we each took turns asserting and denying women's equality and subordination, sometimes reversing ourselves completely.

This book and the research on which it is based are the culmination of our efforts to sort through the contradictions in women's status and power in Indonesia and to bring some resolution to these debates. Our research results shed light on the ways that gender relations are constructed and reproduced at multiple levels, from within the intimacy of household and community to a project of state and nation. This book contributes to a larger literature on the gender politics of development, demonstrating the power and limits of an authoritarian state and hegemonic gender ideology. Finally, we have provided a picture of the lives of women and men in a country that is a major power among developing nations and a growing force in a global political economy.

The study is located in two rural Javanese villages in the special province of Yogyakarta, Indonesia, and also more broadly in the island of Java and the Republic of Indonesia. Yogyakarta is a primary center of Javanese culture and power for Indonesia, a country whose existence and importance has only slowly been recognized by the Western world. Indonesia is the world's fourth-largest nation, trailing China, India, and the United States, and has the largest population of Muslims. It is a nation of immense diversity, composed of thousands of islands and innumerable language, ethnic, religious, and cultural groups, but it has been tightly controlled throughout its modern history by a central government seated in the most populous island of Java and steeped in Javanese culture and custom. Although densely populated, two-thirds of Indonesia remains rural, and the crowded landscapes of rural Javanese villages provide the backdrop for understanding central issues in social and economic development and the role gender relations play in this process.

In this book we provide a detailed examination of the ways gender is negotiated in the daily lives of rural Javanese villagers to support and reproduce family life, to earn a living, and to sustain community and the larger society. We focus on the lives of women, but we investigate both women and men to understand how gender is constructed and reproduced, how power is exercised, and how these influence women's roles and status as Indonesia faces the challenges of building a new social order. By placing our tale in a comparative framework, using two research sites that at the inception of the study represented different levels of rurality, development, and state intervention, we are able to examine both the unities and the common features of women's experience and the sources of difference and change in a country that has experienced rapid and sometimes cataclysmic social change from its birth as an independent nation to the current period of reorganization, reconstruction, and stabilization.

The Conundrum

The contradictory views of women's status in Indonesian gender relations are part of a conundrum formed by a gender role ideology that requires active and assertive roles for women in a culture that devalues these qualities. The vigorous participation of women in economic life and village affairs, a long-standing staple of Indonesian society, is matched by a combination of state, cultural, and religious prescriptions that promote domesticity and denigrate women's agency. The discrepancy in perception and interpretation is compounded by difficulties in reconciling the results of past research. In part these difficulties arise from one-sided views that neglect the complexity of gender role ideology and construction and fail to appreciate their multidimensionality. Examples include the failure to understand the meaning and exercise of power and how it is gendered in Indonesian culture, the failure to simultaneously examine power within the household and in the larger society, the failure to distinguish between power in these two realms, and the failure to investigate how the two realms intersect.

In this book we examine how power is defined and manifested in both public and private domains to construct gender roles and practices that transcend any distinction between the two. The research draws on four areas of scholarship: (1) the nature of power relations that focuses on forms of hegemony, domination, subordination, and resistance; (2) gender relations and the role of women in economic development; (3) livelihood strategies, families, and household economies and practices; and (4) detailed knowledge of Javanese history, culture, politics, and gender relations. Thus we merge research traditions from Indonesian culture and area studies with a broader social science and sociological perspective. The result is a greater understanding of Javanese gender relations and women's access to status and power in a Muslim-majority society as well as a case study that provides a window on sources of stability and change to established gender orders.

The Research

The research discussed in this book began in 1993 and is now well into its second decade. Fieldwork in one village conducted by Siti in 1993 as part of her dissertation research was followed in 1995 and 1996 by more-comprehensive research at the original study site and at a second rural village. Subsequent return visits to the field in 2002, 2004, 2005, 2006, 2007, 2008, and 2010 have extended data collection into the present. Both villages are located in the special province of Yogyakarta, Indonesia, and were selected to provide a comparative framework for the study of gender and development. While sharing a regional economy and culture, in the mid-1990s when we began the study, the two villages differed in their degrees of urbanization and isolation and the types of government-intervention programs in use to promote women's roles in economic development.

Research originally intended to be a cross-sectional study grew into longitudinal research that is still ongoing. As the research extended over time, we were able to take advantage of the unique opportunity to study gender relations and practices during a period of immense change in Indonesian society that spanned the time just prior to, during, and after the crises provoked by economic collapse and the end of the New Order government. This work depicts life in the waning years of this period of nation-building, demonstrates the politicization of gender roles harnessed to this goal, and provides a foundation for understanding some of the new developments and issues emerging in the subsequent (current) chapter of Indonesian history. Thus we use the story of gender roles at the end of the old regime as a springboard to examine changes in how gender is discussed and politically mobilized since the fall of Suharto's New Order and the movement toward democratization and decentralization.

We employ multiple research methods: participant observation, secondary and archival data sources, surveys, and in-depth interviews with eighty-three couples, both wives and husbands, including residents and formal and informal leaders of both villages. Interviews were also conducted with representatives of women's organizations and government officials. Much of the study analyzes qualitative data, using the respondents' own words to develop the narrative. Multiple sources of data, however, have allowed us to balance different accounts.

The results of this study underscore the contradictions in women's roles and also the impacts on these contradictions made by modernization, globalization, urbanization, economic development programs, and the Islamic revival. Women's ability to capitalize on their access to and control of resources is limited by a cultural concept of power that devalues material wealth and conflict and elevates spiritual values of nonworldliness and repose. Similarly, a patriarchal gender ideology that is reinforced at all levels, from within the family to the highest levels of government, pervades both daily life and structures of power to restrict women's ability to gain real autonomy. Programs to enhance women's access to resources and opportunities play into these contradictions by bringing women under greater state surveillance and more social and community pressure to conform to gender role expectations. Thus the more urbanized village, with a larger number of economic development programs for women, provides greater opportunities not only for acquiring income and other amenities, but also for social control and pressure to conform to gender role expectations. Women's bodies, beliefs, and capacities become fertile terrain for the unfolding of sometimes competing but more often coinciding nationalist, developmental, and religious agendas.

Our analysis relies on an understanding of gender as fluid, constructed, and multidimensional, entailing both structure (a set of patterned institutional arrangements) and process (ongoing change in action and interaction). The "gender order," or the general pattern of gender arrangements (Connell 2009, 4), and the "structure of gender relations" (Connell 2002, 55) are complex, occur in multiple domains, and cannot be reduced to a simple hierarchy of "institutionalized inequality" or patriarchy, although power differentials and domination/subordination are real and recurring. The exertion of state power, of religious authority, and of cultural norms and values reinforces inequalities that circumscribe the options available to both women and men and that historically have limited women's access to full participation in public life. Gender differences are the outcome of institutionalized practice (J. W. Scott 2007), and persist through an internalized and normalized hegemonic ideology (Gramsci 1971). The state assumes a powerful role in this ideology's formulation and enforcement, deliberately deploying its resources to control women's labor in pursuit of nationalist and developmental goals. At the same time, gender is continuously negotiated and reproduced, an emergent phenomena that changes in the practice both of daily life and of larger institutional realms, suggesting ongoing opportunities to destabilize even the most restrictive gender ideologies.

In order to understand how this takes place, in this study we follow Diane Wolfe's prescription in *Factory Daughters* that household (and by analogy community and societal) processes "should be studied rather than assumed" to "work toward a more satisfactory theoretical framework . . . that analyzes the interactions among local, state, and global structures, intrahousehold dynamics and extra-household networks and groups" (1992, 264–65). Through detailed scrutiny of how power and gender are related within the household and in the larger community in the context of Javanese culture and Indonesian politics, this research builds on recent feminist frameworks and rural development research to gain a greater understanding of women's status and roles in constructing gender and power in daily life.

The Researchers

While this is primarily a tale of two villages and the gender relationships that inform and shape everyday life in Yogyakarta, Indonesia, there is also a subtext that cannot be divorced from the research reported here. It is the story of how this research came into existence—a tale of two researchers from very different cultures and backgrounds whose lives and interests intersected to produce this study. We briefly diverge from our joint account to explain in our individual voices how we each arrived at the scene of this study.

AN AMERICAN GOES TO INDONESIA: ANN TICKAMYER

I did not originally plan to go to Indonesia or to study gender issues in that complex society. My first trip was the result of a fortuitous encounter with a postdoctoral student at the University of Kentucky when I was a young faculty member there. Bambang Suwarno of IKIP Bandung (now known as Universitas Negeri Bandung) had completed his PhD in sociology at UK and had returned for further study. He had read some of my early work on fertility, labor force participation, and gender roles, and more important, from his perspective knew that I was highly trained as a quantitative data analyst. He asked me to consult on a funded research project studying fertility in West Java. At first I wasn't interested. Typical of the cultural insulation of Americans growing up in the 1950s and 1960s (even those for whom Vietnam antiwar protest had put Southeast Asia on the map), I had barely heard of Indonesia, had only the vaguest idea of its location, and knew even less about its culture. It was not on my cognitive map and initially held little attraction for me as a destination, with my knowing only that it was tropically hot, politically suspect, and a very long way away. Bambang persisted, however, and eventually I agreed to be a consultant to his project and a courier for the latest software.

That first trip occurred in the summer of 1986. I was charmed by the country and its landscapes, by the people I met, by its cuisine, by the complexity of its history and culture, and was eager to learn more and, most important, to return. This began an odyssey that has to one degree or another preoccupied my personal and scholarly interests ever since. I did not instantly or even ultimately become an Indonesianist or a Southeast Asian scholar, but sought opportunities to augment my knowledge, beginning with efforts to learn the language as well as extending scrutiny of the issues that had always dominated my scholarly endeavors—gender and work—to the context of Indonesian culture and society. Many years later, I still struggle with these goals, but I certainly have metaphorically traveled an even longer distance since that first journey.

In many ways that first trip not only shaped my interests in Indonesian society but also heavily influenced how I viewed American institutions as well and sealed my appreciation for the value of comparative work, regardless of scale. Indonesia brought together interests in gender, interests in work and livelihood practices within rural communities, and interests in their intersection in the context of economic development. These are issues that are not unique to Indonesia or to developing countries but also are central to the dilemmas facing all countries, including the affluent postindustrial nations of the global North, in an era of uneven development amid increasing globalization. The experiences of villagers in rural Java have implications, if not repercussions, for women and men in many locations. Both explicit and implicit comparisons sharpen understanding of the phenomenon at hand and the larger social picture.

One aftermath of the trip was that I became the automatic choice for adviser to the occasional graduate student from Indonesia. This is how I first met Siti Kusujiarti. Siti arrived at UK in the fall of 1988 with a scholarship to study rural sociology and an interest in rural development and gender roles. The next part of the story is hers.

An Indonesian Contemplates Her Culture: Siti Kusujiarti

As a Javanese woman I have always been intrigued by the ways husbands and wives interact in the family and in the society, as well as how women as mothers are perceived as important figures. From my own experience, I have been socialized to the idea that women as mothers have important roles and a relatively high status in the family. The proverb that "heaven is located on the bottom of your mother's feet" has been instilled in children to ensure that they respect and treat their mothers well. Local legends and oral traditions (e.g., the legend of Malin Kundang, a son who was cursed for not properly appreciating his mother) reinforce this value as well. There is a strong message that we have to pay respect to mothers because they have such important roles in our lives. Women as mothers have been put on a pedestal.

I have always heard that Indonesian women enjoy equal status and have more freedom than women do in other countries, including Western countries. However, I also witness that women, including mothers, are not regarded or treated as well as the traditions suggest. In a family, the father is the ultimate head of his household and makes most of the significant decisions for the family. He may enforce his role as family head both directly and indirectly: directly by making and imposing his decisions and viewpoints on other members of the family, and indirectly through the internalization by himself and family members of the perception that he has the most power, wisdom, and knowledge to make the best decisions for the household.

In the public sphere, despite an absence of formal discrimination against women, significant barriers exist for women in educational and work environments. Women generally do not experience difficulties in achieving educational levels similar to those of men as long as resources are available. When funding is limited, however, frequently men receive priority in education. Women who want to go abroad to get a higher education usually need formal and informal permission from either their husbands or their fathers. Some of my friends who qualify for higher educational training abroad are unable to do so because their husbands or fathers disapprove or family obligations prevent them from going.

Women's participation in politics is generally limited, despite the fact that various efforts have been made to increase women's visibility in political affairs. Women receive different treatment and internalize their role expectations mostly through a more subtle, embedded social construction of gender; yet, because of its subtlety, it is quite challenging to pinpoint the main sources and mechanisms of women's subordination. Moreover, there are various contradictions in expectations and social pressures put upon women, but these contradictions are perceived as "normal" and are taken for granted.

These contradictory points of view of women's status and positions puzzle me and encourage me to seek further understanding of why most women put up with the situation and apparently accept these contradictory positions. I also have wondered why I used to believe that gendered arrangements and perceptions were the best way to maintain harmonious relationships in the family and in a larger context. I myself have been subjected to these situations. I want to unravel the puzzling situations and to better understand the fundamental and institutional reasons that support and perpetuate these gender relations.

I have been interested in gender issues since the end of my undergraduate education in Indonesia in the mid-1980s, when women's studies and gender issues began to be addressed in academic settings. Because of the emergence of various centers for women's studies in universities and exposure to articles, research, and increasing discussions on gender issues, women and gender issues became more visible. Exposure to information and knowledge led me to question existing gender relations and encouraged me to further investigate the issue. However, this effort has been challenging. As a woman who has been socialized in the culture, I tend to accept the established beliefs and norms, yet I want to be critical of the norms to understand underlying reasons and ideologies of gender relations. Opportunities to further my endeavors in understanding women's status, power, and gender relations among the Javanese were realized when I came to the United States to receive my graduate training. During this time, with the encouragement of my adviser (my coauthor, Ann Tickamyer) and increased exposure to feminist theories, ideas, literature, and research, I developed a stronger commitment and curiosity to conduct research to gain more knowledge and understanding of the issue. My dissertation included research in Yogyakarta, Indonesia, my hometown. I did the field research for my dissertation in a village in the district of Sleman. Then, after the dissertation, my adviser and I decided to extend the research and include a second, more urbanized, village located in the district of Bantul for our collaborative research that became the basis of this book.

This book is the result of a long and continuous struggle to comprehend Javanese women's lives and to untangle the conundrum of our contradictory roles, status, and power. With the rapid social change in Indonesian society occurring now, these contradictions are even more apparent as past values and perceptions start to disintegrate and new expectations are instilled. However, Indonesians and Javanese want to retain their unique culture and identities. How we handle this pressure and whether we manage to survive in this era of globalization partly depends on our honest understanding of ourselves; and to understand ourselves, we need to understand the status, power, and roles of women in the society.

Collective Voice: Insider/Outsider Collaboration

While we bring different experiences and perspectives, the study itself is very much a collaborative effort, resting on an emergent shared understanding that would not have been possible individually. Our different backgrounds and complementary division of labor have enabled us to engage in an ongoing dialogue concerning the meaning of our findings and to scrutinize them from different angles. All data collection for the initial field study was conducted or supervised (research assistants from a nearby university assisted in some of the data collection) during the years of 1995–1996 by Siti in her native Bahasa Indonesia and Java languages, building on prior data collected in 1993. These data were augmented during return visits by Siti in 2002, 2004, 2005, 2006, 2007, 2008, and 2010; she was accompanied on many of those visits by Ann, the American researcher. Research design, decision making, and analysis have been our joint responsibility spanning this interval. Supplemental interviews with key informants on women's issues in Indonesia were conducted by the American author in English and Bahasa Indonesia with the assistance of bilingual assistants/translators. The ability to approach this subject from both inside and outside perspectives has greatly enhanced our understanding and ability to interpret what we have found.

There is a substantial amount of debate in the literature about the desirability and liabilities of conducting field research from within—by a researcher immersed in the meaning and uniqueness of a setting by birth and socialization; versus from without—by a researcher whose neutrality, objectivity, and flexibility are enhanced by distance from the setting. The former permits access, cultural sensitivity, understanding, and empathy. The latter provides the space necessary to be able to analyze and detect patterns that may be hidden by the blinders of familiarity.

Diane Wolf (1996) examines the various claims made for inside versus outside knowledge and demonstrates the multitude of both advantages and disadvantages cited for each and their sometimes overlapping nature. Both insiders and outsiders have occasionally asserted the superiority of their standpoint for bringing balanced understanding to the research. Insiders more often claim superior access and understanding, but also more often cite problems arising from divided allegiances and the same dual consciousness that also provides deeper understanding. The problems of the outsider are obvious, ranging from practical obstacles hindering entry into the field to lack of understanding and insensitivity in a variety of forms.

It seems clear from both the past record and our own experience that a combined approach is preferable to either one individually, and, in fact, the distinction itself has been branded as yet another example of false dualism that feminist approaches have taken such pains to deconstruct and overcome (Hesse-Biber and Yaiser 2004). There is limited evidence demonstrating the value of bringing different views to the same research setting with resulting differences in disclosure (Wolf 1996, 15), and even more evidence that demonstrates the variation and fluidity in insider/outsider categories to the point that they appear almost meaningless. A researcher may be an insider in some respects (e.g., language and culture) and an outsider in others (e.g., class and race), and the possible combinations and permutations of different dimensions of these and other categories (or positionalities), even within the same individual, let alone across collaborators, create complex arrays of position and standpoint that both enrich and complicate the research process (Bhavnani 2004; Naples 1999).

In our case, as American and Indonesian collaborators, there are obvious respects in which we each represent straightforward inside-outside positions. This is as basic and as important as facility in the languages spoken by the people in our study. Even if the

American researcher had adequate facility in Bahasa Indonesia, the national language of Indonesia (and she doesn't), the research would be impeded by her lack of Javanese in all its forms, the local language of most families in these communities. It was not just a matter of conducting interviews in the language of home and most comfort for many of the villagers, as was the task of the Indonesian researcher, but also Siti's ability to recognize the important cues provided by how Javanese was spoken and by whom.[1] On the other hand, Ann's tendency to interrogate the assumptions and meanings often taken for granted by the native researcher, Siti, played an important part in the research process and opened areas of investigation that otherwise might not have been available.

This dialogue was enhanced by our experience together in the field. In many cases we saw the same phenomena from different angles and using different lenses. These differences, however, sharpened our understanding and analysis. Many additional questions arise from this dialogue, many lessons learned that further enhanced our interests and commitment to the issue. Our questions and answers were tested and revised through our conversation and exposure to the people, the culture, and the political context in the field. These combined efforts eventually enriched our understanding of Javanese gender relations and women's status and power.

While we cannot claim to know definitively that we were able to transcend all of the very real pitfalls in conducting this research, or that we have no bias, we have struggled for a nuanced approach that combines sensitivity and analysis. Ultimately, it was the dialogue created by our separate standpoints but joint endeavors that created an outcome larger than our individual contributions. In that spirit, while we will refer to separate experiences when necessary to make sense of events or findings, we generally continue this account with one collective voice.

Additionally, we needed to be sensitive to other dimensions of the differences between us and between us and our subjects. These include differences in position, privilege, and life trajectories. Even the "insider" to the culture and society (Siti) was an outsider to the communities in the study, a distinction with real ramifications, both positive and negative, for her ability to gain access and establish rapport. Siti's status as a married woman, university faculty member, and daughter of a prominent urban family with a comparatively high economic and social position had a significant impact on social relations with village residents, sometimes in almost dizzyingly contradictory ways. Despite her intention to be as "native" as possible, her identity and status marked her as an outsider. At the same time, however, she was accorded honorary insider status as a fictive member of one subvillage head's family. The subvillage head frequently mentioned this in conversation and her hosts (this head's aunt and uncle) sometimes introduced her as their child. "Adopted" status in their family opened doors but also created obligations and expectations as well as giving her a defined location in the village social order that at times was at odds with the objectives of the research.

Ultimately, the success of this project was in the hands of the research subjects, who pivotally helped us in this endeavor. We tried to make clear that the main reason for this research is to learn more from them because they are the experts of their own lives. Their willingness to be open to us, to answer our questions, to satisfy our curiosity, and to accept us as part of their families and communities has been a critical part of this process, creating yet another form of collaboration between us and them. They collaborated with us in their own ways and emerge as the subjects and the central voices of this book. We hope that we are able to present their voices as they were presented to us.

Access to the Field

There are numerous practical considerations that influence selection and entry into the field. The selection of the two villages was based on practical considerations of access and proximity, as well as their suitability for this study. Access at both sites benefited from

Siti's personal connections. The more rural village in Sleman was selected because Siti's brother had done research in a Japanese eggplant-processing plant located there, and his familiarity with the location and his good rapport with the village officials and residents facilitated access and further study both in 1993 and subsequently in 1995–1996 and after. The second village in Bantul was chosen for similar reasons of access and established connections with key informants.

Access is not a matter to be taken lightly, as it requires not only the cooperation of research subjects and local officials, but also involves negotiating the many layers of Indonesian bureaucracy for permission to do fieldwork. This was especially important during the rule of the New Order government, which was when much of the fieldwork was conducted. The strong hierarchical structure of the government created a lengthy and sometimes frustrating process that included numerous steps. Good relations with village officials were significant factors for gaining entry to the village since they are the gatekeepers of the community. Without their consent, which was assisted by Siti's local and family connections, the research could not have taken place. In addition to the informal consent from village officials, formal letters of permission from the provincial, district (*kabupaten*), and subdistrict (*kecamatan*) officials were required. These, in turn, required a local sponsor and connections with a local university. A letter from the head of the Center of Women's Studies at that university fulfilled those requirements.

Such negotiations highlight another facet of the complexities of the relationships between the researchers and the researched in this setting. At the same time that it is important to establish intimacy and rapport while in the field, the traditional Javanese and Indonesian social hierarchy places great value on finely drawn distinctions in social status. Access at many stages of research is facilitated by rank and symbols of status that may need to be carefully calibrated to match the expectations of the subject. Thus, in contrast to conducting fieldwork in settings where the challenge is to demonstrate that the fieldworker is not "above" or socially "better" than subjects, but can fit in or become accepted as a plausible participant as well as an observer, in Indonesia, status displays and credentials can provide a currency for overcoming obstacles such as getting permits or a sympathetic hearing from local gatekeepers. Material resources may permit forms of reciprocity that allow the researcher both to display valued status and to offer assistance in exchange for acceptance and inclusion, outcomes that may not seem plausible on the surface.

For example, a priori it seemed obvious that although an automobile was necessary to get to the most rural research site and occasionally could provide valuable assistance to villagers who lacked transportation, traveling on foot within and between subvillages would be preferable as a rule. Walking would provide more opportunity to encounter and participate in informal conversation with people working in their fields or gathering in front of their homes as well as reduce social distance. Furthermore, the state of village roads made driving a car difficult. However, in one village, Siti's hosts had very different perceptions. They urged her to borrow their motorcycle on the grounds that people are more receptive and enthusiastic toward guests who do not come on foot. They claimed that when they hear the sound of an engine they immediately open their door. In contrast, a person on foot will not be heard or welcomed.

Even so seemingly simple a matter as where to park the car can become a matter of complex negotiation and exchange. For practical reasons in one of the villages, Siti planned to park in front of her host's house, but the subvillage head had other plans. Ostensibly for safety reasons, he suggested parking at his house. At first she did not realize the ramifications of this request. However, on reflection it became clear that the parked car symbolized her connection and dependence on him as well as giving him a more direct claim to the car when needed (as he himself acknowledged). During her stay in this subvillage, she frequently and willingly drove him and his family to meetings and visits with other family members. The fact that her car was parked at his house strengthened her connection and rapport with him and his family while simultaneously empha-sizing her dependence on him (since access to subjects was heavily dependent on his approval and permit). His status and power in the community were also enhanced.

Similarly, although somewhat more ambiguously, the existence and presence of the American researcher appeared to open doors by lending prestige and gravity to the research process, serving an analogous function to that of the automobile. Ann's visit to a re-search site generated substantial interest as well as generous hospi-tality that were punctuated with requests for information on how to advance village children's opportunities for education and study abroad. While access did not rest on these interactions, it appeared to provide additional importance and credibility to the research in the eyes of both officials and research subjects.

Other more obvious challenges to access came from gender, age, marital status, and religion. Despite the fact that we were primarily interested in women, all initial access to village sources was controlled by men, typically village and community officials and informal leaders. It was necessary to establish good relations with these men before it was possible to proceed with the study. In both villages, men served as the gatekeepers, and cultivating their approval through use of family and friendship networks played a pivotal role in the process.

Since we were studying gender, not just women, it was impor-tant to include men in our study. However, most social gatherings in the more rural village are segregated by sex. Women and men mostly have separate meetings. In the few meetings open to both, they are seated separately. Because of this, we mainly had to rely on information supplied by male research assistants to understand what was happening in male gatherings. On a few occasions, due to her "outsider and researcher" statuses (another example of the ambiguity of insider/outsider position), Siti was allowed to attend more formal male gatherings after negotiating the terms with vil-lage officials and local religious leaders. However, being the only female in these gatherings created awkwardness and on some occasions, such as a male gathering conducted the night after the birth of a baby, permission was not forthcoming. This was because the gathering was conducted at night right outside the house of the parents of the baby. The men usually played card games or other games until morning, and it was not considered appropriate for a woman to accompany them. Negotiating her position as a relatively young married woman was an ongoing challenge in the field research, subject to frequent reminders from senior males of her dependence on their goodwill and protection.

In contrast, Siti's shared age and marital status facilitated establishing rapport with the majority of the women and enabled discussions of the gender division of labor in the household, family planning, and marriage. Evidence of her success in establishing rapport came not just in the openness of subjects, but also indirectly by comparison to the experience of research assistants hired to assist data collection. Some women indicated to Siti in follow-up interviews necessitated by incomplete information that the reason for omissions was concern over lack of understanding from younger, unmarried assistants.

These examples could be multiplied many times over to further illustrate the complexities of access to and in the field. In general, combining the need to impress officials, satisfy local gatekeepers, and gain the confidence and acceptance of research subjects was a constant balancing act requiring sensitivity to the nuances of the situation.

From the New Order to Contemporary Indonesia

At the very time that we were completing the initial field research in 1995–1996, the social, political, and economic system in which this work is embedded was beginning to unravel. Within a year, the Asian economic crisis and the subsequent collapse of the New Order government opened the way for massive restructuring of the political system and new scrutiny of many social arrangements, including many that affect gender roles. The political and economic upheavals that have characterized Indonesian social life since that time might initially call into question the value of a study that originates within the old regime. In addition to the severe economic hardships experienced by millions of Indonesians, the fall of the Suharto regime, the revelations and subsequent political machinations of *Reformasi* leading to the controversial election of a woman president, Megawati Sukarnoputri, and the rejection of the tightly centralized government for a new democratized and decentralized political structure suggest the magnitude of the changes that Indonesians have experienced.

Unlike the widespread political violence that marked the mid-1960s overthrow of the regime of the founding president of Indonesia, Sukarno, Reformasi was accomplished with much less bloodshed and open conflict. Political protest, while common and sometimes violent, was often localized, and the change in political institutions occurred over a span of years, in many cases reflecting more continuity than change. Among the biggest changes was the progressive implementation of direct elections of political offices, starting at the top with Parliament in 1999 and the president in 2004, and working down to smaller political jurisdictions. Accompanying direct election was the increasing importance of political parties and the massive decentralization of what had previously been a tightly controlled centralized system of administration. As political control loosened and became democratized, there was increasing room for a variety of social and religious movements, new organizations, and new voices and actors in the political process, including women, many of whom were very active in the democracy movement (Collins 2007). At the same time, efforts to hold the old regime accountable and to tackle corruption, collusion, and nepotism often met with little success, suggesting that former centers of power found new avenues to exercise their control.

Especially since one of our objectives is to look at the political dimensions of women's roles in Indonesian society, it is important to understand the foundations of the current situation. Our study begins during the former New Order as the prelude to making sense of current social life. This study makes important contributions to understanding the social and political arrangements that are emerging from the ashes of the New Order.

The recent history of gender roles and relations provides an important window on the social arrangements in place before and during the crisis. It provides an anatomy of a system that defined and reinforced Indonesian gender relations for more than three decades. This study has more than historical interest, however. Situated at the intersection of old and new, it provides both an account of the status quo ante and the foundation for understanding the roots of change. In many ways the society depicted remains very much the same, with social arrangements that are slow to change. Political and economic crises have opened opportunities for increased scrutiny and change in these and other realms, but the impact on other institutions is more muted the further from the source. Although there has been increased discussion and some actual change in the way gender is perceived, conceptualized, and manifested, especially in the political realm with much talk and some action about gender mainstreaming and empowerment, we argue that, overall, there is more continuity than change in dominant conceptions of gender relations and women's roles in society. This is the case in spite of genuine opportunities for political participation as new structures of democratic governance take hold in place of the waning influence of New Order organizations and institutional practices. Finally, our study does not end with the fall of the New Order but continues into the present. We extend this research to consider recent developments with numerous visits back to the research sites, additional interviews with original participants and new informants, analysis of existing data, and evaluation of how recent events shape and are shaped by the gender politics revealed in our research.[2] The results provide a window onto possible futures for gender role ideology, politics, and practice in a new social order.

Gender Roles and Relations in Two Villages

The remainder of this volume traces the gender roles in the two villages and beyond from the end years of the New Order into the current period of consolidation and implementation of reforms. Chapter 1, "Like Our Own Mother: The Limits of Gendered Power in Theory and Daily Life," provides background and lays a theoretical foundation for subsequent work analyzing the contradictions in gender relations by taking a close look at the nature of gender roles in Javanese and Indonesian history and culture. It uses the example of the difficulties encountered by Megawati Sukarnoputri in her bid to become president of Indonesia to gain insight into the cultural barriers to women's achievement and the contradictory expectations all women face. This chapter creates a conceptual framework for examining gendered power in the lives of village residents. It considers the meaning of power in Javanese society and in the context of everyday activities in the household, in the community, and in the economy. We discuss different definitions of power, ranging from Western ideas that frame power within a context of overt or covert coercion and conflict, to the seemingly opposite Javanese concept that emphasizes power in repose and lack of exertion. In each case, these meanings are embedded in gender ideology that influences how power is conceptualized in the abstract and how it is attributed to different social actors. We examine the sources of gender ideology from state proclamation and intervention to culture and religion and its daily reproduction in mundane activities to construct a truly hegemonic belief system. Finally, we explore the resulting conundrum of a gender-role ideology that requires active and assertive roles for women in a culture that devalues these qualities.

Chapter 2, "Two Villages in Yogyakarta," enters the villages that are at the heart of this study and provides a detailed look at the settings as they appeared in our first encounters with the villages, their officials, and their residents, and what they look like now. It sets the scene, describes the differences between the two villages as well as their similarities, and depicts the changes in both material and cultural environments. It provides a window on the physical and social arrangements of village life as it appeared in the mid-1990s and in the present and lays the foundation for the subsequent effort to understand gender roles and relations in this environment.

Chapter 3, "Goats and Doves: Contradictions in Gender Ideology and the Gender Division of Labor," picks up the themes from chapter 1 to show how in practical terms the exercise of power is gendered and the resulting implications for women within rural Javanese society. In this chapter we examine how the seemingly contradictory constructions of gender roles that were discussed in chapter 1 are manifested in the gender division of labor and how they are understood and practiced in daily life for rural Javanese villagers. The purpose is (1) to describe gender role beliefs and behaviors adhered to by rural Javanese women and men; (2) to examine how these beliefs and behaviors are influenced by cultural practices and state intervention; and (3) to determine whether and how the beliefs and behaviors vary by location and state-sponsored development programs. Extensive interviews with women and men in the two villages supplemented by survey data illustrate the ways in which women and men negotiate these roles.

Chapter 4, "Gender and Agricultural Production," scrutinizes the role of agriculture and how it structures gender roles and relations in these two rural villages. The villages vary in the degree to which they are dependent on the farm economy, but even in Bantul, the more urbanized village, agrarian pursuits and traditions permeate village life. This chapter profiles a household in each village to show the role of agriculture in livelihoods and the ensuing gender division of labor. Similarities and differences between the two villages are examined as these play out in gender roles. Both survey and interview data are used to illustrate the power of traditional ideologies in women's work, even in the midst of changing economic circumstances.

Chapter 5, "Involuntary Voluntary Service: Gender and Social Welfare in Crisis and Reform," looks at the way women are used to deliver basic social welfare services in rural areas. Indonesia's New Order government initiated community-based social welfare programs that were designed to mobilize support for the government's domestic policies and agenda while minimizing the cost to the state. Women were the primary targets of these programs, and although their participation was formally voluntary, in fact their time, labor, energy, and other resources were conscripted for these programs. The two villages differed in the numbers of programs and the expectations for women's participation, and we first examine how this affected village life and then how it changed after the demise of the New Order. We illustrate with examples from the two rural Javanese villages that show how official gender ideology serves the state and determines the parameters of women's power and authority in the family and in the larger community.

In the final chapter, "Men's Rib: Women's Power and Empowerment," we examine women's political roles and participation in the village and the nation before and after Reformasi, the political upheaval that ended the New Order and initiated a period of political, social, and economic reform. We use this as a means to return to the issues that guided this study: women's access to power, the ways gender shapes women's roles, the contradictions embedded in traditional and contemporary gender ideology and expectations, and the prospects for change.

Indonesia has experienced immense change. Efforts to build civic institutions that were repressed under the New Order regime have materialized, taken root, grown, and changed. Social movements and popular mobilization in support of a more democratic system have emerged and met with some success, including peaceful transition in the central government, mass electoral support for a woman candidate for the highest office, and her obstacle-ridden ultimate attainment of this post. However, the New Order government was in power for more than thirty years, and produced deep impacts on people's livelihoods and civic culture, and its influence will not change overnight. In many ways the difficulties encountered by former President Megawati in her quest for the presidency parallels the problems faced by women who seek village-level office, and we use village examples of women officials and candidates for office to examine the problems and prospects women face in acquiring power in the larger society. In this book, we evaluate the obstacles and challenges to creating a more democratic society with more balance between the state and the civic institutions and more opportunities for women's full citizenship and participation.

Chapter 1

LIKE OUR OWN MOTHER

The Limits of Gendered Power in
Theory and Daily Life

The Enigma of Megawati

I N 2 0 0 1 , Megawati Sukarnoputri, the daughter of the first president of Indonesia, became its fifth president and the first woman
to hold this office in the country with the world's largest Muslim
population. Her ascendancy to power was not direct or assured; the
twists and turns of her fortunes in pursuit of this office sometimes
resembled a crude melodrama as shifting alliances, public opinion,
and behind-the-scenes maneuvering finally contrived to place her
in office. Her achievement is emblematic of the contradictions that
Indonesian women face in the public arena and in daily life. On
the one hand, Megawati's election represents a widely promulgated notion that Indonesian women have significant power and
equal status to men. On the other hand, the very broadly expressed
doubts about her abilities and preparation prior to gaining office
and the continuing criticisms of her character and actions throughout her term reflect general assumptions about women's character
and their appropriate position and roles. Even after she left office,
she continued to be the target of criticism not just for her policies and administration, but for a specifically gendered perspective
on her performance in this role. Her lost bid for reelection was

undoubtedly the outcome of widespread dissatisfaction with failed policies and mediocre performance as well as continuing feelings of unease with having a woman in the highest office.

These conflicting views have long historical roots. In hierarchically organized Southeast Asian societies, high-born women could outrank lower-status men (Errington 1990, 7), and women occasionally attained positions of honor and prestige in ancient Javanese society. However, such events were rare, and subsequent influences of Hinduism, Buddhism, and Islam reinforced a restricted role for women. Attainment of high position was more often the direct outcome of unique events in association with a prominent husband or father, as in Megawati's case. Her dynastic birthright as the daughter of the founding president, Sukarno, is usually perceived as one of the primary factors that helped her become president.

Megawati's ascribed status is often used to demean her abilities and competence. Her political skills and interests are widely discredited on the basis of gender and a perceived lack of interest in public and political issues. The media depict her as uninterested and disengaged from the political process. She is generally perceived as uninformed, unable to express her opinions or make decisions, heavily dependent on her advisers, and more interested in stereotypical feminine activities such as attending fashion shows and watching cartoons with her grandchildren than tackling the daunting economic and political problems facing the nation (Chandrasekaran 2001; McGirk 2001). While it is not obvious that she received any more criticism than other post-Reformasi presidents, the types of criticisms leveled at her during her time in office were often rooted in gender-based stereotypes and anxieties.

Megawati's case represents the contradictory views and paradoxical status of women in Indonesia in general and Java in particular. Javanese women are perceived to have equal rights and position in the society and demonstrably have major responsibilities in supporting their families, often as the primary earners in their households. They typically control household finances, and they own and manage property in their own names. The women of

Java do not face the seclusion or formal exclusion from public life that typifies the situation of women in many other Islamic cultures and even other parts of Indonesia. They occasionally hold public office. Yet women face structural and cultural obstacles to becoming effective leaders and to gaining access to significant roles in the society. Even in their own households, where their power is most clearly established and asserted, they typically remain subordinate to male preferences and privilege.

This contradiction is also reflected in gender ideology. Women and men espouse a gender ideology that simultaneously asserts women's importance and relegates them to second-class status. The status of women in Java appears contradictory to observers from both inside and outside the culture, yet the contradiction is endured, reproduced, and perpetuated. Why do women tolerate the contradiction, and why is the contradiction perceived as "normal"? These are puzzling questions that will be examined in greater detail and addressed theoretically in this chapter.

Javanese Women's Status and Power

These contradictory views are also reflected in the research on gender relations among the Javanese. Past studies of Javanese society disagree in their analyses of women's status. Prominent early studies, including Hildred Geertz's (1961) *The Javanese Family* and Robert Jay's (1969) *Javanese Villagers*, vividly portray Javanese women's power in the domestic sphere and in nurturing children. Other work in this tradition (Alisjahbana 1961; Koentjaraningrat 1967, 1980; Reid 1988; Willner 1961) further emphasizes women's high status in Javanese society. These studies underscore Javanese women's economic independence, freedom to work outside the home, and relatively higher status and access to resources compared to women in other developing countries. This is achieved through the predominantly bilateral family structure, the widespread belief in the complementarity of men's and women's roles, women's active participation in the economic sphere, and their management of the household economy.

More recent studies question this view and argue that prior accounts do not adequately capture the reality of Javanese women's lives or the limits of their power. Women may be active economically, but this does not automatically confer power and status. The early studies are criticized by more contemporary scholars for overemphasizing Javanese women's autonomy in the economic sphere without balancing description and analysis of the existence of a patriarchal ideology promoted by the state, religious practice, and cultural values. They fail to take into account the tensions and contradictions faced by the majority of Javanese women that arise from the existence of a patriarchal gender ideology on the one hand, and the limited economic resources and power that they, in fact, hold on the other. Issues such as women's lack of control over sexuality, women's lack of power in political and civic activities, limitation of women's economic choices due to poverty, and the contradictions of expectations related to women's economic behavior and "feminine" qualities are not generally addressed (Wolf 1992, 56). Women may, in fact, be highly involved in economic activity and household financial management, but their actions and attitudes are constrained by economic necessity and the existing gender ideology, which despite lip service to equality, denigrates women's position. Appearances to the contrary, women lack significant real power in either the household or society (Berninghausen and Kerstan 1992; Djajadiningrat-Nieuwenhuis 1992; Elmhirst 2000; Errington 1990; Keeler 1987; Locher-Scholten 2000; Manderson 1983; Mather 1982; N. Sullivan 1994; Wieringa 1988; Wolf 1992).

There is disagreement among these studies on the degree of actual autonomy or subordination and the extent to which women are able to resist patriarchal control. However, Norma Sullivan's (1994) image of "masters and managers" captures the basic views of many recent accounts of women's position.

Women are entrusted to manage household resources but are not granted true power to direct their lives or those of their family members. They are the caretakers or delegates of male authority and have only as much control as they are permitted by the true "masters."

The existence of two apparently contradictory views shows that Javanese women's status looks different from different perspectives. Of course some of the contradiction can be explained away by generational and cohort differences in both the researchers and their subjects. Accounts that attribute the most power to women generally predate the upsurge of feminist theories of women in development and the reflexively feminist accounts of fieldwork and analyses. The refinement of feminist theories and the proliferation of new approaches to studying gender relations in developing countries have created a much more critical view of women's status. Additionally, different cohorts are being studied, so that some differences may be the result of the passage of time and genuine changes in either gender ideology or social practices. The options available to Javanese villagers in the decades following independence look (and are) very different from those of the past twenty-five years. Finally, the reference point is important. It matters whether Indonesian women are being compared to women in other developing societies or are being assessed on some more abstract level. It is often argued that Indonesian women appear to have more real autonomy when they are compared to women in other Asian and Southeast Asian countries, or Islamic cultures.[1]

However, the chasm between these viewpoints is deeper than can be simply accounted for as the outcome of generational differences in perspectives, cohort differences in practices, or reference points in global rankings. They do not merely reflect interpretive differences in how the reality of women's lives are seen and explained. Instead, the differences arise from different components of the reality of women's lives and as such embody the contradictions noted above. The different interpretations each capture a piece of the reality, magnifying it, reifying it, and seeing it as equivalent to the (partial) whole, rather than confronting the contradiction directly.

We suggest that rather than trying to explain the contradiction away, it is important to face it head-on. Each account represents different facets or dimensions of women's status that have to be pieced together and scrutinized both separately and as a larger package. Without a multidimensional approach that can embrace even contradictory assessments of women's position, it is not possible to fully understand the fluid, contested, and negotiated aspects of gender roles and relations in which different factors and values are constantly in contention.

Thus assessing the reality of Javanese gender relations raises difficult questions. First, what are the actual circumstances of women's status and roles in different social realms, how have they changed, and how do they vary in different contexts? To what extent are women independent actors who exercise agency and authority in the family, economy, community, and polity? Alternatively, to what extent are women subordinated to male power and privilege, under what circumstances, and by what means? The emphasis here is on issues of degree rather than "either/or" or "all or nothing" judgments. One of our tasks is to examine these issues for the women and men in the two villages.

Second, what are the beliefs about women's roles and status that are prevalent in the society and among these villagers, both women and men. How do they view gender roles? This, too, is one of our tasks. Finally, what is the relationship between gender ideology and gendered relations and practices? In other words, how can the first and second tasks be combined to demonstrate how beliefs are reconciled with the facts on the ground? If there are indeed contradictions between beliefs and practices, how are these perpetuated? For example, if women have access to economic resources and are relatively free to conduct productive activities outside the home, why do they comply with the values and norms that work to the detriment of their status? Why are women unable to use their range of opportunities more to their own advantage? Why does it seem that they "voluntarily" act against their own interests? Why have the Javanese women who experience the contradiction of their lives been able to endure it for so many centuries? Javanese women face these tensions in gender relations in their daily lives. How they resolve these tensions and with what outcomes requires further investigation.

Before investigating women's actual power and practices, we will begin by scrutinizing the sources of gender ideology for Javanese women, both historically and in current times. We argue that difficulties in gauging women's status and power in Javanese society stem from the contradictory facts of Javanese gender relations and the cultural environment in which the contradictions arise. To understand women's situation, it is necessary to examine the concept of power and the meaning of contradiction in Javanese culture, how these are embodied in gender relations and reproduced by state policy. Historically, the Javanese have a unique conception of power and a distinctive way of perceiving contradiction that was adopted and used to further political goals by the New Order government under President Suharto. The state institutionalized centralized government programs for women that assigned formal legal equality while reinforcing subordinate status. The contradiction, however, is accepted as intellectually and logically sound, because it builds on a long history of contradictory gender ideology and even more on a uniquely Javanese approach to conceptualizing power that entails the ability to embrace and harmonize contradiction without obliterating the contradictory elements.

Power in Javanese Culture

Javanese society is hierarchically arranged, and notions of power and status are central to the social order. Understanding the concept of power in Javanese culture will lead to knowledge of how politics and hegemonic ideology work in a Javanese context. Scholars of Javanese culture (Anderson 1972; Koentjaraningrat

1980; Mulder 1980; Moedjanto 1986; Pye 1985; Sutherland 1979) contend that the Javanese view power differently from Westerners. Although there are variations to conceptualizing power in Western and European traditions of political theory, power is generally formulated following Max Weber as some variant on the ability to impose one's will over others', even when opposed. It may be legitimized through tradition, bureaucratic or institutional sources, or in divinely inspired personal gifts of charisma and persuasion, but it is always abstract and relational, inferred from the outcome of contests between opposing interests rather than directly observed or manifested.

According to Anderson (1972, 21–22) in an influential account of the differences between Western and Javanese beliefs about power, the Western approach assumes that power is abstract since it is a formulation of the recurrent pattern of social interaction, its sources are heterogeneous, the accumulation of power has no inherent limits, and power is morally ambiguous. In contrast, Anderson (7–8) also argues that there are four characteristics of the Javanese idea of power that differentiate it from Western political theory. The four attributes of power in Javanese culture are:

1. Power is concrete, not embedded in social relations, but has its own existential reality. It is perceived to come from divine energy, intangible, and mysterious.

2. Power is homogeneous and indivisible, emerging from one (divine) source.

3. The quantity of power existing in the universe is constant. As a consequence, a concentration of power in one person or place leads to the decrease of power elsewhere.

4. Power is not derived from a relationship between human beings; therefore, it does not have an inherent moral implication, nor is there any question of its legitimacy.[2]

As a consequence of this notion of power, power holders must convince subordinated groups that they are divinely and spiritually selected. Once power holders establish their legitimacy, there are few obstacles to the exercise of absolute power and the demand for absolute acquiescence. This concept of power has thoroughly penetrated present-day Javanese society and beyond, having infected Indonesian politics under the New Order government and continuing into the present.[3]

Manifestation of this concept of power in gender relations is represented by the notion that *kodrat*, or one's "God-given nature and spiritual propensity," determines differences in power and status ascribed to men and women. Kodrat is a central concept in Javanese society that emphasizes the importance of fulfilling predestined obligations. This does not eliminate the need to strive to make the best of one's life, but it underscores the obligation to realistically accept limits to this effort and the importance of meeting inescapable obligations.

Kodrat differs for women and men, and the expression of these differences permeates Javanese culture. Gender status is shaped primarily by access to symbolic culture rather than physiological differences, position in relations of production, access to material resources, or access to formal political position—all power sources commonly acknowledged in Western theories. In Indonesian society, women commonly have access to these resources (some more than others), but this is insufficient to provide real power or equality. This is the basis of the master-manager distinction (N. Sullivan 1994). Women may participate and even have major responsibilities in productive, societal, and familial activities without having real authority and cultural power. Women are not viewed as having a strong or powerful spirit, but serve as a *wadah*, or container, while men are perceived as the *isi*, the content or essence of power. As a container, women do not have their own power and intellectual capacity to perform significant cultural and social affairs. While this notion also implies the existence of interdependence between men and women, men are deemed to be more potent and important. This cultural notion creates a fragmented "reality" that imposes restrictions on women. The Javanese concept of power also supports the notion that men's power stems from their "natural" or divinely determined position or kodrat and therefore is predetermined and uncontested.

Another important element in Javanese culture is the effort to maintain order. A Javanese person is obligated to keep the order of life by fulfilling predestined obligations. Denying kodrat also means jeopardizing harmony and order. In social relations, the maintenance of order and harmonious relations is manifested in the pressure to live in conformity with the local norms and to meet social responsibilities.

The Javanese social order consists of an infinite number of hierarchically arranged statuses, with each status bringing specific duties, expectations, and rights to respect and deference. Traditionally the Javanese people are very status-conscious; every social encounter requires the actors to act, speak, and follow strict norms according to his or her social status in this hierarchical constellation and thus to be aware of minute gradations and signs of status. These are expressed in the Javanese language as different levels of speech that are utilized by the speakers to denote their statuses. This vertically oriented social life plays a central role in the Javanese moral order and is legitimized by the idea that superiors are closer to the ultimate truth and therefore deserve respect. Superiors have to demonstrate their superiority by controlling themselves and their circumstances. These controls entitle them to deliver moral guidance and protection to their subordinates. Superiors are expected to know better, to be paternalistic, and to care for their subordinates or followers; they are entitled to make decisions in which subordinates are generally reluctant to interfere (Mulder 1992, 49). This hierarchical view applies to each level of social organization from the state to the local community and to the household and family. In politics and government the ruler has superior position. In gender relations, the superior is the father, who heads the household and protects his wife and children.

The values associated with this Javanese worldview can be traced back at least as far as the Mataram Kingdom and many of the components were evident even far earlier, manifest in the layers of religious belief that mark the history of the region. They assumed special prominence under Dutch colonial rule where they were heavily emphasized and promulgated as a means to extend Dutch power, co-opt indigenous elites, and deflect opposition. Collaboration between the Dutch colonials and the Javanese feudal power resulted in the extension of the Javanese worldview in a manner beneficial for extending the domination of both parties (Brenner 1998). Values underscoring "acceptance," "order," "harmony," "respect," and "hierarchical relations" are used by power holders to legitimize and maintain their position and to pacify subordinates. These values continue to serve as reference points for the Javanese people. Contradictions faced by contemporary Javanese women may indicate the process of accommodation of new values while simultaneously retaining the classical concept of power.

The Influence of Religion and the Importance of Islam

To understand the sources of this worldview as well as its influence on gender ideology, it is important to examine Javanese religion. The defining features of Javanese culture are often attributed to the syncretic incorporation of succeeding waves of religious beliefs exported to the island over the centuries. *Syncretic* is defined as the "aiming at a union or reconciliation of diverse beliefs, practices, or systems."[4] Traditional Javanese culture is seen as a material culture based on irrigated rice cultivation combined with an amalgam of spiritual beliefs and practices, beginning with indigenous animism dating from prehistoric times and followed by Hinduism, Buddhism, and Islam. Each of these religious regimes contributed attributes that reinforced important components of the social organization and belief systems, but also through their combination created a tradition of incorporating and managing a variety of beliefs.

Many of the elements of Javanese culture that can be traced to back before the advent of Hinduism, the first of the world religions to be embraced by the Javanese, remain in evidence today. These include the primacy of the village as a social unit, belief in the divinity and magical power of the political ruler, animism or the belief that all existing things were alive and had souls, the continuity and potency of the human spirit after death, and the importance of harmony between dual spiritual and earthly universes.

A purely Javanese tradition predating the influence of successive world religions was supported by a well-developed belief system that included significant female divine figures, including two goddesses whose mythological presence permeates all subsequent religious and cultural development. These goddesses were Nawang Wulan, the moon maiden associated with rice and cloth; and Nyai Rara Kidul, the sea goddess associated with power and death. Both played important roles in buttressing and legitimizing royal power, and were incorporated into the Mataram Kingdom chronicles (Kumar 2000).

HINDUISM-BUDDHISM

Trade with South Indian merchants brought Hinduism and later Buddhism to Java in the third and fourth centuries CE. Local leaders quickly adopted the Hindu belief system because it gave further ideological support to their rule, reinforcing belief in their divine powers and superhuman status. It also appears to have entrenched a class system based on ownership and access to land and rice production, and encouraged the growth of an increasingly centralized bureaucracy to manage intensified agricultural activities, including irrigation, cultivation, production, and distribution. Some local leaders were able to expand beyond village rule to create hereditary dynasties centered in court systems that ruled over large feudal kingdoms. One such agrarian Hindu-Javanese kingdom was the early Mataram Kingdom, the precursor of the later Mataram Kingdom that preceded modern Yogyakarta.

The Javanese agrarian kingdom based its concept of kingship on Brahmanistic Hinduism, which in some respects closely paralleled indigenous Javanese beliefs. In particular, they both asserted the connection between the structure of the universe and the more restricted realm of human beings. The rulers were believed to be reincarnations of divine power, and they had the duty to preserve the cosmic order by symbolically replicating the structure of the universe in their kingdoms. They were obliged to protect their subjects and maintain universal law and harmony in the world. Their own powers, spiritual and otherwise, emanated from their divinity and radiated outward based on kinship. The closer the relationship to the king, the more power an individual could claim.

What is not totally clear is to what extent this power was available to women. Early Javanese accounts have women remaining active in agriculture and trade, but in the highly patriarchal Hindu system, these mundane activities of rural villagers did not confer high status or power. There are only a few accounts of women rulers in the early Hindu Javanese kingdoms, and these were more likely to be found in coastal trading kingdoms of Java and in other commercial centers in the Indonesian archipelago rather than in the inland agrarian kingdoms, such as the Mataram Kingdom that preceded modern Yogyakarta.

The implementation of Hindu law and values generally disqualified women from gaining high office (Reid 1988, 639). Hindu law prescribed that a woman's first god must be her husband, and that she must refrain from expressing her own wishes and desires. Her main function was to produce sons and gods. By the later days of Hindu influence, only sons could inherit the throne. The clearest picture of beliefs about women's roles from this period comes from their depiction in the Ramayana and Mahabharata epics that are the basis of Javanese shadow-puppet theater and are still influential today. These portray highly stereotyped gender roles for women as servants and helpmeets to their husbands with few rights of their own (Berninghausen and Kerstan 1992, 33). While Hindu influence was most apparent in palace culture, its value system permeated Javanese society.[5]

Islam also came to Java through trade, first brought by South Asian merchants in the fourteenth century and spread widely during the next two centuries. In addition to the merchant carriers, Muslim scholars and mystics (*sufi*) brought a mystical version of Islam that resonated with the preexisting mysticism of Hindu-Buddhist Javanese cultural traditions (Koentjaraningrat 1985, 48). Sufism, or mystical Islam, seeks to regulate mental attitude rather than behavior. Its main tenet is the transformation of the soul by freeing it from mundane interests and desires that prevent human beings from uniting with God (Woodward 1989, 5). In the sixteenth century it provided the core of a state cult and a theory of kingship that enabled the new Mataram rulers to expand their power and further legitimate their rule. The history of Javanese Islam was not simply a matter of conversion, but the gradual institutionalization of Islam at the state level as an imperial religion. Islam quickly penetrated Javanese culture and was embraced by the agrarian kingdom of the new Mataram regime as the basis of a theocratic state.

Mataram court culture focused on mystical practices, exempting rulers from the ordinary duties and practices of Muslims. Essentially they were placed above the law, while at the same time serving as the ultimate arbiters of Islamic law as practiced by the population (Woodward 1989, 150). For ordinary inhabitants of rural areas, Islamic practice was much more embedded in following *syari'ah*, or the codification of behavioral norms found in the Qur'an and the Hadith that regulate every aspect of human existence from family life to business practices (Woodward 1989, 4).

The status of women under Islam is a matter of ongoing debate. Different passages from the religious texts, different historical traditions, and different versions of Islam bring varying interpretations. The Qur'an contains passages widely associated with male prerogative and women's subordination. These include acknowledgment or justification of polygamy, men's unilateral right of repudiation, a husband's right to physically punish his wife, the veiling requirement for women, and unequal inheritance law based on gender (Berninghausen and Kerstan 1992, 40). Yet these stipulations are also highly debated and contested, dependent on the interpretations of a handful of verses that put heavy emphasis on women's roles as wives and mothers and provide justification for demanding wives' obedience to husbands and male authority. There are other verses and passages that are interpreted to justify women's equality with men, and a basic tenet is that all persons, both women and men, are equal before God. This principle represents a break with Hindu and Buddhist traditions in which women are not seen as able to find Nirvana or attain high spiritual position. Islamic law also advanced women's right to own property and to be the recipients of marriage settlements rather than their parents (Berninghausen and Kerstan 1992, 41). All in all, the advent of Islam brought mixed messages about women's status.

In more recent times, the degree to which Islam is incorporated into Indonesian law and policy has been a source of ongoing debate and continued mixed, even contradictory messages for women. At independence, proponents of an Islamic state vied with more-secular forces about the place of Islam and syari'ah law in the new state. A draft preamble to the constitution called the Jakarta Charter included a stipulation of the "obligation for Muslims to follow *syari'ah* law," but ultimately this passage was omitted from the constitution, along with a requirement that the president be Muslim (Noerdin 2002, 180–81).

First under Sukarno and then under Suharto's repressive rule, there were efforts to control and undermine the power of Islamic groups, and all organizations, including religious groups, were required to adopt the state ideology of *Pancasila*, an essentially secular statement of five principles guiding the Republic of Indonesia.[6] Late in his rule, however, Suharto turned to Islam and cultivated religious leaders in an attempt to use religion as a means to bolster his faltering legitimacy. At the same time, the lesser repression of Islamic groups and the sanctity of the mosque provided space for expressing dissident views and developing support for the political reforms that culminated in political crisis and the resignation of Suharto.

After the fall of the New Order, under the political reconstruction of Reformasi, issues of the relationship between Islam and the state once again became a matter of public debate and contention. There were calls to reinstate the Jakarta Charter and to implement syari'ah law either nationally or, more effectively, at a regional level in some of the more autonomous areas created by decentralization. Most notable has been the Aceh region, but increasing numbers of jurisdictions have made some effort to implement syari'ah law. Noerdin (2002, 180) describes ten regions; by 2008, Bush reports 52 out of a total of 470 districts and municipalities (2008, 177). Although the content of this legislation varies, often having only a tenuous relationship to Islamic teaching, a third involves imposition of Islamic dress codes on women and sometimes also men.

The impact of these developments on women is not at all straightforward, continuing the mixed messages about women's status and power. Indonesian women, unlike many of their Middle Eastern and Arabic counterparts, have a long history of studying and interpreting Islamic texts and engage in both debate and activism to promote their understanding of Islam, especially as it applies to women. These debates cover subjects ranging from the most extreme conservative views promoting women's subordination and exclusion to justifications for emancipation and full equality (Van Doorn-Harder 2006). Many of these teachings are not just contradictory between different schools of thought and groups, but incorporate contradictory specifications within the same interpretation. For example, Van Doorn-Harder (2006, 14) juxtaposes a pre–World War II Muhammadiyah teaching that "portrayed a woman simultaneously as a full partner in marriage and as an obedient servant" and a

1999 document produced by Aisyiyah, the women's branch of Muhammadiyah, that "concluded, 'There is no objection to a woman becoming a leader' as long as she does not ignore her main duty 'as housewife'" (14).

Another example comes in the heavily scrutinized (especially among Western observers) practice of veiling. During the last twenty years, women have increasingly adopted the jilbab and other forms of Islamic dress, but the reasons are not always clear. One explanation is *santri*fication, the increase in observance and piety that has permeated middle-class Indonesian society, affecting women and men alike (Barton 2001, 245). Another was that it became fashionable to do so when Suharto turned toward Islam. On the other hand was the almost opposite motivation—as a badge of opposition to New Order policies and practices as women as well as their male compatriots found space to protest government corruption and repression within religious organizations and movements (Hefner 2000). In some areas, wearing the jilbab represents pressure from local formal and informal leaders to define women's place in society within strict Islamist interpretations, as in Aceh and other regions pressing for syari'ah law.

Somewhat paradoxically, a recurring theme is that the growth of Islamic dress accompanies the expansion of women's access to public space. It is evidence of women's efforts to protect themselves from censure as they assume more and more public roles, whether in the economy or polity. The jilbab defines them as virtuous and provides symbolic protection from male predation at one extreme and gossip and disapproval at the other (Brenner 1996; Collins and Bahar 2000). Politically, the jilbab can serve as a prop to advertise party values and policies, as in the case of the PKS (Prosperous Justice Party) in recent elections (Rinaldo 2010, 6). Probably all of these reasons and more are the case, depending on circumstances. The point is that it is not possible to implicate any one cause or any one meaning to this trend, and it is certainly not possible to interpret it as a simple indication of a particular ideology about women's gender roles emanating from Islam.

Other examples come from the contradictory ideology espoused by Islamic women's groups. One of the arguments against Megawati's presidency came from Islamic sources who cited religious texts to claim women's ineligibility for high office. At the same time, religious parties, such as the PKS, while emphasizing women's domestic responsibilities and obedience to their husbands, also have active women's leadership; and both the policies and ideology of PKS promote women's participation in the public sphere, often through the practice of "public piety" emphasizing issues of public morality (Rinaldo 2008, 2010).

The difficulty of pinpointing Islam's influence on women's status is further illustrated by Islam's place in the multilayered legal structure that complicates understanding women's legal rights. Even looking at only the national level, there are overlapping legal systems that place jurisdiction for different aspects of women's rights and legal status in different courts, so that marriage and family law may be applied in religious courts for Muslims, but inheritance issues may be dealt with in either religious or civil proceedings. Different regions also have different systems, predating decentralization, with potential for increasing divergence as this process gains momentum. As stated previously, in a number of areas there is currently an attempt to apply syari'ah with stringent enforcement of conservative interpretations of women's rights (Noerdin 2002). Thus, it is not possible to give a simple answer to the question of "How much has Islam been a basis for the gender order in Indonesia?" (Robinson 2001,18). Rather, Islam provides one important source of the many-layered set of influences that have created gender relations and ideology in Indonesia and for Javanese women.

New Order Government Gender Ideology

Throughout the history of Javanese society, the state has always played a central role in regulating people's lives. Gender ideology not only is reproduced through family values and practice and religious doctrines, but also is re-created and reinforced by state policy. From the Mataram Kingdom through early modern and colonial Java, the tandem development of hereditary state institutions and world religions reinforced subordinate views of women's status and practices of seclusion and exclusion from public life, although the degree to which these affected everyday life and practice always varied by class and proximity to court culture (Andaya 2000). It wasn't until the New Order era that gender ideology was explicitly incorporated into state policy.

To support the primary goal of creating economic development, the Indonesian New Order regime under past president General Suharto built a strong, centralized bureaucracy. The regime created powerful bureaucratic channels leading from the central government down through the village level, controlling popular initiatives and the flow of resources to implement its policies and enforce its power (Bulkin 1983; Santoso 1993). The New Order policies concerning women assumed that women's primary roles are as mothers and wives, and all government policies reinforced this view (Suryakusuma 1991,73). The state was organized on the patriarchal principle that the state is one big family headed by the father figure of the president; women are perceived to be the mother of the state (Suryakusuma 1991, 71). The institutionalization of this ideology variously has been termed "housewifization" (Mies et al. 1988); "state *Ibuism*" (*ibu* means "mother") (Suryakusuma 1996); and "familial ideology" (Barrett 1980). It taught that marriage and motherhood are the ultimate destinies (*kodrat*) for women. Other roles were perceived as secondary, and women felt obligated to meet these ideal values. By any name, this ideology hampered women from full involvement in civic affairs and the development process, but it delivered positive political benefits for power holders by depoliticizing and pacifying women.

It was not enough to have women as quiet subjects, however, and the Indonesian state sought ways to use women to advance its goals, a tactic that characterizes many developmental states

(Mayer 2000; Rai 2008). To enlist women's cooperation in national economic development programs, women were exhorted to follow their *Panca Dharma Wanita*, or women's five responsibilities, listed here in order of primacy: (1) loyal partner and supporter of her husband; (2) caretaker of the household; (3) producer of the nation's future generations; (4) secondary income earner; and (5) Indonesian citizen. The government suggested that these five obligations are parallel with women's kodrat to make them appear as if they are deeply rooted in human nature and endorsed by tradition and religious beliefs. Thus, despite women's heavy involvement in productive activities outside home and the absence of formal barriers to active participation in the public sphere, the state promoted a gender ideology advocating that women's "appropriate" roles are in the home as wives and mothers (N. Sullivan 2000, 1). This ideology has acquired tangible form in social institutions and practices and in social interaction, and therefore "constitute[s] both the experience of social relations and the nature of subjectivity" (Poovey 1988, 3). This also means that those who regularly operate outside the prescribed roles are faced with contradiction and criticism.

The contradictory expectations deepened with the implementation of the second five-year plan of development in 1975, formulated with international pressure from donor agencies to integrate women more fully into the development process. The discourse on women's active involvement, equal rights, and opportunities is stipulated in various government policies and documents such as GBHN, or general outlines of state policy, ratified by the People's Consultative Assembly every five years. The 1993–1998 General Outlines of State Policy (GBHN) states:

> Women, as citizens as well as a human resource for development (*sumber daya insani pembangunan*) have rights, responsibilities and opportunities which are the same as men in all aspects of development. The fostering (*pembinaan*) of the role of women as equal partners of men is aimed at increasing their active role in development activities, including efforts to materialize (*mewujudkan*) a healthy, prosperous and happy family, as well as the development

(*pengembangan*) of children, adolescents and youths, within the framework of the development of the complete Indonesian human (*manusia Indonesia seutuhnya*). The position of women within the family and society and their role within development must be maintained and increasingly stepped up in order to provide the greatest possible contribution towards the development of the nation, while being mindful of their essential nature (*kodrat*) and dignity. (Tiwon 2000, 73)

Contradictory expectations and accounts are all too evident in this and similar expressions of state gender ideology during the New Order government. The formal discourse defined women as *mitra sejajar* (equal partner) and *pendamping suami* (husband's companion), as well as having rights and responsibilities equal to men. Yet the state simultaneously assigned women as primarily responsible for domestic chores and unable to deviate from their "natural" propensities and destiny. The reinforcement of these ideas is not merely a symbolic gesture but is incorporated into the application of government policies. Thus Javanese women face this contradiction and embrace it as part of their lives.

Javanese Culture and Contradiction

Contradictory gender ideologies and policies do not result in either symbolic or practical resistance.[7] This is partly due to the acceptance of contradiction within Javanese culture. For the Javanese, contradictions are not perceived as problematic but are part of the law of life. Even more, the ability to accommodate contradictory or opposite accounts is perceived as a sign of power in Javanese culture. A powerful individual and society should be capable of syncretizing and harmonizing contradictory elements. In a quintessential example, Anderson cites President Sukarno's (independence leader, founding president, and Megawati's father) doctrine of *Nasakom*, an effort to combine nationalism, religion and communism. From an external perspective, Sukarno's formula appears intellectually incoherent since it contains an inherent contradiction. Within the context of Javanese thinking, Sukarno's formula represents the sign of a powerful ruler who can absorb contradictory elements within himself and make a syncretic conquest of the disparate elements (Anderson 1972, 30).

This practice follows from a long history of managing overlapping layers and varieties of religious beliefs. Modern world religions, such as Hinduism, Buddhism, Christianity, and Islam, as well as elements of animism and indigenous beliefs, are accepted and blended even when they espouse contradictory values and practices. The ability to tolerate and harmonize opposing viewpoints is perceived as a sign of Javanese superiority, rather than intellectual irrationality or inconsistency.

Similarly, the discourse that promoted women's active involvement in development created new social pressures on women to perform *peran ganda* (multiple roles) in public, private, and social spheres harmoniously. A good woman is expected to perform her responsibilities as a good wife, mother, and member of the society simultaneously without complaint or problems. Those who fail to meet this expectation are perceived as deficient. Emphasis on the unchanging nature of the kodrat exacerbates women's difficult position. The development process requires them to be active in state-directed programs that consume their time and resources, while their responsibilities as wife and mother must be met satisfactorily.

The contradictions are clearly seen in the mixed messages about "career women" (*wanita karier*) that emanated from the New Order government. The mass media and state-controlled information sources assisted the dissemination of the state's gender ideology. Despite the state emphasis on an ideology of domesticity, Indonesian women of all classes continued to work outside the home in the New Order era by both choice and necessity. Increased educational opportunities, growing demand for cheap female labor by multinational firms, formal equality, and traditional values that endorse women's involvement in the trading and farming sectors enabled and encouraged women to be economically active. At the same time, the New Order government imposed various restrictions and created the contradictory doctrine that emphasized domestic responsibilities and devalued work outside the home.

The New Order also disseminated a negative perception of the "career woman" that still further reinforced the contradictory nature of its gender ideology. The term "career woman" signifies a woman who is admired due to her ability to participate in the modern economy and institutions, but who is at the same time suspected of being self-centered and selfish to the detriment of her family. There was a perception that her role as career woman may interfere with her duties as wife and mother; she may become overly absorbed in her work, causing her to neglect her family. The fear that her independence might lead her into extramarital affairs or that her lack of attention to her husband and children might destroy her marriage and family is continuously expressed in the popular media (Aripurnami 2000; Brenner 1998, 242). At the same time that her competence is judged to endanger her family, she is simultaneously depicted as less able to perform public roles, hampered by domestic proclivities and commitments.

Women with important positions in the public sphere are generally portrayed as less capable due to their domestic nature in the way Megawati was denigrated. This depiction is a means for indicating and reinforcing the ideology that women are less able to harmoniously and successfully encompass and embrace the contradictions in their lives due to their *kodrat*, or natural inclinations and lack of power. Megawati has been depicted as having "motherly" characters and she is called "ibu." An article in *Kompas* during the presidential campaign when Megawati ran for reelection describes her as "*seperti ibu sendiri*," literally, "as if she is our own mother."[8] In short, the Javanese display ambivalent views of women who are involved in the public and political spheres. Formally and historically, many women are actively involved in the public sphere, but their involvement tends to be discouraged and circumscribed through subtle institutional and cultural barriers.

Tolerance for contradiction may be part of Javanese cultural heritage, but by itself it cannot explain how gender roles are inculcated into individual and collective consciousness or why Javanese women who face daily contradictions in gender relations nevertheless endure these contradictions over a long period of time. Gramsci's (1971) theory of hegemonic ideology provides a powerful tool for understanding the process by which ideas become hegemonic and repression is neutralized and internalized, thus explaining the persistence of the contradictions of gender relations in Javanese society. Ideology is a distorted and fragmented reality, but it prevails and is normalized because it becomes part of everyday thought. It also promotes social cohesion by representing contradictions as unitary and representing "necessity" as "freedom." Through ideology, particular interests of powerful dominant groups are perceived as general interests, and are "voluntarily" accepted by the subordinated groups (Komter 1991, 58). As a result of the influence of hegemonic ideology, the contradiction faced by Javanese women is represented and perceived as a unity necessary for women and society.

Javanese patriarchal and bureaucratic institutions under the New Order government successfully inculcated their gender ideology so that this ideology became hegemonic. To support, reproduce, and strengthen the ideology, the government manipulated and used existing Javanese cultural concepts of power and specific values. This ideology penetrated the main social institutions and found common ground with existing religious norms and customary values, and therefore was "accepted" by the members of the society as part of their daily "reality." The role of the state is to create active consent to the hegemonic ideas. Yet the state does not do so in a mechanistic, direct manner, but instead works on and through existing beliefs, values, religion, and social norms and customs to create a gendered belief system.

Ideological hegemony is built through a long social process in which "consensus" about norms and values is developed between dominant and subordinate groups. Consensus is manifested in the approval of the dominant values, symbols, beliefs, and opinions by the subordinates. From this view, primary social institutions such as the educational system, family, religion, state, and mass media carry significant roles in building social consensus. The state apparatus, public opinion, and prevailing cultural practices make actions or attitudes conducted by subordinated groups appear to emerge from their free will, while in fact they reflect a necessity derived from existing relations of domination. Women seem to endorse their own subordination and act as responsible agents for reproducing and enforcing the gender ideology. The New Order government reshaped and strengthened the elements of the gender ideology that had been in existence in the culture and society for centuries. Therefore, old values were transformed and translated to fit with new development, but their essence was maintained.

The concepts of order, acceptance, hierarchical relations, respect, harmony, and the Javanese beliefs about power served as a fertile breeding ground for enhancing and reproducing the state's gender ideology. Acceptance of inherent contradiction as a fact of life for the Javanese helped create an atmosphere where the contradictions of Javanese women's lives were perceived as normal.

Conclusion

Difficulties in analyzing the position and status of Javanese women stem in part from the contradiction inherent in their lives. To unravel the source of these difficulties, it is important to understand the cultural, historical, and political mechanisms and structures in which contradictory accounts take place. This chapter provides an analysis of the sources of gender ideology consolidated during the New Order that revitalized and reinforced local cultural concepts of power, gender differences, and inherent Javanese hierarchical structure. These factors help clarify women's active consent to the terms of their contradictory lives. New sources of gender ideology and the repackaging of old themes that followed the collapse of the New Order feed into and reinforce many of these values and practices. In the following chapter we enter the study sites and examine local culture as a prelude to the analysis of how these contradictions are manifested in the gender division of labor within the household, the family, the community, and in livelihood practices, and how these are negotiated, maintained, and reproduced.

Chapter 2

TWO VILLAGES IN YOGYAKARTA

DAERAH ISTIMEWA (D. I.) YOGYAKARTA, the special region of Yogyakarta, is located in south-central Java. It is "special" both by history and by political designation. From ancient times to the present, Yogya, as it is more familiarly known, has been recognized as the center of Javanese culture and society, the product of a long syncretic accumulation of religious and cultural movements that include animism, Hinduism, Buddhism, Islam, and indigenous Javanese elements. Although Islam has been fully entrenched for three centuries as the dominant religion and social influence, the area remains heavily permeated with the remnants of its predecessors. Islamic values and practices often merge with traditional elements of Javanese culture.

Politically, the region has a pivotal place in Javanese history, from the time of its founding in 1755 as part of the Mataram Kingdom, through its prominent role in the fight for independence from the Dutch. The city itself served as the Indonesian capital from 1946 to 1950 when the Dutch reoccupied Jakarta in an attempt to reclaim its colonial control after World War II. After independence, its place and the role of the sultan, Hamengku Buwono IX, in the revolution were rewarded with its special status as a province of the Republic of Indonesia and the appointment of the hereditary

sultan as governor for life. To this day it remains the only function-
ing sultanate in Indonesia, governed by a descendant of the hereditary rulers.[1] While it has changed dramatically from a tightly
structured, feudal, and autocratic society to a more democratic
system, many traditional values dating from feudal times have not
been completely washed away.

Currently, Yogyakarta serves as a regional commercial center
and, with its many public and private colleges and universities,
as an educational destination for the entire nation. It has changed
since its founding more than 250 years ago, but it is still, as it was
in 1755, an area concerned with formal religion, mysticism, and
the quest for magical power. It also remains a symbol of Javanese
power and culture. Given the dominance of Java in modern Indonesian history, Yogya by extension also has a central place in
Indonesian society.

In the mid-1990s, at the time we initiated this study, the province had a population of more than three million people[2] spread
across four districts (*kabupaten*) and the municipality (*kotamadya*)
of Yogyakarta, the provincial capital. Between the 1990 and the
2000 censuses,[3] the population increased by only 7.2 percent, but
shifted from primarily rural to majority urban (56 percent rural in
1990; 42 percent in 2000), marking this time as one of rapid population change (BPS 2004). As in all of Java, there is high population
density, even in agricultural and rural areas. The two study villages
selected were a more remote agricultural village located in the *kabupaten*, or district, of Sleman, in the northern part of the province;
and a more urbanized village, located much closer to the center
of urban life, in the district of Bantul in the southern part of the
province.[4] By the 2000 census, both districts averaged population
densities of more than fifteen hundred persons per square kilometer (BPS 2004).

We chose these two villages for both theoretical and practical
reasons. They each matched the requisite characteristics of being
fairly typical rural villages that share Javanese culture and history.
They have ethnically homogeneous and stable populations whose

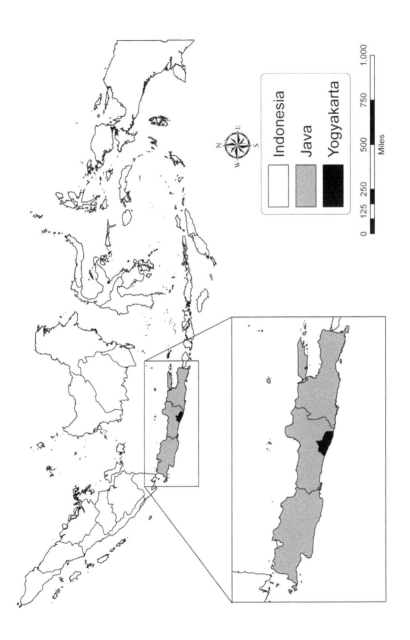

Indonesia

Java

Yogyakarta

N
W E
S

0 125 250   500   750 1,000
Miles

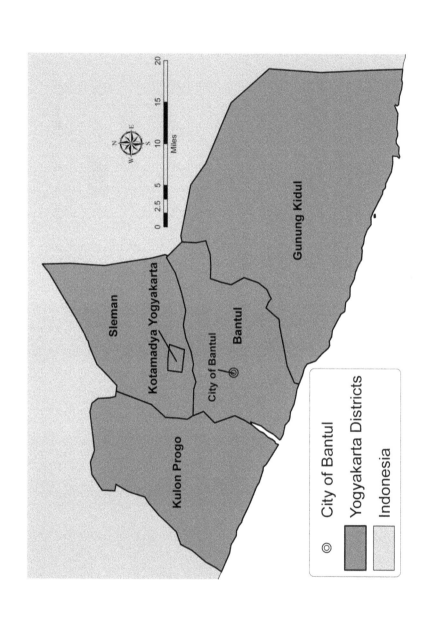

City of Bantul

Yogyakarta Districts

Indonesia

members have deep roots in their communities. Most villagers are practicing Muslims; and the two main Islamic organizations, Muhammadiyah and Nahdlatul Ulama (NU),[5] are well-represented in both villages. But the villages varied dramatically in their degree of isolation from urban influence and the amount of state intervention involved in their economic development. One village remained more physically isolated, more agrarian, and slower to shed traditional social and cultural practices. The other was heavily influenced by its proximity to urban centers and the cultural influences of urbanization and modernization. They each had active women's and community groups whose contributions to village life could be observed and studied, but the degree of state intervention in women's activities also varied in the two villages. Finally, they both were accessible and receptive to our inquiries and had officials who were willing to give the necessary authorization to conduct field research.

Village Structure

In D. I. Yogyakarta, as in the rest of Indonesia, a village, or *kelurahan* (formerly *desa*), is an administrative classification that typically encompasses a series of rural settlements or subvillages called *pedukuhan* (formerly *dusun*),[6] as well as the agricultural and open fields that are incorporated into its boundaries. Village lands may stretch for a substantial distance, and the pedukuhan, or subvillages, serve as the communities or neighborhoods that are most salient to daily life. In each village and subvillage, in addition to the individually owned plots, some of the fields are public lands whose use is politically or administratively allocated, usually as part or all of the compensation for kelurahan and pedukuhan officials. The village is administered by a head (now known as a *lurah* but formerly called a *kepala desa* or *kades*), who is directly elected by its residents for a term of six years.[7] He is paid a salary and may also get use of village lands. Each subvillage (pedukuhan) also has a head known as *kepala dukuh* or *dukuh*, who formerly was appointed by district officials in consultation with the lurah,[8] but now is elected following changes in the law after the end of the New Order. The dukuh is not paid a salary but is compensated with use of pedukuhan land. While the village lurah's job is largely administrative and ceremonial, the tasks of the subvillage dukuh are more diverse. He (or she, although usually a man) is expected to be on call around the clock to deal with any community issues or residents' problems. The intensity and more personal nature of this official's responsibilities are indicated by the fact that most do not have a formal office; they use their homes to conduct their business.

Previously, there was no formal limit to the dukuh's tenure; usually he served until he was ready to retire. Post-Reformasi, there is mandatory retirement at age sixty. The wives of village and subvillage officials also have important roles in village life. Although unpaid, they automatically become the heads of local women's organizations, both in name and (usually, although not always) in fact, and they are expected to be active in community affairs.[9]

Village and subvillage officials act as gatekeepers to village life. As described previously and detailed further below, establishing relationships with the officials was an important part of gaining access to the field. In each village, we selected three subvillages to be the sites for our research. As in village selection, they were chosen for both practical and theoretical reasons. The former include access and accessibility—ability to establish relationships and rapport with both leaders and residents and the ability to get around and travel between sites. The primary theoretical issue was to make sure that subvillages fully represented the range of social and economic variation among village residents since patterns of spatial stratification varied. Some subvillages were homogeneous in the social and economic status of their residents; others had a mixture of classes. In order to provide a complete picture and enhance understanding of village life in each location, we include detailed descriptions of the subvillages used in the study. However, when reporting results, we generally make no distinction between subvillages, focusing on the much larger differences between villages.

Our field research was initiated during the mid-1990s in the last years of Suharto's New Order government, with numerous subsequent return visits to collect new data and observe new developments. During this time there have been many changes in the political system, including village organization and administration. The New Order was a hierarchically organized and centralized administrative system that was tightly controlled from Jakarta, the capital. One of the biggest changes since the end of the New Order has been an ambitious decentralization plan that gives greater authority to local areas, most notably regions and districts, but also local communities. Shifting control to local areas has been a long, complex, and continuous process that has involved much jockeying for position and ultimate authority between regions, provinces, districts, and even local communities. By the mid-2000s, however, with the exceptions noted, the basic outlines of local Javanese village administrative authority had been determined.

The Village in Kabupaten Sleman

The district (kabupaten) of Sleman adjoins the city of Yogyakarta to the north and encompasses valuable property and affluent neighborhoods including Gadjah Mada University and other schools for which the area is known. However, Desa Danau,[10] the study village in Sleman, was poor, relatively remote, and isolated, located twenty-five kilometers north of the city of Yogyakarta and five kilometers from the nearest main road connecting Yogyakarta to another midsize city, Magelang. In the mid-1990s, only small dirt roads connected village settlements or subvillages to the secondary and main roads. There was no public transportation directly to the subvillages, but it was available at a secondary road approximately one kilometer away. Work, marriage, and social activities were contained mostly within village boundaries, and travel to Yogyakarta was rare.

At the time we started the fieldwork, village records placed the population at 4,542 people in 1,026 households; 873 households were headed by males and 153 were headed by women. Women head households in the absence of an adult male because of the death of their spouse, divorce, desertion, or migration to other areas to seek employment.[11] There were four primary schools located in the village, but no junior highs or high schools. The majority of the population (72 percent) had attended primary school. Education was valued and increased among younger cohorts, but the travel beyond the village required after primary school added expense and difficulty.

The village covers an area of 326,000 hectares, with 70 percent of the land used for agricultural production. Proximity to the active volcano Merapi creates fertile soil for agriculture as well as periodic crises for inhabitants. Village records are inconsistent and contradictory, but it is safe to say that agriculture is the primary occupational sector, employing as many as 70 percent of individuals who reported occupations[12] and dictating the rhythms and schedules of village life. The raising of crops was also a source of local pride, status, social relationships, and values.

Small landowners predominated (720 persons, or 77.5 percent of those who are involved in agriculture), but their holdings were very small, averaging 2,500 square meters or one-quarter of a hectare of land or less, an amount that cannot supply adequate yield or income for most families. Almost 17 percent of the landowners owned between one-quarter and one-half hectare of land, while only one household had more than two hectares of land. Another 133 persons were land operators, and 76 people were farm laborers. Land operators are those who do not own land but have access to land by sharecropping or renting, while farm laborers do not have any direct control of land.

The farmers in this village usually independently chose the varieties and types of plants to be cultivated. Farmers' groups were not very active and had little influence on agricultural production practices. Dry-season crops included vegetables and fruits such as eggplant, watermelon, green beans, corn, peanuts, and soybeans. An eggplant-processing factory constructed and owned as a joint Japanese-Indonesian venture provided a market for local produce and employment for some young villagers.

Other jobs were found in trade, services, and handcrafts. Agricultural products such as rice, tobacco, and vegetables dominated trade. The handicrafts sector consisted mostly of plaited mats, of which women were the primary producers. This activity was one of the lowest-income-generating activities, since each mat marketed at only Rp 125 to Rp 150 (6.25 to 7.50 cents at the value of the currency at the time). Because of this, many women participated in this activity as a secondary job. Multiple job holding and utilization of the labor of most household members was typical of this village.

Most of the population (4,400 people, or 96.9 percent) were Muslims; six persons (0.1 percent) were Protestants; and 136 persons (3 percent) were Catholics. According to many of the people in the interviews, before 1965 (the date of the failed bloody coup that ultimately brought Suharto to power), most of the people in the village were believers in Javanese mysticism. The village was among some regions in Yogyakarta where many disciples of Javanese religion were allegedly also members of or closely affiliated with the Communist Party. Since the Communist Party was banned after the failure of the attempted coup and most of its members were incarcerated or killed, people were apprehensive about being affiliated with the religion and, by extension, the party. Thus many adherents of the Javanese religion converted to one of the five formal religions accepted by the Indonesian government, and most of these converted to Islam for political expediency—Islam has the most followers in Indonesia, and Muslims were among the most active advocates for banning the Communist Party. Conversion to Islam was viewed as the safest way to avoid the accusation of being an ex-communist.

Despite the fact that village records did not indicate any current adherence to the Javanese religion, in some subvillages, traces of Javanese religion still persisted. This was very apparent in one of the subvillages where this study was conducted. Many people asserted that official religious organizations were not very active. According to our informants, the Muslim religious gathering *pengajian* was held only once a year, on *Idul Fitri*, the day after the end of Ramadan, the Muslim fasting month. In comparison, in the other two subvillages, pengajians were held routinely and the mosques were well maintained. Although formally Muslim, some households openly maintained practices associated with Javanese mysticism. They kept pictures of their deceased mystic teacher and claimed to communicate with him before making important life course decisions, such as getting marriedor finding a job. They visited his grave regularly to get his blessing and absorb his mystical knowledge, and they contacted him in their dreams or meditations, seeking spiritual messages to guide their course of action. These beliefs and practices are legal because authorities consider them cultural practices or a way of life, not a religion. At present, when the pressure of being accused of being a communist has lessened, people are able to talk more freely about their mystical practices.

In recent years, with the Islamic revival and the resurgence of influence of more-orthodox Islam, there has been a decline in mystical practice and growth of Muslim religious observation and organizations. However, in this village, and especially the subvillage where Javanese religion was widespread, the NU is somewhat more popular, because of the perception that even though NU is usually identified as the more traditional Islamic organization, it is also seen as more open to Javanese cultural influence, including the mysticism that was prevalent there. In general, however, people say they want to be good Muslims and avoid overt declaration of affiliation with one group or another.

Other signs of increased Islamic piety common elsewhere post-Reformasi were relatively rare in this village. For example, few women wore the jilbab except on special occasions, such as for weddings or religious gatherings. They pointed out that it was inappropriate and uncomfortable for farmwork and also too expensive. They generally viewed it as a primarily urban practice and a luxury available for women who did not have to engage in physical labor.

There were numerous religion-based social activities available in the village. Village records indicated that there were 33 Islamic religious groups with 660 members. If this accurately reports participation, it indicates that only 15 percent of the total Muslim population was actively engaged in religious gatherings and practices. These numbers most likely reflected formal membership rather than actual participation. Undoubtedly, the figures would be much higher now, but these data are not available. There were no data on the activities of other religious groups, but from the interviews we learned there were several active Catholic groups that conducted regular meetings and *arisans* (savings associations that work like a fixed lottery).

Other social activities in the village included health improvement activities, family planning, the Family Welfare Program (Pemberdayaan dan Kesejahteraan Keluarga, or PKK), a youth group (Karang Taruna), and sports and art groups. In fact, these social activities could be found in most Indonesian villages, since these were programs sponsored and coordinated by the government. The central village organization in which all groups of the society were represented and through which all social activities were organized and controlled was the LKMD (Lembaga Ketahanan Masyarakat Desa), literally the Village Resilience Organization.

Under the New Order, the LKMD served as the primary channel between the state and the citizens, propagating government ideology at the village level. It emphasized the idea that people have to improve their future conditions with help and guidance from the government (Gerke 1992, 29). Local formal and informal leaders organized the LKMD. Women were formally represented only in the family welfare (PKK) section of the LKMD, the only official role they have, since women are not usually appointed to represent any other section. Most LKMD meetings were attended by men only since the meetings mainly deal with public affairs, which are considered men's domain. Since Reformasi, the LKMD has been disbanded and partially replaced by Badan Permusyawaratan Desa (BMD—Village Representation Board).

Women were underrepresented in the village government; all village offices, except one subvillage head position, were held by men. According to informants, women have never been selected as village officers. There were several women candidates in previous elections, but none of them had ever won.

ENTERING VILLAGE SOCIAL LIFE IN SLEMAN

In the mid-1990s, the first views of Desa Danau village life conformed to a scene typical of rural Java. The access road was heavily traveled, crowded with bicycles, motor scooters, ox carts, automobiles, and pedestrians carrying heavy loads. Far fewer people were evident in the actual settlements, and the first impression was of the village's pastoral nature. Agricultural fields dominated the setting, and it was apparent that the area has fertile agricultural land, attributed to proximity to an active volcano, Mount Merapi, whose silhouette looms in the background. This volcano periodically erupts, forcing some village residents to temporarily seek refuge away from the path of destruction.

The village was divided into eleven *pedukuhan*, subvillages or hamlets. We selected three of the pedukuhan located relatively close to one another to conduct the research. The first stop on entering the village was at the village head's office. This was located along a secondary paved road, surrounded by agricultural fields with only a few houses nearby. Most residences were located in separate settlements, with the nearest subvillage residential compound located approximately two hundred meters away. The office was a relatively old and modest building with a main room used for local meetings and several offices for village officials who conduct

daily business there. Official duties include providing identification cards, birth certificates, and similar documents and services.
The village branch of the nationally organized Family Welfare
Program (PKK) also had a small room as its office in this building, but it was not well maintained. It contained a few documents,
books, and reports of the PKK's activities. These reports and books
looked dusty, and the room appeared to be infrequently used.

Approval from the village head was a necessary requirement for
conducting the research. The village head granted formal approval,
even though he appeared to have reservations about the project
and a hidden agenda. He clearly hoped that Siti's connections with
a prestigious local university could assist his children in gaining
admission there. He also was eager to learn what people said about
him and his conduct. Later on he resisted being interviewed separately from his wife, and interfered with his wife's interview, frequently answering questions for her. Although ultimately he did
not create a serious obstacle to the larger research project, he had
to be handled carefully to prevent interference with the research.

SUBVILLAGES

The first subvillage, Gunung Kayu, is located approximately three
kilometers from the main road between Yogyakarta and Magelang,
and four hundred to five hundred meters away from a secondary
paved road, but only dirt roads lead directly to the subvillage. The
formal entrance road through the village gate was narrow and
rough, with bumps and clumps of grass creating a surface that
could be traversed only by bicycle, motorcycle, or buffalo cart (buffalo carts had disappeared by 2002). The other access was actually
the back road that led past the eggplant-processing company. This
road was in better shape, accessible to cars and trucks that trans-
ported goods to and from the factory. Located on the left, immediately after passing the eggplant-processing company and entering
the residential part of the subvillage, was the subvillage cemetery.

The cemetery's location also marks this as having originally been a back road, since the cemetery is usually located at the very back part of a settlement. People now prefer to use this better back road.

On entering this subvillage, Mount Merapi can be clearly seen in the north, with rice paddies and fields of watermelon and other dry crops in the foreground. The eggplant-processing plant is located on the left at the end of the paved road. The plant stands by itself, surrounded by agricultural fields and separate from the compound where all the houses in the subvillage are located. Its gray paint is in stark contrast to the lush green of the paddies. The company employs some younger people (men and women between eighteen and forty years of age) from the adjacent subvillages, but most employees are from the subvillage where it is located. Employment of local youth was stipulated by the subvillage as partial compensation for allowing the company to build its facilities on its land.

At the suggestion of the subvillage head, Siti stayed with his uncle and aunt, Bu and Pak Simbah, while doing fieldwork. Quite unusually, this couple lived by themselves; their children were grown and lived apart. Their three-bedroom brick house was relatively large and well-maintained, considered one of the best houses in this subvillage. It had a large living room, a spacious family room, and a dining room in the main house. Besides the main house, an area containing a well (equipped with an electric pump by 1995, but not in 1993), a bathroom, and a toilet connected the main house and an older structure with bamboo walls and dirt floors that contained the kitchen. This was the original house and this couple's living quarters before they renovated and added the newer sections. The kitchen was fairly rudimentary. The stove consisted of wood placed between two stacks of bricks. To keep the fire going, Bu Simbah blew through a long piece of bamboo to produce a draft that fans the flame. The house was renovated several times, and by 2010 contained a more modern kitchen.

Bu Simbah was the second wife of Pak Simbah and the younger sister of his first wife. His first wife died many years ago when his children were young. All of the children are from the first marriage. Bu Simbah reared the children after her sister's death and maintained very close relationships with all of them. Yet she still worried that her stepchildren would not properly care for her in her old age. In an effort to secure her future and make village and family life more attractive to the children when they retire or return to the village, she sold land she had inherited from her own family and used the money to renovate their (originally her husband's) house. In addition to enhancing the value and comfort of the home, this action represented an investment of her personal resources in her husband's property to give her a bigger stake in her husband's and stepchildren's holdings. It was a transaction designed to create a moral as well as an economic obligation for the children.

Many members of this extended family (including the subvillage head, his siblings, and his father) resided in the subvillage and made up one of the most influential families in the area. The subvillage head's own house was located on the same property as his parents' house. There was a connecting veranda between the two houses, and they shared a well, a bathroom, and a kitchen that were located at the back of his house. Both of these houses were of brick construction and were considered to be among the best houses in the subvillage. His parents' house was a little bit bigger with a large living room that could hold sixty to seventy-five people. This room usually was used to hold local meetings. In 2002 during a return visit, we discovered that this house had been inherited by the sister of the subvillage head after their father died. This sister previously lived in a modest bamboo house located behind her father's house.

One important local gatekeeper was a highly respected religious leader. He was the imam of the local mosque located on his property next to his house. He did not originally come from the village but settled there because of his wife's connections. In addition to his moral authority, his prestige and influence were enhanced by his education (he had two college degrees) and his wife's social standing. She was the only child of a family that owned substantial amounts of land and other property, which she inherited. As the moral and religious arbiter for the majority Muslim population, he was able to exert substantial influence over pedukuhan life through his sermons, advice, and daily practices. Informally, his power and influence exceeded those of the dukuh, who regularly consulted him before making important decisions. His approval and cooperation were vital in the field research.

Social activities in this subvillage were dominated by several socially prominent women. Foremost was the wife of the subvillage head, who quickly became an important key informant and facilitator for the research. She was a very active and self-confident woman and the main driving force behind almost all women's activities in the area. Even though she married before finishing high school, her broad social networks supported by her husband's social status, her outgoing personality, and her leadership ability placed her in a leading position in both the subvillage and the village. She was only in her late twenties during the time we were first there, but she managed to interact well with both older and younger generations. She almost always led and spoke at local women's gatherings and served as an important intermediary between village and subvillage levels of government and other less formal activities.

She and Siti established an immediate rapport that resulted in numerous sources of information and access to village activities and residents. Her central role in so many meetings and activities provided ready and convenient access to village social life. However, this assistance had to be carefully balanced with relationships with other local leaders as well. The vigor with which the subvillage head's wife pursued her activities to some extent created tension in her relationships with a few other active and prominent women who competed with her for influence in village affairs.

One of these women had served as the acting chair of the subvillage PKK branch during the administration of the previous subvillage head. She performed this role in place of the former head's wife, who was older, illiterate, and not able to perform the necessary tasks. Since the appointment of the new head, she had to step down from the position and assume a more subordinate role. Another woman who competed for recognition and social status came from the wealthiest family in the subvillage. Her family controlled the most agricultural fields in the area and had several profitable businesses, including tractor rental, tobacco trade, and a fleet of mini pickup trucks used to provide public transportation. This woman herself was active in trade.

These two women resided at one end of the subvillage, while the subvillage head and the wife of the prominent religious leader, who was also active in women's affairs, lived at the other. These two women got along and worked well together. The distance between the two ends of the pedukuhan was not very far, no more than a couple of city blocks, but marked a division in village social life. However, the competition between these women tended to be subtle. They avoided open conflict by separating women's activities in the two sections of the subvillage. In each section, two women served as coleaders, and this arrangement actually encouraged women's activities. Both areas had relatively active women's participation initiated locally and not always directly connected to formal PKK programs.

The second subvillage, Bukit Kayu, was located adjacent to the first, separated by only a small dirt road. There were two elementary schools attended by most of the children from these and several other subvillages in the area. Soccer fields fronted the schools, and many younger males from the area came there to play. However, during the dry season, from April through September, this field was sometimes used for drying tobacco leaves.

The subvillage head at the time of fieldwork in 1995 and 1996 was the son of the previous incumbent.[13] The family of the subvillage head was influential and possessed significant landholdings. Partly because of the family's background and his charisma and connections, he managed to obtain the head position, conveniently replacing his father when he retired. This also indicates that he already had established strong connections with local government officials and both formal and informal leaders.

A few years earlier, during his father's administration, there were no active women's social organizations. In part this was because the father's wife showed little aptitude for initiating and leading women's activities. However, it was also partly the result of her husband's strong reservations about his wife's involvement in social activities. He pressured her to spend most of her time in household and agricultural work, leaving her little time for village affairs. This situation gradually changed with the advent of the younger and more educated new leader. His wife began to reactivate various women's groups, and despite some challenges, she managed to organize several routine meetings and programs. These efforts were supported by the wife of the village head, who also lived in this subvillage, as well as by the wives of other prominent residents.

Revitalizing these groups was not always easy. Social activities were often conducted between 1:00 and 2:00 p.m., during the lunch break of agricultural workers who usually stopped work at noon and returned to their fields around 2:30 after the sun had lowered slightly. Other meetings were held at night after dinner. Meetings often started later than scheduled. In an indication of either lingering resistance or lack of interest in the renewal of organized activities, women would straggle in as much as an hour late or have to be prompted and rounded up by group leaders.

As in other subvillages, most of these meetings were held in the house belonging to the subvillage head. This house commonly functions as a residence, office, and meeting venue and tends to be bigger with a larger living room that can accommodate official functions. In this subvillage, the head had a new house just across from his parents' house (his father was the former head). Even though the incumbent's house was not quite as large as his parents', the living room was divided into two parts: a smaller room to receive guests and a bigger room used to hold community meetings. It was a modern brick house with a tile roof and floor.

The third subvillage, Pedukuhan Kayu, is located next to the second subvillage to its south. It had the oldest head among the three study subvillages and probably the oldest among all eleven of the subvillage heads. Most subvillages have gradually appointed (and now elected) younger and better-educated subvillage heads in the past few years.[14] This man was in his sixties and had a middle school education; his wife was a few years younger and had a similar level of education.

One unique characteristic of this subvillage that set it apart from the other two was the persistence of belief in traditional Javanese religion. This subvillage used to be a stronghold for adherents to the religious beliefs closely associated with core Javanese values. However, while the number of residents who held these views had decreased significantly from the time of the abortive coup in 1965, and continued adherence was both stigmatized and dangerous, some subjects still clearly expressed their affiliation with these beliefs and practices. One person mentioned that he met his wife through a vision when he meditated. In his vision his late spiritual teacher endorsed the relationship and suggested that his wife would make a suitable mate. Other similar stories were common. The strong influence of this belief in the past also manifested itself previously in the existence of performing arts groups such as a gamelan (a traditional Javanese musical instrument) orchestra and a Javanese dance group. However, these groups were inactive at the time of the research.

Women's social activities were present and there were regular meetings, but they were not as intensive and organized as in the other two subvillages. In general, there was less contact and we gained less information from residents of this subvillage, possibly a legacy of insecurity after 1965. The wife of the subvillage head was not very active in women's groups or village affairs, and she was not very forthcoming with information. Similarly, not many other women were active in the local and village-level social activities.

Social relations in Desa Danau, Sleman, are very tightly hierarchically structured, as is generally true in Indonesian society. Social identity and status determine the nature of relationships with others, and these are heavily influenced by social class and access to and use of status markers. Ownership of a motorcycle, a car, a nice house, fashionable clothing, jewelry, or land is an outward sign of high status. People, especially outsiders, are judged by their appearance and display of status symbols.

Within the village, housing both reflects and establishes social and economic positions. The more affluent residents have modern houses made of brick and tile. The living room is at the front of the house and serves as the showcase for the family. It is usually the biggest and best room in the house, with family portraits, awards, and other items that demonstrate the family's status on display. The kitchen and bathroom are located in the very back part of the house (the expression for going to the bathroom or toilet is *kebelakang*, "going to the back") and are usually the least attractive and least well-maintained parts of the house. Especially in the better houses in the area, there is usually a sharp contrast between the condition of the living room and the back part of the house. Those who have higher status in the community tend to maintain their "front-stage" by renovating the front part of their houses and their living rooms. Limited funds and the perception that it is not socially important to renovate other rooms mean that other parts of the dwelling are not as attractive or well-kept as the living room.

Less-affluent persons or families who can be defined as "middle class" commonly have a house that is half brick and half bamboo with a tile roof. The floor is usually made of portland cement, or part of the house may have dirt floors. Bamboo-walled houses with more-modest tiled roofs or even thatch roofs and dirt floors signify lower-class houses. Since the residential area of a subvillage is a densely populated compound surrounded by agricultural fields, these different types of houses are located adjacent to one another. People from different social classes interact daily and intensively in these subvillages and to some degree are interdependent on one another. More-affluent villagers may employ poorer residents as household helpers and field hands. Because of this proximity and intensity of relations among different social classes, status display is important from the point of view of those who are in a higher status to reinforce the differences.

The use of different levels of language is another important mechanism to maintain status differences. In this village, Javanese is the main language used in daily conversations and also in formal meetings. Some older people do not speak Bahasa Indonesia, the national language, which is not as sensitive to social status as Javanese. The Javanese language finely differentiates speakers based on their social statuses. Those who have lower social status have to use a high level of language to address those who have higher status, while the higher-status people use a lower level of language to address lower-status subjects. Because of the common use of Javanese, some interviews in this village were conducted in that language. The use of Javanese, however, not only served as a reminder of relative social status but also maintained the boundary between outsider and insider. Villagers addressed Siti mainly in high-level Javanese. In return, as an outsider and to be polite, she addressed them the same way. However, conversations in high-level Javanese tend to maintain formality and social distance between the speakers and therefore prevent informality and intimacy between the subjects and the researcher. Only the subvillage head and his family, who treated her as a family member, occasionally spoke to her in low-level Javanese. Depending on the situation and speaker, Siti sometimes initiated conversations using Bahasa Indonesia or a mix of the two languages. For example, this dukuh had previously lived in Jakarta where he had become used to speaking the national language. This is in marked contrast to a highly respected religious leader who always had to be addressed in high-level Javanese.

The Village in Kabupaten Bantul

Although the district of Bantul is a poorer and generally more rural area, Tanah Kaya, the study village located in this district, was (and is) more affluent and much more influenced by urban activities and values. It is only eight kilometers from Yogyakarta, the center of the province, and three kilometers from Bantul, the district center. It is connected to these cities by a main road, the Yogyakarta-Bantul road, and there are various forms of public transportation from the village to both cities. Despite the persistence of an agricultural sector, proximity to the two cities permits many village inhabitants to work, shop, attend school, and seek entertainment in the two urban centers. Presently, almost no physical distinction remains between the village and the cities, with urban sprawl turning it more and more into a bedroom community.

This village was larger than the Sleman village in both land and population. It consists of sixteen pedukuhan, or subvillages, and covers an area of 6,980,170 hectares. Although it had less land devoted to agriculture, the majority was still used for semi-irrigated rice fields (3,633,066 hectares, or 52 percent), followed by residential areas (2,769,104 hectares, or 40 percent). The remainder was classified as plantation and dry farmland. The total village population at the time of initiating fieldwork there in September 1995 was 16,229 people in 3,836 households; 3,039 (79 percent) of the households were headed by men, and 797 (21 percent) were headed by women.

Educational attainment was higher than in the Sleman village, with the majority of the residents having more than a primary school education and even higher aspirations for their children. Schooling through high school was readily available, with seven kindergartens, ten primary schools, two junior high schools, and one high school available within the village boundaries. There were also two traditional Islamic schools (*pesantren*) run by NU.

The population that reported holding a primary job was 7,313 persons, or 45 percent of the total population. According to village statistics, a much smaller but still substantial number of residents were classified as having primary work as either land cultivators or farm laborers (approximately 40 percent of those with reported occupations). Farmers' groups were more active in this village than in the first village; most farming activities were coordinated by these groups. People also planted more homogeneous varieties and types of plants. Unlike Sleman, however, agricultural labor was not highly valued. It was seen as demanding work, to be avoided if possible by persons with higher education and middle-class aspirations, and especially by women. Factory and construction work were the next-biggest categories of employment, often requiring travel to one of the cities. There were many other forms of employment pursued by residents of this village, but somewhat paradoxically, despite diverse opportunities, fewer than half the population reported a primary occupation. According to informants, it was more difficult for men to find nonagricultural employment than for women, because women had a variety of opportunities to obtain credit to start their own enterprises, usually some sort of small-scale production and market trade, whereas men sought mostly waged labor.

Most of the village population (15,446, or 96 percent) were Muslim, 502 (3 percent) people were Roman Catholic, and the remainder (less than 1 percent of the population) included 42 Protestants and 23 Hindus. Religious activities played significant roles in village social life. In sharp contrast to Sleman, almost half the Muslim population was actively engaged in *pengajian*, the Islamic religious gathering, and nearly all other religious believers also participated in organized religious activities. These religious meetings served both spiritual and social purposes, providing places for villagers to meet and communicate. For Muslims there were forty-eight mosques available in the village. Many of the men and a few of the older women went to a mosque several times a day to pray and to socialize. There were also several *kyais*, Islam's traditional religious teachers, who resided in the village. They led two *pesantren*, or traditional schools for studying Islam. The religious schools also served social and cultural functions as well as their educational mission. The schools, however, were located in different subvillages than where the research was conducted. As in Sleman, participation in religious activities has increased since the initial fieldwork. Here Muhammadiyah tends to be more popular than NU, although affiliation varies across subvillages. Informants suggest that rising affluence has made Muhammadiyah more attractive to upwardly mobile villagers who are eager to demonstrate their orthodoxy. However, many villagers participate in both organizations, and often there are combined ceremonies and religious observations in the same mosque. For example, in the evening prayers (*tarawih*) during Ramadan, the fasting month, Muhammadiyah followers conduct eleven prayer cycles, while NU adherents continue to complete the twenty-four cycles prescribed for them. In recent years, it has become increasingly popular for villagers who can afford it to go on the Hajj, the pilgrimage to Mecca, prescribed for observant Muslims as a sign of their orthodoxy and devotion. It is now common practice for women to wear the jilbab in public for all the reasons outlined in chapter 1, including piety, security, social pressure, and fashion. In Bantul this practice is made easier by women's greater affluence and lower participation in agricultural labor than in Sleman. Despite these outward signs of increasing religious observance, there is little interest in more extreme or radical Islamic groups. The few examples that villagers identified were marginalized outsiders who had moved to the village from elsewhere.

Religious gatherings were not the only social activities present in the village. There were various other social activities. Similar to what has been described in the Sleman village, LKMD functioned as the primary institution organizing almost all formal social activities in the village. One of the main roles of this institution was to mobilize the rural people to support the government's development programs through *gotong royong*, or mutual self-help. Government-sponsored social organizations were active in directing women's social and civic activities and providing access to credit for women's enterprises. We selected three subvillages for fieldwork where active programs were located, including P2WKSS (Peningkatan Peranan Wanita menuju Keluarga Sehat dan Sejahtera, or Program to Improve Women's Roles in Healthy and Prosperous Families) and the PKK programs, since one of the aims of this research is to understand the impacts of these programs on women's livelihoods, roles, and status.

Entering Social Life in Tanah Kaya, Bantul

It is much easier to reach the village in Bantul than the village in Sleman, both then and now. It is readily accessible from the main road connecting the city of Yogyakarta in the north and the city of Bantul in the south. This road is also the route to a popular beach in the south Indian Ocean or Indonesian Ocean, Samas. Public transportation abounds, with both city and regional buses regularly traveling this road as well as every sort of private vehicle. Since this is also the main road used by the many commuters who reside in Bantul to travel to Yogyakarta, students, government officials, traders, and others regularly start their day early in the morning going from Bantul to Yogyakarta and returning in the afternoon. Traffic flows reflect this pattern, packing the northbound lane in the morning and the southbound lane in the afternoon. In the past, most commuters rode bicycles; however, now motorized vehicles crowd this modest two-lane road. Some relief came in the late 1990s when a ring road was built to channel traffic and reduce the burden on this road. The western part of the ring road is located approximately 1.5 kilometers away from the village, cutting across the Bantul-Yogyakarta road. This ring road connects to different parts of the city of Yogya and reduces travel time significantly between different corners of the city and different districts in the province. Proximity to these urban centers, and the consequent increased mobility of people, information, and goods, has facilitated more rapid urbanization in this village. It also is widely perceived to have increased social problems such as consumerism and substance abuse.

Coming from Yogyakarta, the village head's office is located on the right-hand side along the Bantul-Yogyakarta road, two kilometers away from the formal border between the district of Bantul and the city of Yogyakarta. The area is highly built up. Few fields can be seen from this road; instead, there are schools, businesses, houses, and shops. Similarly, only a few plots of agricultural land can be spotted adjacent to the office, and this scene, too, is dominated by residential homes, businesses, and school buildings. Agricultural fields are located behind these buildings, away from the main road. As in any other village head office, this facility has a flagpole in front, an enclosed office for the *kades* (head), a large main room for holding community meetings, and other offices for conducting the village governmental business. Compared to the first village, it appears to be better maintained and looks busier, with people continually coming and going.

During the New Order government, the layers of village government were constructed to serve as important gatekeepers for Indonesian society. Members of the community were required to obtain a variety of letters and documents from the village head for conducting their lives and livelihoods. Marriages, divorces, and deaths all had to be reported to this office; the more dynamic and mobile the people in the village were, the busier this office. However, before coming to this office, they must first obtain signatures from lower-level governmental officials, such as the head of the neighborhood association and the *dukuh*, the head of the subvillage. These layers of bureaucracy were used to monitor and control members of the community and to create dependency on government agencies, reinforcing government power.

This became especially evident in the process of negotiating the layers of local bureaucracy. Getting access and establishing rapport in Bantul were more challenging than in Sleman. The village is larger and more diverse, with a more heterogeneous population than in Sleman, which by itself would make it more challenging to identify those who have influence and power in the community. In addition, however, Bantul was experiencing political turnover and tension that both complicated the situation and provided opportunities for a firsthand view of local politics. The previous elected village head had been dismissed for corruption. He had been replaced with an interim head, who, in turn, was slated to be replaced in an election to select a permanent incumbent toward the end of the initial fieldwork. The interim head had been a sub-district government official who was appointed[15] to conduct daily governmental business in the village, but he was an outsider who lacked any direct connection to village life. He did not live there or have any personal or family connections. He exercised formal authority over governmental and daily affairs without having strong local cultural, social, and political networks.

This political instability made it difficult to gauge who had power in the community and, especially, who had formal and informal authority over women's social activities. The standard practice during the New Order was for the wife of the village head to organize and administer women's social activities. However, since the interim head did not reside in the village, his wife was not available to serve as the chair of local women's organizations and the Family Welfare Program (PKK). Instead, the first wife of the previous (discredited) village head maintained her previous position, serving as the interim chair for these organizations. At the time of our field research, she was the formal and highly influential leader of the local PKK, continuing her previous service.

However, her position was tenuous and controversial, highly colored by the scandals that had caused her husband to step down and his generally unsavory reputation. In addition to the charges of corruption that ended his term, he also had a shady reputation for his keen interest in gambling and other illicit activities. Finally, he had two wives who periodically lived under the same roof. The first wife lived in this village and performed the formal obligations as the wife of a village head, including chairing the local women's organizations and representing the village in formal women's meetings inside and outside the village. The second wife, along with her children, lived mainly in the city she had originally come from, but she sometimes came to the village and lived with her husband's first wife.[16]

The uncertainty and controversy surrounding her leadership created a degree of apprehension and tension that influenced the dynamic and atmosphere of the women's social activities. Despite a very high level of activism in the local PKK branch, some respondents mentioned that there had been even more vigorous activities before the scandal of her husband's activities and corruption trial became commonly known. All of this was slated to soon change with the impending election of a permanent village head.

SUBVILLAGES

The ecology of this village also presented different issues for selecting subvillages for intensive study. The village is bisected by the main road, and residential location has important effects on the economic activities and social status of village residents. We conducted the field research primarily in three different subvillages selected to reflect these differences (with a few additional informants, who play important roles in the village PKK branch, coming from a fourth subvillage). Two subvillages in this study are situated on the east side of the main road and one subvillage is on the west side. Two of the subvillages are partially located on this road, whereas one of the subvillages to the east is located farther out with no direct access to the main road. Persons who live along the main road are usually wealthier and have higher social status than those who live relatively far from the main road. Main-road property has higher property values; those who reside there have greater access to capital for more lucrative business ventures. Some of these property owners inherited their land and homes, others acquired them later, but either way, most of these residents come from affluent families and live in comfortable circumstances.

The subvillage of Pedukuhan Tengah was marked by sharp contrasts. Parts of this subvillage are located along the main road with a substantial number of wealthy upper-class residents. This area is mostly flat. The other end of Tengah is a rough, mountainous area inhabited by much poorer residents. There is also a middle ground between these two contrasting areas, but this area does not occupy a very significant amount of the landscape. Even though this pedukuhan is located not very far from an urban center, its terrain has had an important influence on the economic and social situations of those who live there. No public transportation was available to access the less developed and more isolated parts of the subvillage. Roads were not paved, and during the rainy season they became quite muddy and hardly passable. Cars and larger vehicles could get through only limited parts of some of the roads, and outsiders rarely wanted to take the risk of getting stuck in the mud. This further isolates the area. To conduct research in this area, it was necessary to park the car at the bottom of a steep and muddy hill and walk the rest of the way to people's houses. Local leaders initially tried to discourage us from interviewing these subjects, ostensibly because of the difficulty in reaching their homes.

The differences between the two areas were obvious in the residents' housing and standards of living. Houses in the poor area had dirt floors, bamboo walls, few windows, thatched roofs, and no electricity. In contrast, houses in the more affluent area were two-story brick houses, equipped with tile roofs, ceramic-tile floors, gas stoves, and electronic appliances. These housing conditions also reflected the economic and educational status of their residents. The illiteracy rate was quite high in the hilly poor area. There was a history of tension and problematic relationships between people in these two contrasting areas. Despite living in the same subvillage, each group occupied its own world and had limited interactions with one another. This had started to change, however, with the selection of the current dukuh.

This subvillage had (and still has) a woman head who was relatively new to the job (approximately three years at the time of the initial fieldwork). It was and still is extremely rare to have a woman subvillage head and also somewhat controversial because of the nature of their duties. These include taking an active role in village affairs that might require paying night visits to distressed households, officiating at funerals, and similar work that is seen as unsuitable for a woman. Even more remarkable, this woman resided in the poorer section of the subvillage, the first person from this area to occupy this prestigious position.[17] Previous subvillage heads had always come from the more developed and affluent part of the subvillage, reinforcing the division between the two areas. Although she had a middle-class background, her residence and close relationships with the people from the "hinterland" increased participation and involvement of the people from this group in governmental programs and local community gatherings. She managed to serve as a mediator between the groups. Her social class enabled her to relate to the higher-class people who live in the other part of the subvillage; her residence made her part of the less developed region. As a result, these two groups were often seen side by side in local community gatherings.

Despite demonstrating the ability to integrate different segments of the community, leadership positions in the local PKK were retained by members of the affluent group. In fact, preserving their privilege seems to have been one of her promises to local leaders when this woman ran for the position. The position of dukuh was closely contested, and there were numerous stories and rumors about the process used to make the appointment. Her nearest rival was a woman from the more affluent part of the subvillage. Although the losing woman did not want to discuss the matter herself, her husband was quite forthcoming with his views of the affair. By his account, his wife believed that she had actually scored first place in the qualifying exam for office and consequently should have won the appointment. He claimed that the decision was abruptly changed when financial and political interests favoring her rival interfered.

Not surprisingly, this account was at odds with the views of the woman who actually won the dukuh appointment. She claimed that she was the true winner and the best candidate who rightfully deserved and earned the position. A particularly important component of this claim was her connections to the more depressed area of the subvillage, putting her in a better position to represent this group without neglecting or threatening the more affluent residents.

Regardless of who was the rightful winner, under the leadership of this dukuh, PKK programs and other women's groups have been very active, creating venues for different factions of the community to meet. She has also taken a direct interest in improving women's circumstances in this village and has been especially proactive in programs for poor women farmers and those engaged in small home-based production such as making *emping*, a kind of cracker made from the *gnetum gnemon* nut. This subvillage was selected as one of the sites for P2WKSS or the Program to Improve Women's Roles in Healthy and Prosperous Families. One of its main objectives was to improve women's economic standing and facilitate access to credit for their existing economic activities. The P2WKSS deliberately recruited women from this depressed area to improve their situation. Although the majority of the population and its leaders were Muslim, there were also several Catholics active in women's activities.

The next subvillage, Sungai Bengkok, is located away from the main road in the middle of the village surrounded by agricultural fields. While it was accessible by several different roads, with the exception of one semipaved road, they were narrow and unpaved. This subvillage covers an area half the size of the first subvillage with a little more than half its population. As in other subvillages, people's homes were clustered together to make a residential compound surrounded by farmland and open fields. However, population pressure and economic development have resulted in many plots of agricultural land being converted into residential areas, with the result that a few houses are located somewhat apart from the main housing compound. The area is mostly flat, and it is divided by a river that periodically floods parts of the residential area. Residence near the flood-prone area reflects the inhabitants' social position; they are usually lower class. There were no significant differences between the two areas divided by the river, although there were class-based social divisions. The entire population identified as Muslim.

This subvillage was the residence of a number of village officials, including the former village head and his wives (especially the first wife). These women held the positions of leadership in women's organizations, giving this community a very active set of organizations, and making it a target group for the P2WKSS. However, this subvillage was also the site of strong negative opinions on these activities.

The subvillage head had held this position for only a year before the field research began. He was from a middle-class background with strong connections to prominent community members in both the subvillage and the village. His wife graduated from middle school and came from a lower-middle-class background. She was not active in a women's social organization before her husband's appointment to the post. Her modest education, knowledge, and background placed her at somewhat of a disadvantage, despite her formal position as the head of the subvillage PKK branch, and she was largely superseded by several local women who had important village-level PKK positions. This followed a historical pattern in this subvillage. The wife of the previous subvillage head was illiterate and somewhat older, and she, too, did not actively take part in women's activities. Instead, she was represented by her daughter-in-law, who had several years of college education. This daughter-in-law still maintained an important role in some women's activities even after her father-in-law retired. The acting head of this subvillage PKK branch was a close companion and distant relative by marriage of a woman who became prominent as a candidate during the election for village head. Her appointment to head the PKK branch was the outcome of a complicated web of social, political, and economic obligations between these couples and upper-echelon district officials. In particular, the PKK chair assisted the subvillage head in gaining his appointment. She then argued that the subvillage needed an acting PKK chair because of his wife's lack of experience. Giving her the acting chair position was part of the way that the subhead paid his debt to her and her husband for their assistance in the acquisition of his job.

Pedukuhan Barat is the third subvillage for this research. It is flat and located east of the main road, accessible from both the main road and a secondary paved road. There were seven neighborhood associations and an active subvillage PKK branch as well as other social activities. The population in this subvillage was heterogeneous but not as much as in Pedukuhan Tengah. Higher-class houses were located side by side with more-modest homes. The better houses usually belonged to government officials, civil service workers, military officers, and more-successful businesspeople. These houses ranged from fifty to several hundred square meters with both front yards and backyards, brick and cement walls that were usually painted in white or other light colors, and ceramic-tile floors. Typically, these households were affluent enough to own several motorcycles, and in a few cases, they also possessed automobiles.

Access in this subvillage was facilitated by a somewhat tangled web of connections between Siti and the dukuh. A friend of Siti's sister and his wife, who was also a distant relative of Siti's family, hosted Siti during the research. This man was also a distant relative of the dukuh. These connections opened many doors in the community, including providing easy informal access to the subvillage head and his family. The subvillage head was young, in his early thirties, and relatively new to the post (approximately two years). His upper-middle-class family had a long history of residence in the area and extensive connections with local government officials, connections that secured his appointment. He married a widow who was a few years older with a child from a previous marriage. This was quite uncommon in Javanese society and was a subject of daily conversation in his family (including Siti's host). The wife had several businesses including ice-making and a small stall at their house that sold toiletries, rice, cooking oil, and other daily household needs. They also produced concrete blocks. These enterprises gave the family a good income. In fact, the dukuh stated that one of his main motivations for taking the position was not to get economic benefits for himself but because of social pressures from his extended family, especially his parents and siblings. As a subvillage head, he received no cash compensation. Instead, he got the right to use a plot of subvillage agricultural land. He let his father cultivate the land and profit from selling its output. He saw serving as subvillage head as more of a family obligation and a means to sustain their social status.

The elected village head came from this subvillage, and his wife was quite active in the local PKK programs. The wife of the subvillage head was both the formal and the actual chair of the local PKK branch. There were also several other women from middle-class and upper-class households who were active in both subvillage and village PKK branches, including the subhead's mother, who worked in a local Family Planning office and was very active in various social programs.

Village Life and Lifestyles

The house Siti stayed in was located in a nearby subvillage (in Pedukuhan Hijau). Although this subvillage was not one of the research locations, the description of her hosts' home and family provides a representative picture of solidly middle-class life in this village at the end of the New Order.

The house was situated on a narrow secondary paved road, accessible by car, only five hundred meters from the main road. The couple inherited the house from the husband's adopted parents, a childless uncle and aunt, who both died several years ago. He also maintained close ties with his biological parents, who lived in

Central Java. The wife came from a different village in the district not very far from where they lived. Her relatives frequently came to visit. The formal members of the household were the husband, the wife, and their daughter, but the house saw a continual stream of visitors that included numerous relatives, friends, and close neighbors. Members of the husband's extended family who lived in the village dropped by daily for a variety of reasons. There was little privacy, although this did not appear to be very important to household and family members.

The house was brick with a concrete floor, tile roof, and wood-framed windows. It was a relatively big house, yet at the time of the initial field research seemed to be a bit dilapidated. Some parts of the floor plan were open, and a heavy rain resulted in leaks. The house had been renovated and was in much better condition when we revisited in 2002, but still retained the pattern described previously of a sharp distinction between the well-kept front or "public" rooms and a less-well-tended rear portion where family functions prevailed.[18] Thus, there was a formal living room at the very front of the house with two sets of sofas flanking the entrance. Across from this entrance, another door connected the living room and the family room, where members of the family and regular guests were entertained. A television set and a couch were found in this room. The master bedroom was located to the right of the family room. Straight ahead were the dining room and the kitchen. The kitchen had a gas stove and a cupboard. There was a prayer room located just to the left after entering the dining room. On the far right side of the dining room, a door led to an open area where the well was located. The bathroom and toilet were located in the far corner of this area. The door of the bathroom had a large opening that was not completely covered by an attached small board. There was also a garage next to the open area where the well was located. Beyond this was an addition to the main house that had a bedroom and a small living room where Siti stayed.

When we conducted the field research, the husband did not have a regular job, despite having an undergraduate degree from a well-respected state university. He had previously held various jobs; the most recent was as a low-level administrator in a state-operated plantation in East Java. His family, however, pressured him to come back to the village, because his father was very sick. His wife had some college and worked as a civil servant in a state research institute in a different district. She commuted from Bantul to the city of Wates, which was twenty-five kilometers away, using public transportation. Their only daughter was in middle school and usually took care of herself after school. They hired a neighbor as a household helper to cook and clean for them.

As in the village in Sleman, people from different classes lived side by side in Bantul; different types of houses corresponding to the social and economic status of their owners were located next to one another. The house Siti stayed in was fairly typical of middle-class houses in the area. Higher-class houses are usually bigger, better maintained, and have more up-to-date designs, while lower-class housing is smaller and rougher with bamboo walls and dirt floors. The contrast between rich and poor, higher class and lower class, was even more apparent in this village than in the village in Sleman. These differences could be observed from their housing conditions as well as from daily interactions. This made for more-complex and volatile social relations and more community conflict. This also made it more challenging to navigate among the different segments of the community.

Village Similarities, Differences, and Change

How similar or how different these two villages appear depends on the lens and focus used to examine them and the time frame in question. From the beginning, in their broad outlines, they were very similar. They both were composed of stable, ethnically homogeneous populations who shared language, culture, history, and, to a large degree, a way of life. They had been shaped by a shared climate and landscape and by the political and economic events of both recent and distant pasts. They both had power structures that were formally and informally dominated by men and values that emphasized family and communal welfare. Yet there were important differences that led us to select them for comparative purposes. One village was (and is) more urban and urbane. The other was sleepier and remained more rooted in agrarian traditions. These differences were reflected in variation in educational attainment and opportunities, occupational choices, the importance of agriculture as both a living and a way of life, access to urban environments, state investment in economic development, and the activities and activism of village women.

Of course, close scrutiny also magnifies minute variations in social, demographic, and economic conditions and highlights the idiosyncrasies of village landscapes and history as well as power structures, social relations, and even personalities. Some of the differences were random or meaningless for this study; some reflected the accident of place and space; others, however, seemed to put the villages on different development trajectories. What was not clear when we began this research was what, if anything, these differences might mean for gender roles and women's status and power, a topic that is the focus of this study.

Differences in village life were evident in gender roles and practices, as will be seen in subsequent chapters. However, as the study progressed, it became increasingly clear that the two villages, initially seeming so different, were more and more on a path toward convergence. Both have been swept up in the political and economic upheavals that changed the course of Indonesia's development with the Asian economic crisis in 1997 and the subsequent downfall of the New Order government in 1998. Democratization and decentralization, in opening up the space for new political movements, participation, experimentation, and communication, somewhat ironically, have resulted in increasing similarities between the two study areas as both have been subjected to political reform, urban development (and sprawl), economic change, and incorporation into the global marketplace.

In one of our many subsequent visits, we interviewed the elected bupati of the kabupaten of Sleman and Bantul, the districts in which these two villages are located. While they were very different in their backgrounds, capabilities, styles of administration, and plans for the future, we were struck by how much the bupatis' views nonetheless reflected shared understanding of Indonesia's past and a convergence in the development of their districts. The same holds for these villages and their residents. We suggest there is a similar process of convergence in the lives and views of the women and the men at the heart of this study.

Bird's-eye view of village in Sleman (1995)

Women planting paddies in Sleman (1995)

Close-up of women planting paddies in Sleman (1995)

Trading next to the field in Sleman (1995)

Washing clothes in Sleman (1995)

Women vendors in the market in Sleman (1995)

Bu Simba's kitchen before renovations (1995)

Arisan *in Sleman* (1995)

Siti and village head in front of village office in Sleman (1996)

Subvillage head and wife in Sleman (2004)

Subvillage head, Ann, and colleague in Sleman (2004)

Prosperous farm family in Sleman (2007)

Woman harvesting rice with sickles in Sleman (2007)

Loading a rice-hulling machine in Sleman (2007)

Women at pengajian *in Bantul* (2004)

Candidate for village head in Bantul (1996)

Gathering for arisan *in Bantul* (2007)

Winning money at arisan *in Bantul* (2007)

Kitchen in Bantul (2007)

Bu Muji in her kitchen in Bantul (2007)

Judging a PKK food-preparation contest in Bantul (2007)

Chapter 3

GOATS AND DOVES

Contradictions in Gender Ideology and the Gender Division of Labor

> *But we have equal rights, even though men tend to be better, but we have equal rights.*
>
> —Bu Tifa

THE SOURCES of Javanese gender ideology in history, culture, religion, and state policies are further elaborated by examining how beliefs about gender roles are manifested in daily practice. Making sense of the relationship between the ideological construction and the material practices of gender roles remains problematic, especially when investigating non-Western societies. There is a lingering tendency for Western and Eurocentric analysts of gender roles to associate women's economic activity, especially paid labor and access to financial resources, with higher status for women and greater gender parity, even within deeply patriarchal systems. Alternatively, it is often assumed that cultural practices alien to Western norms of appropriate gender display, such as Muslim rules of dress, automatically signify inequality and subordination. These contradictory interpretations are especially evident when the impacts of modernization and development programs on gender roles and women's status are investigated. Casual assumptions about gender roles and women's well-being often are challenged by empirical evidence.

In this chapter we examine how the seemingly contradictory constructions of gender roles that were discussed in chapter 1 are manifested in the gender division of labor and how they are understood and practiced in daily life for the rural Javanese villagers in Bantul and Sleman. The purpose is (1) to describe gender role beliefs and behaviors adhered to by rural Javanese women and men; (2) to examine how these are influenced by cultural practices and state intervention; and (3) to determine whether and how they vary by location and state-sponsored development programs.

In the introduction and chapter 1, we discussed the contradictory views of Indonesian women's status and position. This is particularly evident in the disjunction between women's actual economic autonomy and the ideological construction of women's status and roles (Hatley 1990, 180). In fact, Javanese women's lives embody a basic experience of contradiction, and in some accounts multiple layers of contradiction (Brenner 1998). Many previous studies emphasize theoretical deconstruction of this contradiction to show that in some way it can be unraveled or that it is less paradoxical than it first might appear (Keeler 1990). We argue instead that the contradiction is real and, in fact, fundamental to notions of gender in this society, and that embracing contradiction is a deeply seated part of the gender roles for many Indonesians—women and men. In this chapter we demonstrate empirically the ways this contradiction is manifested in Javanese gender relations. In particular, we investigate the gender division of labor in the household and the family, the relationship between gender ideology and the division of labor, and whether these vary by proximity to more urban development, market opportunities, and state-sponsored development interventions.

This chapter draws on both quantitative and qualitative data from interviews with eighty-three couples in the two villages conducted during the early fieldwork, as well as numerous follow-up observations and interviews with both the original participants and other informants over the subsequent years. We focus on the connections between the gender division of labor in the family economy and gender role perceptions to gain a better understanding of the contradiction between gender role perceptions as the manifestation of gender ideology and the actual practice of the gender division of labor in household and income-producing activities among Javanese villagers. Of particular interest in our studies is the differences between the two villages in order to determine the impact of urbanization and state intervention.

Gender Relations and Ideology

Numerous analytic schemes characterize the study of gender. The complexity of the topic is such that it can be plausibly characterized as a manifestation of individual belief and behavior and as a feature of a society and its institutions. Important distinctions are made between gender as identity, behavior, and discursive practice; gender as structure that creates the boundaries for expression of male and female differences and similarities; and gender as social relations that emerge interactively from its "doing."[1] Ultimately, gender must be conceptualized and analyzed as multidimensional phenomena in which practice and belief interact continuously. Thus widespread belief in a dichotomous system of gender roles based on biological difference conflicts with actual practice in everyday life. Similarly, policies and practices promulgated by cultural and political authorities may be widely and popularly subscribed to but still bear only nominal resemblance to the intricacies of the social order.

In this account we focus on "the structure of gender relations" (Connell 2002, 55), or the enduring patterns that characterize relations between women and men in Javanese society as they emerge from daily life. Different classification schemes have been proposed to analyze the structures and processes that construct gender relations. For example, Mitchell (1971) identifies four spheres in which women's subordination takes place: production, reproduction, sexuality, and socialization of children. Each of these spheres may have different weight at any particular historical moment, but they combine to determine women's status at a given point in time. Similarly, Walby (1990) identifies six structures that promulgate patriarchy: paid employment, household production, culture, sexuality, violence, and the state. Others focus on how gender operates within distinct societal institutions such as education, the economy, and the polity (Epstein 1988; Lorber 1994). More recently, Connell (2002, 2009) argues that the multidimensionality of gender relations requires recognition of social relations beyond "institutionalized inequality" or patriarchy. She proposes that gender relations are manifested in four sets of social relations: power relations, production relations, emotional relations, and symbolic relations. These may entail different forms and degrees of inequality for women, varying over time and place and with different levels of stability and susceptibility to dynamics for change.

All of these schemes attempt to identify analytical distinctions between different forms of gender relations located in distinct institutional spheres. None are completely satisfactory, because they tend to harden what are ultimately fluid and dynamic social processes. Furthermore, despite the efforts of these analysts to avoid creating polarities within and across different dimensions, the act of naming them and describing the different forms of interaction within each tends to fix these relations into categories that imply oppositional forms. Of course, in practice, it is unavoidable to divide different activities into recognizably different structures and processes—household vs. labor market, reproduction vs. production, and so on—but the point is to avoid turning these into "separate spheres" conflating fluid reality with immutable analytic scheme. As Connell (2009, 85) points out: "In a real life context, the different dimensions of gender constantly interweave, and condition each other." For this reason we examine the gender division of labor in household and income-generating activities together as part of the family economy, in the process incorporating elements of all four of Connell's dimensions and recognizing their fluidity.

Kodrat and Woman's Natural Destiny

Regardless of the particular analytic scheme and whether social relations within each sphere are more or less uniformly unequal, an ideological element of women's subordination takes the form of representing women's place and status as women's natural destiny rather than as a cultural construction (Wearing 1984, 20). The existence of this ideology renders women's roles and status in each sphere as biologically and metaphysically determined and therefore "inevitable." In this context, *ideology* is defined as a "natural" presentation of a culturally constituted structure, institution, or character (Wearing 1984, 21). Pak Janaka, a *dalang* (puppet master) from Bantul, uses a combination of sexual, emotional, and cultural imagery in this long, evocative discourse on gender differences:

> Oh, it's clear now that you want me to explain the essential differences of men and women. Based on Javanese belief, it's very clear that there are differences: Men are goats and women are doves. These are natural differences. Because of this, goat does not marry with another goat. Based on their emotional characters, women are more emotional; and based on behavioral differences, women tend to keep their true goals hidden while men [tend] to be more open about what they want to do. Those are the three main differences between men and women. Why do we use goat and dove symbolism? Because of the differences in their sexual drives. Goats are more aggressive and it is difficult to restrain their sexual drives; that's why some men want more than one wife. Polygamy is usually coming from men; because of this sexual drive, they have different biological sexual organ. So the main thing for men is their ability to restrain their sexual drives. Good men such as Janaka[2] still have their sexual drives.
>
> Now emotional character. Men are more able to express their

emotions; they tend to get bored easily with one woman. While for women, once they fall in love with a certain person, it's difficult for them to forget this; the feeling sticks for a long time. For men, it's the opposite; it's easy for men to forget their feelings and emotion for somebody when they look at other people who are better, because men are like goats . . . they like to wander around. While for women, it's difficult for them to express their feelings openly; they tend to hide their true feelings or emotions, while men tend to vulgarly express their feelings. There are different cultural perceptions about men and women; if men wander around at night or go somewhere, nobody will look for them, but when women do the same thing, their husband and children will look for them.

In Javanese society, beliefs about women's roles in each sphere are derived to some extent from their perceived biological characteristics, and there are strongly held views about differences in sexuality. However, unlike many Western representations of gender differences, biology alone is not the source of distinctly feminine and masculine characters. In many Western accounts, both popular and scientific, sex differences and, by extension, gender roles are assumed to be rooted in dualistic anatomical and physiological developmental processes based on genitalia and hormones.[3] As discussed in chapter 1, in Javanese culture, the concept of gender differences rests as much on a spiritual as on a biological dimension. Women's and men's natures, including their differences, are assumed to be their *kodrat*—their fate or destiny—and therefore are inevitable and inevitably lead to distinct social roles.

The inevitability of gender difference is further elaborated in the concepts of *wadah* and *isi*, female and male principles respectively. As noted in chapter 1, *Wadah* is the container, the essence of what being female means in the culture. It is receptive, providing the vessel in which something is deposited, protected, sheltered. *Isi* literally means "seed," and is given priority as the source of life. Unlike the more phallic imagery of Western sexual narrative, it does not necessarily connote action and penetrative power, but is in fact vulnerable, requiring the protection of the wadah. As a seed, it is life-giving but also exposed and susceptible to harm, requiring the protection of its female counterpart. Clearly there is a strong biological element to this imagery, but it is not biology alone, not directly attached to real or imagined physiological function in the form of specific anatomical structures and biochemical processes, that defines kodrat. It is embedded in the *idea* of women and men, not just the material forms.

The emphasis is on complementarity rather than on contrast or opposition, and gender roles are often explicitly described in this manner, resulting in a distinctly different although mutually reinforcing gender division of labor. Pak Janaka elaborates:

> Men are responsible for those [tasks] related to public functions, but it does not mean that they have absolute power; we have to differentiate between responsibilities and power. Women manage the money, but men earn it; this is quite complicated, but this is a natural law. There is a division of labor and division of responsibilities; some are earning the money, some could eat or buy things from the money. If only those who earn the money [could] eat from the money [there would be a problem]. There is a gap between the givers and the receivers, but we have a division of labor where those who earn money [the husbands] give the money to those who manage the money and buy things [the wives]. That is the division of responsibilities.

In practice, though, despite the complementary natures and functions assigned to women and men, they are often subtly assigned different values, even while professing equality, as is also illustrated by Pak Janaka:

> That is the responsibility of a husband in the household; he has the biggest reponsibility. However, the power is equal. But the main responsibility for the household has to be dealt with by the husband as his destiny; his "kodrat" is as the head of the household. Each gender has its own boundary; even if a woman has power, she has certain limitations. For example, if the house is dirty, both of us have to clean it up. But principally each has responsibilities based on the destiny [*kodrat*].

Numerous observers of Javanese culture note this discrepancy, and it is at the heart of the contradiction so many analysts, including us, report. Complementarity does not necessarily imply parity or equality (Hatley 1990, 182), although it is often portrayed that way. Superimposed on the supposed complementarity are notions of hierarchy that privilege men and subordinate women. Women's subordinated position comes less from ideas about the inferiority of their intrinsic nature and more from layers of patriarchal practices, some historical, some from more contemporary influences, that take advantage of ideas of gender differences to legitimate inequalities. Factors such as religious doctrines and state regulations play important roles in promoting a subordinate view of women at the same time that traditional beliefs maintain the fiction of gender complementarity and parity.

This view is expressed quite directly by a prominent and respected religious leader in Sleman, Pak Mahmud, who laments women's independence from their husbands:

> I think adherence is created by a hierarchical [order of] relations so that those who are in the weaker or lower positions are afraid to oppose or feel pressure to obey. So there should be pressure to force someone to obey. This also applies both in the households and formal relations. I have a prediction that the wives obey their husband[s] because they are in the disadvantaged positions; their lives depend on their husbands. So when the wives can be independent [financially] from their husbands, they do not obey their husbands anymore. Based on religion, a husband should have more power and strength than his wife. But in reality, some men do not have such a privilege.

Pak Mahmud uses religious authority to justify a distinctly patriarchal view of the relationship, but it should be noted that he is very much in the minority in expressing his view this openly and directly. Much more common among women and men alike are the rhetorical gymnastics that maintain women's equality and willing subordination simultaneously.

The state and religious institutions, directly and indirectly through other institutions that they heavily influence and control, such as education and the media, are especially important sources of patriarchal power. Especially in politics, economics, and religious and ritual spheres,[4] men are dominant, and their domination is legitimized by traditional, legal, and charismatic authority. Their authority confers the right to impose their definition of the situation on other members of the society. The dominant gender ideology defines women primarily as mothers and wives, releases men from doing many arduous tasks in the household, and frees them to be involved in more-prestigious civic activities and public spheres. This ideology is institutionalized in daily life, legitimating male lack of responsibility for routine parenting and household maintenance and justifying their authority in the household.

The New Order State's Role in Constructing Gender Ideology

As outlined in Chapter 1, during the history of postindependence Indonesia, and especially during the New Order government, the state and its constitution were built on the principle of familialism. To recap and further elaborate, this coincides with deeply rooted views that the family is the basic social unit. The state is assumed to be a family, with the president (at that time invariably male) accorded the role of the patriarchal father, who wields absolute power and spiritual influence over other segments of society (Suryakusuma 1991, 71). As a corollary, women are mother of the state, imagery that draws on deeply entrenched beliefs about the primacy of motherhood (Blackburn 2004; Martyn 2005).[5] Thus it was a short step to extend this imagery and base state policies on an assumption that a woman's primary roles are as mother and wife (Suryakusuma 1991, 73). In promulgating this view, principles of complementarity and hierarchy are simultaneously incorporated into the organization of the state and the practice of gender relations.

Indonesia is not alone in constructing a gendered state that harnesses both the idea of women and their actual bodies for political ends. It joins a long list of colonial, nationalist, and developmentalist struggles, variously pursued by both emerging and existing nations as a means to create statehood and as a strategy to remake old states (Eisenstein 2000; Rai 2008; Ranchod-Nilsson and Tétreault 2000; Yuval-Davis 1997). Whether violent, brutal, and degrading or "merely" constricting in definitions and options for the practice of citizenship, gender becomes a weapon of war and resistance, a tool of nationalist agendas, and a means to achieve development goals. In Indonesia, it was explicitly elaborated and embedded in state institutions and policies during the New Order (Mayer 2000).[6] This will be seen most clearly in the analysis of women's state-sponsored social welfare activities in chapter 5, but this deployment of gender ideology permeates all institutional spheres and creates the context for understanding gender relations and the limits to women's exercise of power.

The New Order government directly and formally defined women's roles and functions in the development process, beginning with the REPELITA II (Second Five-Year Development Plan, 1974–1979). In REPELITA III (1978–1983), a "Junior Minister for Women" was appointed, and in 1983, this position was elevated to the "Minister of Women," with responsibility for coordinating government-sponsored women's programs and organizations (Wusananingsih 1994, 31). Since the fall of the New Order government, the ministry has been renamed: first as the Ministry for the Empowerment of Women (Menteri Pemberdayaan Perempuan), to match new international emphasis on increasing women's active participation in the political process; but more recently as the Ministry for the Empowerment of Women and Children (Menteri Pemberdayaan Perempuan dan Anak), reverting to the emphasis on reproductive roles. Throughout the New Order, the state gradually restructured the forms of Indonesian women's involvement in the development process to correspond to male organizations and institutions and to coordinate with the broad purposes of national development. We first focus on gender role regimes during the New Order and then consider subsequent developments.

Semigovernmental organizations centrally monitored and organized by the government, such as Dharma Wanita (organization of government officers' wives), Dharma Pertiwi (organization of military wives), and KOWANI (Kongres Wanita Indonesia, or Indonesian Women's Congress), were officially supported and had national recognition. These organizations were dominated by middle-class women. Even the Family Welfare Program (Pembinaan Kesejahteraan Keluarga, or PKK), generally aimed at rural women, was centrally organized by the wives of high-ranking government officers. These organizations had major influence in reproducing and enforcing the ideology of familialism. Their activities were derived from an assumption that women as wives and mothers contribute to nation-building through their unique roles and participation in the development process, primarily through support of their husbands' careers. Women were continuously reminded that their families had to be their primary focus; their participation in public life and civic institutions should not interfere with their roles in the family sphere. At the same time, these organizations provided an avenue for participation in public affairs and experience in bureaucratic roles and practices.[7]

The biggest mass organization for women, sponsored by the government, underscores women's contributions to the national development process through their roles as wives and mothers. The PKK, or state Family Welfare Program, founded especially for women and promoted through a national organizational network encompassing every village in Indonesia, defined women's major tasks in social and economic development in terms of the five roles promulgated by the New Order regime as described in chapter 1: (1) loyal partner and supporter of her husband; (2) caretaker of the household; (3) producer of the nation's future generation; (4) secondary income earner; and (5) Indonesian citizen.

According to this doctrine of women's five roles or responsibilities, *Panca Dharma Wanita*, women are defined by the state to be primarily homebound followers of their husbands' initiatives, with any nonfamily roles of income earner and citizen relegated to secondary status. Item 4, women as secondary income earners, is a relatively recent change to replace a previous version stating that women are the children's primary socializers. The label "secondary earner" doesn't match the reality that many women are in fact the primary income earners, although they maintain the fiction that this is exclusively men's role. Nevertheless, this view continues to be maintained and codified in law, by Articles 31 (3) and 34 (1, 2) of the Indonesian marriage law, which explicitly specifies that women are responsible for caring for the household, while men are officially household heads and breadwinners.

For the Javanese, this ideology is both new and predicated on deep-seated cultural beliefs and practices. On the one hand, it is an adaptation of kodrat ideas that differentiates women's and men's natures and roles. The ideology also mimics views of proper upper-class womanhood held by the *priyayi*, originally the aristocracy but now including all individuals of high status. On the other hand, in both the past and the present, this gender ideology does not reflect the daily lives of most Javanese women and especially poor rural women. They do not have the luxury of leaving productive activities in order to be "good" mothers and wives, even if they should aspire to follow this path.

The power holders, who reside mostly in urban areas and close to the center of the state, have distorted historical traditions to claim cultural grounds for imposing this ideology. The concept of "separate spheres" builds on the cultural belief in complementarity and thus finds strong formal and informal official support. The institutionalization of the ideology implies that being a mother and being a wife are the ultimate destinies (*kodrat*) for women. Women are considered full social and cultural beings only after they have performed these roles. As a consequence, their other roles are perceived as secondary, and women feel obligated to meet these ideal values. The form of familial ideology (Barrett 1980) identified as "housewifization" (Mies, Bennholdt-Thomsen, and von Werlhof 1988) or state ibuism (Suryakusuma 1996), both promotes and circumscribes women's participation in public life and involvement in the development process, and it does so in a manner that is politically advantageous for power holders since it depoliticizes women while utilizing their labor. In policies like the Panca Dharma Wanita, the domestication of women has been institutionalized.

There is divergence between the beliefs promoted by the gender ideology and the everyday lives of women. Although the specific class and status locations women occupy determine how gender relations are manifested, nevertheless, the hegemonic gender ideology is very influential because it presents a view of women's roles that appears to be deeply rooted in culture, religion, and historical experiences, even if many elements are recent reformulations. While we do not assume that women necessarily passively and automatically accept the ideology, the extent to which contradictions are experienced or grievances surface depends on the multiple effects of political, historical, and material conditions that exist at a particular point in time.

Throughout Javanese history, from feudal times to postindependence, a hegemonic gender ideology that both elevates and subordinates women has been reproduced, redefined, and maintained. The dominant ideology embraces and correlates with religious and customary values, so it has received broad "consent" from members of society—Javanese women as well as men. Due to the influence of the hegemonic gender ideology, the contradiction faced by Javanese women is perceived and presented as a unity and a necessity for women and for the society. Even now, with the dissolution of the New Order and the rise of democratic politics and numerous forms of women's activism, views of gender roles and relations remain little changed. New Order gender ideology formed an especially tight and influential grip on public perceptions that lingers long after the end of the regime. Although the post-Reformasi state has relaxed much of the official apparatus the New Order used to inculcate its version of proper gender roles, this belief system remains embedded in the culture and is further reinforced by the growing influence of the Islamic revival with views of proper womanhood that are largely in accord with New Order priorities.[8]

Gender Role Ideology and the Division of Labor in the Family Economy

How does official gender-role ideology match with actual practice in daily life? In our initial field research, we collected extensive quantitative and qualitative information on the gender division of labor in household chores, respondents' primary income-producing activities, and gender role perceptions. We used these data to investigate the commonalities that characterize life in rural Java as well as the differences unearthed by taking a comparative view of gender roles in the two villages. Most previous studies focusing on this issue dealt only with the gender division of labor in household chores and productive activities. They did not take into account how the actual division of labor relates to the beliefs about gender held by women and men. We examine the extent that the dominant gender ideology is embraced by rural Javanese people and whether it differs in the two villages. The rest of this chapter focuses on both gender role perceptions and the actual gender division of labor inside the household and in paid labor for both women and men in the two villages.

GENDER ROLE PERCEPTIONS

To get a more precise measure of how villagers perceive gender roles in the family, we asked respondents whether they agreed with the following eight statements:

1. The husband is the household leader.
2. The husband is the primary income earner in the household.

3. The husband is the primary decision maker in the household.
4. The husband should have a permanent job.
5. The husband is the wisest person in the family.
6. The husband is the person with the highest knowledge in the family.
7. The wife should do most of the household chores in the family.
8. The wife should stay at home more than her husband.

We created an additive scale of gender role perceptions by scoring agreement with each statement as 1, disagreement as 0, and then adding the number of agrees. Scores on the scale of gender role perceptions range from 0 to 8, with higher scores indicating agreement with more "traditional" gender role perceptions that give husbands primacy. We compared the gender role perception scores across the two villages and sexes. We also compared results for those who had different employment status to determine whether they differed in their gender role perceptions.

Table 3.1 provides t-test results of the comparison of gender role perceptions for women and men and the two villages. There is a substantial and significant (p<.01) gender difference. Contrary to expectations, in both villages, men have scores that show less "traditional" gender role perceptions than women. However, there is no significant difference between the villages in gender role perceptions. Men in the more urbanized village in Bantul have slightly less "traditional" gender role perceptions, but the difference is not statistically significant.

TABLE 3.1: Gender Role Perceptions by Gender and Village

	Male		Female
Sleman	5.33	***	6.72
Bantul	4.98	***	6.73
All respondents (both villages combined)	5.15	***	6.72

*** p<.01 (but no difference between the villages)

Thus women have embraced a gender ideology that emphasizes their roles as mothers and as the main household workers, while men are the household leaders, the primary income earners, decision makers, and all around heads of household. Yet this view is often at odds with these villagers' actual lives and daily activities and even seems to be more traditional than the attitudes of their husbands. Furthermore, the existence of various governmental programs to improve women's status in the village in Bantul does not change women's perceptions of gender roles. If anything, it appears to put greater pressure on women to adopt the traditional gender ideology, since these governmental programs are the main channels used to inculcate the official view of gender roles for women.

Panca Dharma Wanita signs could be found in many corners of this village to remind the women of their obligations and responsibilities. During social activities, women were also constantly exhorted about these obligations by their leaders. As the head of the many women's organizations in the more urbanized village in Bantul, Bu Tinah stated: "Women should treat their husbands in accordance to their status as the head or chair of the family. I think kodrat cannot be changed; if we change kodrat, the harmony in the world will be destroyed. Women should not fight to win over men, but we have to give in voluntarily so that we do not lose either."

Bu Tinah describes the contradiction faced by many Javanese women when they have to deal with the hegemonic gender ideology, professing equality and subordination simultaneously. In Bu Tinah's words, "Women should treat their [men/husbands] in accordance with their status. So women should respect men. Even though women have the same rights with men, it doesn't mean that women could challenge men." To save face, women avoid fighting a battle they are almost certain to lose. Instead, they give in "voluntarily" to keep their dignity intact. The word *ngalah*, meaning "to give in voluntarily," instead of *kalah*, meaning "to lose," was used by Bu Tinah and many other women during the interviews to describe their status relative to their husbands'. This is one of the strategies women use to resolve their contradictory positions, one that is very much in keeping with Javanese values of the importance of maintaining harmony and order.

Central to the contradiction is the discrepancy between the importance of women's livelihood activities and the belief that these are part of a constellation of secondary roles. In table 3.2 we compare the gender role perceptions of those with and without paid employment for all respondents and for women only. Table 3.2 shows that there is a significant difference in gender role perceptions between the two groups, both for all respondents and for women only ($p < .05$). Respondents who work at paid employment have lower scores and thus less-traditional gender role perceptions. Although employed women have less-traditional gender role perceptions than women who are not in the labor force ($p < .05$), their scores are more traditional than all nonemployed respondents together; in other words, than scores that include men.

TABLE 3.2: Gender Role Perceptions and Paid Employment Status

	Employed	*Not Employed*
All Respondents	5.80**	6.55**
Women Only (n = 83)	6.54**	7.17**

** $p<.05$

PAID EMPLOYMENT

"Now, women's roles are not only having children, dressing up, and cooking, but also earning money." Bu Mira's sentiments are echoed by many others. The official state view of women's responsibilities outlined in Panca Dharma Wanita explicitly acknowledges women's employment, although it is given secondary status behind family and household responsibilities. Most wives and husbands in the two villages indicate agreement with women's right to employment outside the home, whether or not the husbands or the wives are formally employed. However, they tend to equivocate about how important such employment is and whether it is a woman's responsibility to earn income. Bu Tini expresses very traditional views about women's roles and responsibilities; nevertheless, she is quick to assert the importance of a woman's ability to earn money and support her family:

> Even if I earn more money, I won't disrespect my husband. It's not good to do that; it is our responsibility to serve and respect our husbands because they are our spouses. If we are understanding to others, others will be understanding to us as well. I don't want to talk about others because it is the fasting month, but for example, Pak Yadi's wife, Bu Mimi, her husband is able to earn a lot of money now. She should not just depend on him and ask for money from her husband; if I were her, I would not just stay home and sleep, I would try my best to do something to earn some money.

Most women work to earn money; their income is necessary or important to the household finances, and in a substantial number of cases, they are the primary earners. However, the last situation can create considerable unease and dissonance. Bu Ria is a market trader by day who also runs a *satay* stall at night, working very long hours as the primary income provider in her home. Yet she is not comfortable with her dominant role. While she describes her primacy in the family with great candor, she also maintains a traditional view of men's and women's roles and responsibilities: "A man should earn money to support his family and give the money to his wife so that the wife could manage it to meet the family's need. . . . Her family is her main responsibility; at home she should wash clothes, cook, iron, serve the husband," affirming that she does, in fact, serve her husband, despite his lack of employment. She wistfully describes the ideal family: "A good and prosperous family is the one where the couple work together; both of them earn income to support the family, discuss things together. I wish I had that kind of family but . . . reality is different."

The extent to which both women and men contribute to income through paid employment in each village is demonstrated in the survey. We asked village respondents to identify their primary job (i.e., their most important job as they perceived it). Although rural Javanese frequently have multiple jobs and income-generating strategies, we used the primary job to determine whether a person had significant paid employment. We categorized their responses into five alternatives: (1) does not work in paid employment; (2) works in the trading sector; (3) works in the farming sector; (4) works in the formal sector (primarily government and civil service jobs); or (5) works as a laborer (mostly industrial and construction workers). We compare responses for each category across the two villages and by gender in table 3.3.

TABLE 3.3: Primary Job by Village and Gender

Job Types		MALE (n = 83)		FEMALE (n = 83)	
		Sleman	Bantul	Sleman	Bantul
Does Not	#	—	5	7	17
Work	%		11.4	17.9	38.6
Trade	#	—	8	3	14
	%		18.2	7.7	31.8
Farm	#	15	4	20	1
	%	38.5	9.1	51.3	2.3
Formal	#	16	19	4	10
	%	41.0	43.2	10.3	22.7
Laborer	#	8	8	5	2
	%	20.5	18.2	12.8	4.5
Total		39	44	39	44

The results show that in both villages the majority of women identify a primary job, but that most of the women without a job and all of the men who do not work come from the more urbanized village of Bantul (75.8 percent of all nonworking respondents). In this village, people face difficulties in finding employment that meets their expectations. The trading sector often serves as a safety net when other jobs are not available. Most traders in rural Javanese villages run very small businesses that need only small amounts of capital. More women are involved in this sector since trade is perceived to be more appropriate for women. In Bantul, the trading sector is the most important source of income for women who work. At the same time, more men (eight persons, or 18.2 percent) are now found in this sector, reflecting the lack of job opportunities outside agriculture. In the more rural village in Sleman, no men are involved in trading. In this village, formal and farming sectors are the important sources of income for men. The majority of women work in the farming sector. Fewer people state they "do not work" in this village, and no men will admit to being unemployed. For both women and men, but especially men, agriculture represents a "safety net" or at least a way of saving face to avoid having to be labeled as unemployed.

To see if type of job influenced gender role perceptions, we compared gender role perceptions across job types. Those who work at trade have somewhat more-traditional gender role perceptions than those who work in other sectors (farm, formal, and laborers in manufacturing, construction, and industry). The difference, however, is not statistically significant. Since the majority of women who are not employed or who work in the trade sector are from the more urbanized village in Bantul, these factors explain why women in this village have more-traditional gender role perceptions than women in the rural village in Sleman. During the interviews many women respondents who worked in the trade sector expressed their difficulties in resolving the conflicts between their gender role perceptions and their crucial income-earning activities. In some cases their inability to solve this dilemma almost cost them their marriages. For these women, the pressure from the "official" gender ideology is difficult to resist and to accommodate. They have to reconcile the normative view—that their husbands are the heads of the household and primary decision makers—with the reality of their lives, in which their (the women's) income-generating activities dominate household affairs.

In a few cases there is little difficulty despite the contradiction. Pak Muji from Bantul explains:

> Both of us work and earn money, but my wife has higher income. My wife manages all of the money. It is okay for me to have lower income than my wife; I am not ashamed. It is good for me because my wife has enough income so that I just look for an additional or secondary income. I have never controlled the financial management of the household. I trust my wife; it is up to her to decide. She is the one who decides. I just agree with her. She is the one who has more opinions; I usually agree with hers. *But I am the one who has the power.* Even though my wife has more income, it doesn't make her to have power. (emphasis added)

His wife, Bu Ani, readily agrees: "He is the king and I am the prime minister."

In other outwardly similar cases, the discrepancies between the "ideal" and the "real" are too big to be resolved. Bu Margini, a very active trader from Bantul whose husband works for her as one of her employees, explained her situation as follows:

> I don't know how I feel about my husband. I earn much more money than he does, and he always agrees to whatever I say. He does whatever I want; many people said that he doesn't have any power when he faces me. But I don't feel that I win over him; I still perceive that he is the head of our family. It is difficult to handle this situation, but what should I do?

Her words express her difficulty in resolving contradictory positions. Income and employment are necessary but not sufficient to improve women's status and position or to change hegemonic gender ideology.

Nor does greater urbanity necessarily create a change in gender role perceptions. On the contrary, it can reinforce more-traditional patriarchal gender role perceptions, especially when employment opportunities are scarce for women. This is evident from the lack of differences between the two villages during the initial fieldwork, and it is reinforced by the lack of evidence for any real change with subsequent events—the economic and political crises that ensued in the years immediately following the fieldwork. During the crisis, when finding employment became even more difficult, women may have become even more susceptible to the hegemonic gender ideology.

HOUSEHOLD CHORES

The existence of a dominant gender ideology that defines women primarily as wives and mothers presumes that women perform most of the household chores while men are primary income earners for their families. Women's heavy involvement in productive activities and paid employment does not release them from doing most household chores, nor does it encourage their husbands to be more active in these tasks, regardless of whether either of them has employment or an income-generating role.

Past research illustrates this pattern. In many Javanese rural families, women's work is in the form of unpaid household labor, income-producing employment, and informal exchanges of both productive and reproductive activities. Studies conducted in Yogyakarta and in other parts of Java consistently find that women spend long hours doing both productive and reproductive tasks, while men spend relatively little time on the latter and often not that much more on the former (Sajogyo 1979, 12; 1983, 124; White 1976a, 275; 1984, 24). Cooking, preparing meals, and going to the market or grocery are assumed to be women's work, while men are more likely to be involved in outdoor chores such as taking care of the garden.

These studies also show that women's performance of household chores varies with the types of jobs they hold and their social class and status. Women traders whose work often requires long hours and travel beginning very early in the morning and lasting late into the day are able to spend only minimal time on household chores (Peluso 1984, 37). They often are helped by other female family members, but rarely by their husbands (Kusujiarti 1995, 165). Women who work in unskilled activities, have low education, and come from small landholding families spend less time performing household chores than those who work at skilled activities, have a relatively high education, or come from big landholding families. Several factors explain this occurrence. First, hours spent doing productive activities by unskilled women workers are more numerous, leaving only limited time for performing household chores. Second, the values stressing the importance of housewife and mother roles are more prominent among educated, middle-class women, pressuring them to spend more time on domestic chores (Kusujiarti 1995,175).

To explore the household division of labor in these two villages, we asked both husbands and wives in surveyed households who primarily performs the following twelve tasks: (1) washing clothes; (2) ironing; (3) washing dishes; (4) cooking; (5) preparing and arranging meals; (6) buying daily needs at the market; (7) cleaning the house (inside); (8) cleaning or sweeping the garden or yard; (9) taking care of plants in the garden; (10) buying household utensils and furniture; (11) buying clothes for household members; and (12) taking care of the children.

There were eight possible responses: (1) husband; (2) wife; (3) son; (4) daughter; (5) paid household helpers; (6) together (more than one family member); (7) other family members; or (8) nobody in the household performs the particular task. From this information we can determine who performs which types of household chores in each village and whether there are differences between the two villages.

When asked about household chores, almost everyone agrees that these are primarily women's responsibility, although in interviews many men claim that they are willing and able to help. Table 3.4 shows each chore that we asked about and to whom respondents attribute these tasks. Household chores are clearly divided across gender lines. No husband or son is involved in cooking, food preparation, buying groceries or going to the market, while the wives' participation in these three tasks is very high. In both villages, more than 80 percent of husbands and wives together perceive that the wives perform these three chores. Only one husband (in the more urbanized village of Bantul) washes dishes; otherwise, this task is left to wives. These chores are perceived to be absolutely women's chores; men's involvement in these chores is considered "abnormal" and creates uneasiness. Household chores that involve substantial numbers of husbands (and to some extent sons) include cleaning house, sweeping the garden, and taking care of garden plants. These three chores are assumed to be permissible for men since they are regarded as "outdoor" or physically more demanding chores. Yet table 3.1 shows that even for these tasks, wives still have the highest involvement. In the majority of families, wives perform most of the household chores, although sometimes with the help of other family members. This trend is more pronounced in the more urbanized village, where the category "together" has higher numbers.

We can quantify just how extreme the differences are by averaging the number of chores attributed to each possible household member and also calculating what percentage of all tasks this represents for each village. For example, in Sleman, thirty-six husbands are given credit for doing a total of seven types of household chores. That means on average, husbands perform .46 task, or less than half a task. Similarly, those seven tasks represent 4 percent of all tasks reported by all respondents. Table 3.5 shows these averages for each possible household member who might perform this task in each village. The results show that women in general (both wives and daughters) do many more chores than men (husbands and sons) or other family members, with wives doing far more than anyone else. There is no task that is not performed by a large number of women, including those that are more likely to have some male representation. Daughters are assigned more chores than sons, but neither do very many. Wives report responsibility for an average of just over nine chores in Sleman and somewhat more than seven in Bantul. Even though, on average, they still take responsibility for a

TABLE 3.4: Gender Division of Household Chores by Village
(Chores Performed by Types of Household Members in each Village)

Sleman (n = 78)

Household Chores		Husband	Wife	Son	Daughter	Helper	Together	Family Member	N.A.
Wash Clothes	(#)**	1	56	—	4	5	12	—	—
	%	1.3	71.8		5.1	6.4	15.4		
Iron	(#)	2	47	2	7	4	13	—	3
	%	2.6	60.3	2.6	9.0	5.1	16.7		3.8
Wash Dishes	(#)	—	59	—	7	3	9	—	—
	%		75.6		9.0	3.8	11.5		
Cook	(#)	—	69	—	3	2	4	—	—
	%		88.5		3.8	2.6	5.1		
Food Prep	(#)	—	70	—	4	1	3	—	—
	%		89.7		5.1	1.3	3.8		
Go to Market	(#)	—	65	—	4	—	7	2	—
	%		83.3		5.1		9.0	2.6	
Clean House	(#)**	5	50	—	5	1	15	2	—
	%	6.4	64.1		6.4	1.3	19.2	2.6	
Sweep Garden	(#)**	9	44	2	6	—	15	2	—
	%	11.5	56.4	2.6	7.7		19.2	2.6	
Garden Plants	(#)	14	39	2	3	—	14	3	3
	%	17.9	50.0	2.6	3.8		17.9	3.8	3.8
Buy Clothing	(#)	4	40	—	1	—	33	—	—
	%	5.1	51.3		1.3		42.3		
Buy Utensils	(#)	1	61	—	—	—	—	1	—
	%	1.3	78.2					1.3	
Child Care	(#)	—	31	—	—	1	6	—	39
	%		39.7			1.3	7.7		50

Bantul (n = 88)

Household Chores		Husband	Wife	Son	Daughter	Helper	Together	Family Member	N.A.
Wash Clothes	(#)**	3	44	—	6	3	32	—	—
	%	3.4	50		6.8	3.4	36.4		
Iron	(#)	8	39	—	9	5	24	—	3
	%	9.1	44.3		10.2	5.7	27.3		3.4
Wash Dishes	(#)	1	52	—	9	3	23	—	—
	%	1.1	59.1		10.2	3.4	26.1		
Cook	(#)	—	78	—	2	2	5	1	—
	%		88.6		2.3	2.3	5.7	1.1	
Food Prep	(#)	—	76	—	2	4	6	—	—
	%		86.4		2.3	4.5	6.8		
Go to Market	(#)	—	78	—	1	2	7	—	—
	%		88.6		1.1	2.3	8.0		
Clean House	(#)**	11	31	3	9	4	28	2	1
	%	12.5	35.2	3.4	10.2	4.5	31.8	2.3	1.1
Sweep Garden	(#)**	18	26	3	9	5	24	2	1
	%	20.5	29.5	3.4	10.2	5.7	27.3	2.3	1.1
Garden Plants	(#)	21	27	2	6	4	21	2	5
	%	23.9	30.7	2.3	6.8	4.5	23.9	2.3	5.7
Buy Clothing	(#)	—	48	1	1	—	35	—	2
	%		54.5	1.1	1.1		39.8		2.3
Buy Utensils	(#)	1	55	1	2	1	27	—	1
	%	1.1	62.5	1.1	2.3	1.1	30.7		1.1
Child Care	(#)	2	26	—	—	3	7	—	50
	%	2.3	29.5			3.4	8.0		56.82

% based on each village total

much larger number, wives perform significantly fewer household chores in the more urbanized village in Bantul than in Sleman. Conversely, the husbands do more household chores in Bantul than in the rural village in Sleman. Finally, more families perform household chores together in Bantul than in Sleman.

These results support previously cited studies showing that wives do the majority of household chores. In both villages, the second-highest category is that in which more than one family member does household chores. All the results imply that household chores are still considered the wives' primary responsibility. Men perform these chores only when they have time. This view was confirmed by almost all the respondents in the interviews. Even when women perceive that their husbands help them in doing household chores, in fact, the husbands perform only very small tasks such as turning

TABLE 3.5: Average Numbers and Percents of Household Chores Performed by Types of Household Members in two Javanese Villages

	Sleman (n = 78)	Bantul (n = 88)
Husband (# of chores)	.46	.74
%	4.00*	6.50*
Wife (# of chores)	8.09***	6.59***
%	70.00***	58.30***
Son (# of chores)	.07	.11
%	.70	1.00
Daughter (# of chores)	.56	.63
%	5.00	5.70
Helpers (# of chores)	.22	.42
%	1.80	3.70
Other Family (# of chores)	.14	.08
Members %	1.00	.70
Together (# of chores)	1.87**	2.71**
> 1 Family Member %	16.60**	24.20**

* p<.1, ** p<.05, *** p<.01

on the stove, reheating a meal, making their own glass of tea, or taking out already cooked meals from the cupboard when their wives are not at home.

There is a discrepancy between the rhetoric of responsibility for household chores and the actual performance. Many respondents, both women and men, claim that tasks are divided fairly equally, although both usually admit at some point that it is primarily women's responsibility. Perhaps a more honest picture is provided by Pak Modin when he describes the division of labor in his family:

> There is nothing good for being a wife. She has to cook, wash clothes, clean up, manage the children; all are her responsibilities. She has to go to bed the last but has to wake up the first, and if she does not cook well her husband may get mad at her. So to be honest, and in reality based on my experience having been married for twenty to twenty-two years, it is hard to be a wife.

RELATIONSHIP BETWEEN PAID EMPLOYMENT AND HOUSEHOLD LABOR

Type of job has little impact on the gender division of household labor. We found almost no difference (except for daughters) when we examined the proportion of household chores attributed to each actor controlling for type of job (analysis of variance not shown). Of the respondents who work in the trading sector, daughters are responsible for a higher proportion of household chores. As found in previous research (Peluso 1984, 37; Kusujiarti 1995, 165), the amount of time required in trade jobs results in wives who perform the fewest household chores compared to those who work in other types of jobs. The involvement of paid household helpers is also the highest. These differences were not statistically significant, however, and are not shown.

In table 3.6 we look at the responses of women only to determine if paid employment influences amount of chores and who they say performs them. As expected, women who are employed have a significantly lower proportion of household chores (63.8 percent) than those who are not (73.5 percent); but, in fact, the employed women perform only one less chore on average compared to their nonemployed counterparts. Therefore, even though working women nominally perform fewer chores, the fact that they are engaged in paid labor outside the home does not release them from household labor. They still have to perform the majority of chores, while other family members (husband, son, and daughter) help only minimally.

In the families where the women are employed, the participation of paid helpers in performing household tasks is significantly higher (.53 chore, or 4.4 percent) when compared to the nonworking women (.08 chore or .8 percent). The involvement of other family members (extended family such as mother or aunt) is also significantly higher for employed women (.14 chore, or 1.1 percent) compared to those who are not in the labor force (0 chores). Therefore, employed women reduce involvement in household chores by substituting the labor of paid household helpers or extended family members who are mostly women, while their husbands do not significantly increase their share of household work. In contrast, men's performance of household chores is unchanging regardless of their employment status. The double day and double standard are very much in evidence in these results.

During the in-depth interviews, many working women alluded to this asymmetry. They stated that even though women's work is an obligation (even if formally only as secondary income earners as suggested by the *Panca Dharma Wanita*, five women's responsibilities), they are not released from their obligation to perform the household chores. Bu Tinah, who is very active in social and political activities as well as in the trading sector, asserted:

> Even though women should do all of the five roles as suggested by the Panca Dharma Wanita, it doesn't mean that we can ask our husband[s] to perform household chores as well. It is okay for men to help a little in the chores, but these are not their main

TABLE 3.6: Household Chores Performed by Types of Household Members by Women's Paid Employment Status (Women Only, n = 83)

	Employed (n = 59)	Not Employed (n = 24)
Husband (# of chores)	.49	.45
%	4.30	4.07
Wife (# of chores)	7.31	8.33
%	63.79*	73.45*
Son (# of chores)	.25	.08
%	2.27	.76
Daughter (# of chores)	.96	.42
%	8.64	3.69
Helpers (# of chores)	.53*	.08
%	4.43*	.76
Other Family (# of chores)	.14*	.00*
Members %	1.14*	.00*
Together (# of chores)	1.90	1.80
%	16.94	15.75

* p<.1

responsibilities. Women should have equal positions to men, but we have to separate which roles and responsibilities are appropriate to each gender according to our *kodrat* and *harkat* [nature and destiny as well as dignity].

Bu Tinah is not alone; most of the respondents expressed similar views when they were asked about wives' responsibilities. Regardless of their other activities, household chores are considered women's main responsibility with little obligation to help from husbands or other immediate family members. Internalization of gender ideology stressing women's obligation to perform household chores makes some women feel guilty or ashamed when they see their husbands doing these chores. Bu Idah asserted her feeling about this during the interview: "I don't want my husband to do the household chores. I don't feel right to see my husband doing these chores. It is the wives' destiny to be that way. Society makes fun of husbands who do the household chores."

In these two villages, household chores are very time- and energy-consuming. This was especially true at the time of the initial fieldwork, since electrical equipment and laborsaving devices were rarely available. Even with more extensive electrification in subsequent years, however, household chores remain labor-intensive. This means that women spend most of their time working in both productive and reproductive activities.

Conclusion

Patriarchal gender role ideology is shaped and reinforced by deeply ingrained beliefs and practices institutionalized in the state, religion, family, and cultural traditions. This becomes apparent from the strong adherence to both a highly gendered and inequitable division of labor in household tasks and gender role perceptions held by both women and men, regardless of other work or location. The similarities among different groups outweigh the differences in both the division of labor and beliefs.

On the other hand, there is some evidence of accommodation to changing circumstances. A comparison of respondents from the two villages, one more remotely rural with few active women's programs, the other more urbanized with numerous programs to enhance women's status, demonstrates there are small differences in the actual gender division of labor in performing household chores in the direction of alleviating wives' (if not women's) household tasks. Wives in the more urbanized area report fewer household chores than those in the rural village, while their husbands perform more chores than the husbands in the rural village. Women with paid employment do less than those who are not employed, but this does not mean that their husbands correspondingly increase their household work. The inability of women who have paid employment to do all the household chores is compensated by the higher involvement of paid helpers or members of the extended family, who are mostly women. Daughters' involvement in the house chores is also higher than sons' involvement in these tasks. The results largely support previous research that shows women are mainly responsible for household work, but also provide evidence of change.

For gender role perceptions, however, there is less evidence that differences in material circumstances have an impact on beliefs. There is little difference between the two villages in the respondents' perceptions of their gender roles. In addition to the analyses described here, we also explored multivariate analyses of influences on gender role perceptions, but found that other variables—such as age, age at marriage, education ,and number of children—do not significantly explain differences in the gender role perceptions. The results confirm bivariate findings that only gender (male versus female) has a significant influence on gender role perceptions and the more general conclusion that there is very wide acceptance of the normative view. This may suggest that the hegemonic gender ideology is so internalized that factors such as age and education do not change gender role perceptions. These results suggest that the influence of hegemonic gender ideology is difficult to resist, regardless of circumstances. The women in this study adhere to traditional gender role perceptions. These views are reinforced by state policies, government programs, and social activities as well as through the force of history and culture.

One curious finding that on the surface seems contradictory is the slightly less rigidly traditional views expressed by men. Although purely speculative, this may reflect the greater effort made to reach women with official policy views through state-sponsored programs. Men have not been not the targets of the same state effort to reinforce gender role ideology that the *Panca Dharma Wanita* (women's five principles) represents or that the various government programs for women provide. It also suggests that the amount of effort used to shore up patriarchal ideology reflects the underlying contradictions in women's status and perhaps even ongoing, if subtle, resistance on their part. It is noteworthy that these beliefs persist long after the fall of the New Order. Interviews with village women suggest little change in explicitly articulated views of gender roles.

We also found that job type does not significantly influence the gender division of labor in household chores or gender role perceptions. Women's employment status, however, has more meaningful effects for these two issues. Besides performing fewer household chores, women with paid employment also have less-traditional gender role perceptions. Despite the fact that to some extent paid employment makes women better off, economic position per se is not able to resolve their problematic position. Without a change in official gender ideology, it may even create a greater dilemma for women since it reinforces the contradictions in their daily lives.

The contradictions in the literature reflect the paradoxes of real life for these Javanese women. The resources they control, the autonomy they experience, and the esteem they command in some realms are undermined by institutions that reinforce patriarchal practices and beliefs at the same time that social change makes them harder to maintain. Men remain goats; women doves. Moreover, the contradictory components of traditional beliefs became more explicitly and uniformly expressed by the New Order government's systematic efforts to promulgate this view of women's roles. One of the most noteworthy occurrences in the interviews was the speed and uniformity with which respondents would refer to the Panca Dharma Wanita when asked about appropriate gender roles, regardless of what else they said, suggesting the effectiveness of government propaganda.

The legacy of these practices remains even after the fall of the New Order. Amid new talk of gender empowerment and mainstreaming in official circles, and as the differences between the two villages diminish with the construction of new roads and development, villagers reaffirm the views they first expressed in the early fieldwork. Thus, as areas that once were relatively remote are drawn more and more into the urban centers and as more efforts are made to intervene with development programs and modernization efforts, it may be that women's space to negotiate gender roles becomes even more circumscribed. On the other hand, it may be that new opportunities to contest traditional authority will arise from these changes.

Chapter 4

GENDER AND AGRICULTURAL PRODUCTION[1]

Most of the women here work as farmers, only a few of them are involved in trading. If you come here during the planting season, you will hardly find any woman at home; most of the women work on the farm.
　　　　　　　　　　　　　　—Bu Andi in Sleman

I went to the farm before going to work, so I do it routinely early in the morning. I wake up at 4:00 a.m. then go to the farm and go home at 6:00 a.m., then I work in the city. In the evening, I get back from work in the city at 4:00 p.m. and then I take care of the chickens and cows, so if we suddenly need a lot of money we can sell the cows.
　　　　　　　　　　　　　　—Pak Sudi in Bantul

THE TWO VILLAGES are part of a rural economy, deeply embedded in agricultural production. However, in addition to the differences between the two villages already noted—remoteness, proximity to urban centers, state-sponsored development programs, and so on—they differ substantially in the degree to which agriculture represents the primary livelihood for their residents. The village in Sleman is much more dependent on agriculture, and some form of farm production is a mainstay of most household economies. The village in Bantul, located close to two large urban centers, has a more diverse economy, and many residents find other ways to earn a living, a trend that increases as urban development creeps farther and farther into the countryside. Nevertheless, agriculture remains an important component of its economy and of the livelihood practices of many of its residents. Virtually all households in both villages engage in complex versions of income packaging, combining multiple jobs across multiple members, including the women in the family, with some form of agricultural practice often making up part of the mix.

Javanese gender relations are further dissected in this chapter by examining how households allocate agricultural labor in the two villages and how this has changed over time. To illustrate village differences, we describe village agricultural practices and profile a "typical" family from each village and the changes they have experienced over the duration of the study. While each household is unique, and no one family or household can fully represent all village families, the descriptions of the daily lives of a representative family from each village and the changes they have experienced provide a picture of life and livelihoods in Sleman and Bantul. These descriptions also clearly capture the differences between the two villages and the lives of their inhabitants. Finally, they illustrate the types of accommodations between gender roles and economic roles made by households in each village and provide further insight into how women and men negotiate their gender roles, including the contradictions in their practice.

Village Economy

Land ownership is important in both villages for status and livelihoods, although with few exceptions, holdings are very small. Both women and men inherit and hold title to land, with inheritances often either equally divided between siblings regardless of gender or allocated according to parents' views of fairness and secular inheritance laws rather than by religious prescription. Respondents in both villages were aware that these inheritance practices conflicted with Islamic law, but this didn't outweigh secular or sentimental reasons. Pak Zulkar in Bantul stated: "It is true that based on Islamic law men get two portions and women get one portion (*segendong sepikulan*). But the government has a different rule: It stipulates that women have the same rights to inherit so they should get the same portion of inheritance. The Islamic law was the old regulation, but now it [has] changed."

A woman who inherits land from her parents is seen as having an especially legitimate right to hold the title in her own name. Women are counseled to retain personal title to their property as insurance against a marriage that doesn't last.

Views are more mixed about property acquired after marriage, with a minority asserting that landholding is a male prerogative. Generally, however, both daughters and sons are valued, although often for different reasons, and sometimes this results in different forms of inheritance. According to Bu Mahmud in Sleman,

> It is better to give both sons and daughter[s] the same amount of inheritance, but according to the Islamic law, the son gets twice as much as the daughter [*segendong sepikulan*]. I think a daughter will take care of their parents' property better than a son, so it is better to give the daughter the same size of inheritance as the son. Most of the people here want their daughter to stay at this village [home] and encourage the son to go out because they want the daughter to take care of their property when they are old or dead.

In fact, fairness and the need to keep harmony and avoid family conflict frequently were alluded to as important reasons for equal division.

Land is just one component of the rural economy, and both women and men are active in diverse livelihood practices that frequently combine agricultural production with other income sources. At one time, the highest involvement of women in economic production occurred among the rural Javanese, with 60 percent of women reporting income-earning activity (Hugo, T. Hull, V. Hull, and Jones 1987, 252), primarily in the agricultural sector. Labor force participation has declined for both women and men, but most notably in rural areas for women, especially after *krismon*, the Asian economic crisis (Asian Development Bank 2006, 10–12). In the special province of Yogyakarta, at the time of the initial field research, 43 percent of women and 41 percent of men in the labor force worked in the farming sector, making it the leading economic sector (BPS 1995, 37). By 2002 the figures had decreased slightly to 41.3 percent and 37.5 percent (Asian Development Bank 2006, 92). In chapter 3 we saw that among the villagers in this study, 51.3 percent of women and 38.5 percent of men in Sleman identified agriculture as their primary job, compared to only 2.3 percent of women and 9.1 percent of men in Bantul, clearly delineating the large differences in village economies and notable for the reversal in gender roles in agriculture across the two villages.

In addition to their primary occupations, the jobs respondents perceive to be most important, we also asked them to identify their secondary jobs. Using the same five categories discussed in chapter 3: farming sector, trading sector, formal sector (mostly government jobs), laborer (mostly industrial and construction workers), and none (does not work), table 4.1 describes the primary and secondary jobs reported by the couples in the study by village and by gender. The most common primary occupational category for both villages combined is formal employment (typically government jobs; 29.5 percent), followed by farmwork (24.1 percent). However, another 38.6 percent of villagers report farming as a secondary job. Combined, almost two-thirds of residents report some form of agriculture as one of their jobs. The figure would be higher if all forms of agricultural labor were included.

Both village and gender differences are evident and obvious. Agriculture is the occupational category with the largest number

Table 4.1: Primary (1st) and Secondary (2nd) Job by Village and Husband/Wife+

1st Job	Total	%	Sleman*	%	Bantul	%	Husband*	%	Wife	%
Farm	40	24.1	35	44.9	5	5.7	19	22.9	21	25.3
Trade	25	15.1	3	3.8	22	25.0	8	9.6	17	20.5
Formal	49	29.5	20	25.6	29	33.0	35	42.2	14	16.9
Labor	23	13.9	13	16.7	10	11.4	16	19.3	7	8.4
None	29	17.5	7	9.0	22	25.0	5	6.0	24	28.9
Total	166	100.0	78	100.0	88	100.0	83	100.0	83	100.0
2nd Job										
Farm	64	38.6	48	61.5	16	18.2	40	48.2	24	28.9
Trade	13	7.8	4	5.1	9	10.2	8	9.6	5	6.0
Formal	1	1.0	0	0	1	1.1	0	0	1	1.2
Labor	5	3.0	0	0	5	5.7	1	1.2	4	4.8
None	83	50.0	26	33.3	57	64.8	34	41.0	49	59.0
Total	166	100.0	78	100.0	78	100.0	83	100.0	83	100.0

* p ≤ .001

+ numbers may not add to 100% due to rounding error

of workers in the more rural village located in Sleman, in stark contrast to the more urban village in Bantul, where far fewer residents identify this as either a primary or a secondary job. Gender differences are also obvious. Wives are more likely to report farming as a primary job; husbands are more likely to report it as a secondary job. Many more residents of rural Sleman and more men report having both primary and secondary jobs, regardless of sector. These differences are elaborated by examining how agriculture combines with other employment in each village, beginning in 1995–1996.

DESA DANAU IN SLEMAN

As described in chapter 2, more than two-thirds of this land is used for agricultural production with soil that is especially fertile because of its proximity to the volcano Merapi. Village records are inconsistent and contradictory,[2] but there is little doubt that agriculture remains the primary occupational sector, employing more than two-thirds of villagers with occupations. It also provides the central organizing principle for village life, determining daily schedules and community values as well as livelihoods.

Small landowners predominate, but their holdings are very small, averaging twenty-five hundred square meters or one-fourth hectare of land or less, an amount that cannot supply adequate yield or income for most families. Only one household has more than two hectares of land. The farmers in this village usually independently choose the varieties and types of plants to be cultivated. Farmers' groups are not very active and have little influence. In addition to rice, dry-season crops include vegetables and fruits such as eggplant, watermelon, green beans, corn, peanuts, and soybeans. Apart from farming, other jobs are found in trade, services, and handcrafts, but even here there is often a link to agricultural production. Commodities such as rice, tobacco, and vegetables dominate trade. The handicrafts sector consists primarily of plaited-mat production, in which women are the major producers.

Bu and Pak Yitno typify village agricultural practices as they existed in the mid-1990s and as they persist now. This couple has five children, who ranged in age from twelve to thirty-five years when we first interviewed them. At that time, they all lived in the same household, including a recently married son and his pregnant wife. Agriculture was their main source of income, and every member of the family played an active role in agricultural production. They augmented their own landholdings with rented plots. Each year they planted rice twice and other crops once. At the time of the initial interview, they had a successful and lucrative watermelon harvest, a crop freely selected by this family for its profitability at that time. Other years they planted tobacco and raised chickens.

Pak Yitno was in charge of preparing and cultivating land with assistance from his sons and sometimes hired male neighbors. He delegated pesticide application to his sons. In rice cultivation, his wife took charge of planting, harvesting, weeding, drying out paddies, getting the rice hulled, and marketing the product. Her daughter and daughter-in-law assisted. For planting and harvesting, she usually hired a group of eight to ten women neighbors who worked together on most plots of land in this settlement. They used the traditional *bawon* system of hiring local and family laborers paid in kind to harvest rice, typically receiving a kilogram of rice for every ten harvested. Hired labor was not usually employed in nonrice cultivation, and gender divisions in task allocation were less distinct, although they followed the same general pattern. There was high involvement of all household members, especially when large amounts of land were cultivated. In this household, as is the case throughout the village, differences in tasks were allocated to husband and wife, with daughters and other women family members assisting wives, and sons or men assisting husbands.

Pak Yitno was the most powerful figure in the family. He made the majority of important decisions both in the household and in agricultural activities. He decided what crops to cultivate, and he controlled the earnings, especially from nonrice cultivation. Because she marketed rice, Bu Yitno had greater direct access to rice income, whereas her husband controlled nonrice marketing. He gave his wife an allowance for daily household maintenance.

The household relied on agricultural production to provide basic needs. They consumed some of their crop, especially rice, as well as garden produce and livestock. In the past both husband and wife had other economic activities: Pak Yitno drove a minibus (from Yogyakarta to Semarang), and Bu Yitno had a stall selling chicken feed and supplies, but agriculture was always the backbone of their household economy, a pattern typical of this village.

Twelve years later, the composition of the household had changed as its members matured, and in some cases established their own households, but the general pattern held. Three of the grown children still lived in the same home as their parents—including a disabled daughter and a pregnant daughter, who was married to a policeman who commuted to his job in a neighboring district. Two sons lived close by, one across the road in his own home with his wife and two children and another in the same village. These two sons and one of the wives worked in agriculture. The youngest son had not yet married, although by 2010 he, too, had married and established his own household. After completing training in Japan, he had obtained a lucrative job as a production supervisor in a factory in Semarang. Semarang is too far for daily commuting, but he returned to the family home most weeks on his three days off. He had the opportunity to work in Jakarta, but sought out the Semarang position in order to be closer to the family.

Little has changed in production processes in the years that we have followed this family. They still use the bawon system of hiring agricultural labor, plant the same crops, and maintain the same gender division of labor in the household and in the fields. Pak Yitno complains of rising prices of inputs without corresponding increases for his yield, corruption in administration of subsidy programs, and the difficulties in finding farmworkers for planting and harvesting; but in his view, "Things stay the same; always have to work hard." The biggest change is that some of the children of this successful farmer have moved outside agriculture to find jobs in the new economy.

Tanah Kaya in Bantul

This village covers a much larger area, but has less land devoted to agriculture (less than 60 percent). Farmers' groups are more active in this village than in Sleman; most farming activities are coordinated in these groups. People also plant more homogeneous varieties and types of plants.

According to official village statistics, a much smaller but still substantial number of residents with primary work were either land cultivators or farm laborers. In the mid-1990s this group represented approximately 40 percent of those with reported occupations; by the mid-2000s their number had fallen to 23.5 percent, substantially more than reported in our sample. Unlike Sleman, agricultural labor was not highly valued. It was seen as demanding work, to be avoided if possible by persons with higher education and middle-class aspirations, and especially by women. The account by Pak Dayat, although not typical, is also not remarkable: "I've never worked at the rice field even though I have a rice field; I don't have time to do it. Some of my rice field is rented out as an orchid garden and some other is cultivated by my brother." It was a point of pride for another resident, Pak Mul, to assert, "My wife has never helped on the farm," a statement contradicted by his wife, Bu Arti, when she described her work on the dry-season bean crop. However, she reinforced his underlying meaning when she reported, "My husband doesn't allow me to work in the rice field."

Factory and construction work were important sources of employment, often requiring travel to one of the cities. There were many more types of employment pursued by residents of this village, but somewhat paradoxically, less than half the population reported a primary occupation. According to informants, it was more difficult for men to find nonagricultural employment than for women, because women have a variety of opportunities to obtain credit to start their own enterprises, usually some sort of trade, whereas men mostly seek waged labor.

Bu Ani and Pak Muji are a representative family in Bantul. The Mujis[3] have two daughters; one was in junior high school and one in senior high school when we first met them. They had multiple sources of income to cover the high costs of schooling and living. Pak Muji previously worked as a mason, then drove a *becak* (pedicab) as well as farmed; while Bu Ani ran a stall from their home that carried food items, soap, toothpaste, and other daily needs as well as cooked food and snacks that she prepared. She began her very long day by rising at 3:00 a.m. to prepare the items for sale.

At 5:30 a.m. she would ride in her husband's becak to the market to buy goods for the stall. The stall opened at 6:00 a.m. and stayed open a minimum of twelve hours, often longer as neighbors came by to make late purchases and to socialize. Pak Muji began his day driving his wife to market and then driving the becak in the cities until returning home around 3:00 p.m. During busy farming periods, he drove less and worked more in the fields.

The stall provided the main and most dependable source of income, and Bu Ani perceived herself as the primary income earner and decision maker. Her daughters sometimes assisted her in the stall, but their primary responsibility was their education. Mother and daughters had little involvement in agricultural activities, although Bu Ani sometimes helped with dry-season crops. With help from his father-in-law, Pak Muji farmed a tiny inherited plot of land that could not provide enough income to meet family needs. They hired labor for planting and used the *tebasan* system for harvesting, therefore selling the entire crop prior to harvest. In the tebasan system, farmers sell rice while it still stands in the field to intermediary traders. The traders supply their own permanent group of *penebas*, or harvesting laborers, reducing farmers' freedom to choose their own workers. They also had less general control over agricultural production. The local farmers' group determined what type of crops to plant and organized fertilizer and pesticide use.

Trade conducted by the wife was the primary source of income; farming and driving were at best supplemental sources, but to a large extent, farming was subsidized by other income sources. Pak Muji freely acknowledged that his wife's income financed his farming. Twelve years later, this was even more the case. Although Pak Muji no longer drove the becak, he still worked in the field and assisted his wife's marketing, typically by motorcycle and by helping to care for ducks, goats, and, up until recently, chickens,[4] whose eggs and meat were used in his wife's stand.

This vending business has become even more successful over the years, and Bu Ani struggles to manage a higher volume of meal and snack preparation as demand increases. She has taken advantage of microfinance loans to boost the business. She also gets both labor and financial help from her daughters. Both daughters have grown up, completed their educations, married, and have what are considered good jobs, one in a retail shop in the city and the other as a bookkeeper in a nearby prep school. Nevertheless, they still regularly assist their mother by helping her prepare food and snacks, tending the stand, and especially by using their automobiles to access larger markets where produce is cheaper. Bu Ani expects that they and their families will eventually move back to the village, one to her recently renovated house and one to an adjoining house.

Even though many people remain nominally active in agriculture in Bantul, increasing consumerism and monetization, even before the crisis, have made it necessary to have other income sources. The inroads of urbanism, capitalism, modernization, and globalization, combined with the very tiny plots of land inherited by most residents, have made agriculture less viable and less desirable as a livelihood source. For many residents, such as the Mujis, agricultural work is subsidized by work in other sectors. These trends have accelerated in recent years, but some form of participation in agricultural production remains a way of life for many.

Agriculture and the Gender Division of Labor

These profiled families indicate the importance of agriculture in the livelihood practices of families in each village and the differences in labor allocation between them. They also reflect much larger processes of change unfolding in agricultural production and the rural economy that in turn reach down to influence household livelihood practices. Macrolevel shifts in the structure of the economy are played out in intrahousehold processes of labor allocation and decision making.

It is not always obvious, however, how this occurs. In this chapter we look more closely at how the participation of husband and wife in agricultural labor is related to decision making within households in the two villages. We begin with a historical overview of the changes in Javanese agricultural production that have impacted the gender division of labor and then examine the ways agricultural practices are experienced within households in the two villages. The interviews, surveys, and field observations conducted in 1995 and 1996, supplemented by follow-up interviews and observations in 2002, 2004, 2005, 2007, and 2010, provide the data to examine the extent of participation in agriculture in each village and how agricultural activities and decision making are divided between husbands and wives who work in that sector. The results indicate how village differences are reflected in intrahousehold allocation of agricultural labor and the consequences for wives' and husbands' roles in agricultural production.

Change in the Gender Division of Agricultural Labor

Studies of women in agriculture in developing countries find that in regions and cultures where women are active in agricultural production, the development process has detrimental effects on women's status, roles, and participation. In particular, colonial and capitalist domination, new technologies, new labor and production processes, and modernization and economic development programs "masculinize" the production process, depriving women of their traditional roles and status. Ester Boserup (1970) specified three ideal types of agricultural societies in her groundbreaking studies of women and development: female systems, male systems, and mixed male and female systems. In each of these systems, introduction of new technologies and differential access to training and knowledge elevate the status and power of men at the expense of women (Boserup 1970, 57). In the "mixed system" typical of

Indonesia, for example, even though men and women initially work together, the increasing use of new techniques controlled by men marginalizes women and even pushes them out of the agricultural sector altogether. Although subsequent analysts have criticized Boserup's overreliance on technology and modernization frameworks to explain these developments (Beneria and Sen 1981), and outcomes vary over time and place, there is little disagreement that the cumulative effect of both internally and externally generated change is an increasingly marginalized position for women in agriculture in developing countries (Sachs 1996).

Indonesian Agriculture. The mixed male-female system is typically found under conditions of intensified agricultural production of irrigated land, where population pressures result in highly labor-intensive land-cultivation practices on very small plots. Small landholdings require immense inputs of family labor to supply basic necessities. Men and women often share tasks, resulting in relatively equal status and power in agricultural production (Boserup 1970, 35). Indonesia, particularly densely populated Java, exemplifies this system, historically giving women a significant role in agricultural production compared to women in regions with other farming systems (Williams 1990, 14).

Rice is the primary crop in the labor-intensive agricultural sector in Java. Tasks in rice cultivation are traditionally divided along gender lines (Berninghausen and Kerstan 1992, 81; Schiller 1978, 30; Stoler 1977, 75; White 1976b, 302). Field preparation and other preplanting tasks are predominantly men's activities. These include preparation of the seedbed, plowing, hoeing, harrowing, growing the seedling, uprooting and replanting it, maintaining the water supply or irrigation system, and applying fertilizer and pesticides. Major tasks for women are planting and harvesting. Other tasks such as weeding, repelling birds and animal pests, and marketing are more flexible and variably conducted by both women and men depending on tradition and place, but in Yogyakarta, these tasks are generally performed by women (Suratiyah, Hariadi, Sudibia, and Sudarta 1991, 69–78).

Even when women don't engage in physical labor, they may play a significant role in running the farm, but there is little consensus on the relationship between gender and decision-making power in the agricultural sector in Java. In an early study conducted during late 1950s, Hildred Geertz (1961, 123) found that Javanese women had substantial power in decisions regarding marketing of the agricultural product, payment of hired labor, and distribution of rice shares for the harvesting labor. Men were more influential in the areas of land use rights and choice of plant varieties to be cultivated, but even here they usually consulted their wives. Three decades later, research with a similar design found that in a more rural village, women dominated in only a few areas, including making decisions on the method of marketing, hiring of paid labor, and investing capital, while men prevailed in all other decisions. In a more urbanized village, there was more mutual decision making between husbands and wives (Sajogyo 1983, 225–26).

New Production Processes. In the 1970s, the New Order government, as part of its general development policy, inaugurated a massive "Green Revolution" in rice cultivation that introduced new rice varieties, new technologies, and a reorganization of the rice production process. The government provided subsidies for fertilizers, pesticides, new rice varieties, irrigation, and agricultural credit. Intensified capitalist relations of production replaced traditional familial or patron-client relations (Wolf 1992, 47). These changes came with a political price of increased state control over villages and farmers' lives extending far beyond agriculture. The government dictated crop varieties, fertilizers, pesticides, and farming methods and simultaneously used the opportunity to extend its control through surveillance of daily life and political activities.

Changes promoted by Green Revolution development policies also influenced the gender division of labor in agricultural production. These included both laborsaving technologies and new production processes. Thus the substitution of the sickle for the traditional *ani-ani* (a single-bladed razor used to cut individual rice stalks) to harvest the new short varieties of rice and the widespread use of the rice-hulling machine reduced the demand for women's labor and shifted task allocation between women and men, Similarly, a push to substitute a system of middleman-controlled contract labor for family labor and the adoption of the coordinated production processes termed the *Insus* affected both gendered labor and decision making.

The switch from the ani-ani to the sickle exemplifies the complex connections between technology and the social relations of agricultural production. Sickle use reduces labor up to 60 percent and reduces costs up to 50 percent (Collier 1980,145). Sickle harvest also stimulated the widespread use of a tebasan system, displacing the traditional bawon system of local and family labor paid in kind. In the tebasan system, farmers sell rice while it still stands in the field to intermediary traders. The traders supply their own permanent group of *penebas*, or harvesting laborers, reducing farmers' freedom to choose their own workers.

There is disagreement about the overall impact of these changes. Some observers argue that where the tebasan system was implemented, there was widespread replacement of women with male labor (Huesken 1984, 10). Others dispute this finding and point out that even in the tebasan system, women still are the majority of workers (Berninghausen and Kerstan 1992, 84; Sajogyo 1983, 142). Either way, there was a reduction in the demand for labor that affected women's employment opportunities. Harvesting traditionally was a very important source of income for women, especially for women from poor families (Stoler 1977, 81), and change that reduces demand for their labor has a substantial impact on their economic status and power, in both the household and the society.

The rice-hulling machine also has deprived women of employment opportunities (Berninghausen and Kerstan 1992, 86; Collier, Colter, Sinarhadi, and Shaw 1974, 108; Schiller 1978, 119; Wolf 1992, 49). The machine usually is operated by men, replacing the traditional rice pounding done by women. In a five-year span from the late 1960s to the mid-1970s, the use of women as hired labor in Java to hand-pound rice went from 90 percent of rice production to 50 percent (Schiller 1978, 119). Within the next twenty years, virtually all rice was hulled by machine.

In an effort to increase agricultural production, the New Order government pressured local landowners to implement the Insus, or Special Intensification, which emphasized organization of farmers' groups to cooperate and coordinate crop selection, procurement of fertilizer and pesticide, planting, cultivating, harvesting, and marketing. Insus enforced a uniform production process, and in doing so created problems for both farmers and hired laborers. Farm laborers found it difficult to obtain farmwork outside the scheduled activities; farmers had problems finding labor during busy seasons since all the farmers had to schedule the same activities at the same time (Suratiyah, Hariadi, Sudibia, and Sudarta 1991, 2). This was especially true during the harvesting season, forcing farmers to recruit scarce labor from outside the village or even the region.

This system transferred the agricultural decision-making process from individual family farmers to state organized farmers' groups, almost always reserved for men. By inserting another layer of decision making between the government and the household, Insus reduced the participation of landowners' wives in production, particularly in planting and harvesting, and obscured their participation in decision making. It also decreased the number of opportunities for women from small landowner families to find farming jobs on other people's farms, since they had to expend most of their efforts on their own land, actively supervising farmworkers to ensure that work was performed correctly and on time (Suratiyah, Hariadi, Sudibia, and Sudarta 1991, 67).

Insus was not universally or uniformly adopted. In our study, the village in Bantul was much more heavily affected. After the fall of the New Order, and especially as decentralization was implemented with consequent diminishment of centralized forms of agricultural assistance and intervention, Insus declined or disappeared in many areas where it had formerly prevailed.[5] However, local farmers' groups still exist in many of these areas, and they still coordinate production processes. In Bantul, for example, a few notable examples of women's farmers' groups can be found, but they focus on food processing rather than agricultural production. In general, farmers' groups are sex-segregated, men-only groups, with the same implications for women's knowledge and participation as Insus.

Impact on the Gender Division of Labor. There is general agreement that Green Revolution developments resulted in a declining role for women in agricultural production. Research conducted in the 1970s and 1980s following its implementation documents that more women left the agricultural sector than men (Berninghausen and Kerstan 1992, 84; Collier, Colter, Sinarhadi, and Shaw 1974; Oey 1985, 39; Schiller 1978, 123). Yet both national and regional data show that women have remained the slight majority of farmworkers. It may be that the earlier trend of declining female participation reached its peak but has subsequently stabilized. The initial effects of new technology led to more women than men leaving the agricultural sector, often involuntarily but also by choice, especially where other opportunities for women in manufacturing and service industries expanded and appeared more attractive. Nevertheless, it is difficult to imagine Javanese agriculture without women's involvement in planting and harvesting. Even when women do not directly engage in physical labor, they frequently oversee and manage the process. Furthermore, rural Javanese women generally develop multiple income strategies, often retaining some involvement in the agricultural sector even if the majority of their time is allocated to other work. Finally, agricultural work provides something like a safety net when other jobs disappear for women and men alike (Booth 2000; World Bank 1999). Both national studies of the impact of the krismon and reports from residents of these villages describe the influx of former residents seeking agricultural work after losing their jobs in other sectors.

The Gender Division of Agricultural Labor
and Decision Making in Sleman and Bantul

The history of Javanese gender division of labor in agriculture demonstrates that women's power in labor and decision making varies over time with technology, production process, type of crop, and degree of urban development. It can also be inferred from previous studies that women have more power in decisions related to their traditional roles and activities such as planting and harvesting. We further explore the relationship between women's actual involvement in the agricultural activities and their roles in the decision-making process by investigating two central problems in Sleman and Bantul:

1. **Wife-husband participation and division of labor:** What is the wife-husband division of labor in rural Javanese villages in the agricultural sector? How does the participation of wife and husband vary by task and crop (rice and nonrice cultivation) in each village? Are differences in the forms of economic development and degree of rurality between the two villages reflected in differences in the types of agricultural activities wives and husbands perform?

2. **Wife-husband decision making:** What roles do wives and husbands play in agricultural decision-making processes, and do these differ in the two villages?

Village and gender differences in employment patterns that were described in table 4.1 are reinforced when examining gender differences within each village as shown in table 4.2. In Sleman, farm labor makes up the majority of wives' work, whether first or second job, confirming the observation made by a village newcomer that the place to find women is in the fields. For the husbands' first job, farm labor is a close second behind formal sector work; more than two-thirds report it as a second job.

   This contrasts sharply with research results in Bantul, the more urbanized village, where wives' involvement in the farm sector is minimal. This sector is considered particularly unsuitable for women but less so for their husbands. Thus, as exemplified by the Muji family, some husbands keep working in the agricultural sector while their wives find work and income elsewhere. In Bantul, this is often in the trading sector. Trading is perceived as more suitable and lucrative for women, since it provides more access to urban lifestyles, information, knowledge, and financial resources. Wives who work in the urban market attain higher social and

Table 4.2: Primary (1st) and Secondary (2nd) Job Controlling for Village and Husband/Wife+

| | Sleman | | | | Bantul | | | |
| | Wife** | | Husband | | Wife** | | Husband | |
Job	1st Job*	2nd Job	1st Job*	2nd Job	1st Job*	2nd Job	1st Job*	2nd Job
Farm	20	21	15	27	1	4	4	13
%	51.3	53.8	38.5	69.2	2.3	6.8	9.1	29.5
Trade	3	1	0	3	14	4	8	5
%	7.7	2.6	0	7.7	31.8	9.1	18.2	11.4
Formal	4	0	16	0	10	1	19	0
%	10.3	0	41.0	0	22.7	2.3	43.2	0
Labor	5	0	8	0	2	4	8	1
%	12.8	0	20.5	0	4.5	9.1	18.2	2.3
None	7	17	0	9	17	32	5	25
%	17.9	43.6	0	23.1	38.6	72.7	11.4	56.8
Total	39	39	39	39	44	44	44	44
%	100	100	100	100	100	100	100	100

* $p \leq .001$ for gender differences in primary jobs by village

** $p \leq .001$ for village differences in jobs by gender

+ numbers may not add to 100% due to rounding error

economic status. There are fewer alternatives to the farm sector for their husbands, however. It is more difficult for men to enter trade, since it is traditionally women's domain. Many of the men find their way into construction jobs as masons, carpenters, brick-layers, and so on, but these jobs are unstable, depending heavily on economic cycles and capital investment. The lack of alternatives and a general assumption that men must provide for their families' needs force some husbands, as a point of pride or as a last resort, to work in the farm sector.

The pattern is clear: As farming becomes less important in the village economy, as in Bantul, wives are more likely than their husbands to withdraw from agricultural production to follow other pursuits. However, not all agricultural work is pursued or identified as an occupation. In keeping with the multiple liveli-hood strategies employed by many rural households, some level of agricultural activity is common for household members with other livelihood sources. Some villagers, especially those in Ban-tul, overlook their labor in this sector even as they describe work they perform. As many as 58 percent of the villagers in Bantul who participated in this study reported involvement in agricultural tasks, a much larger proportion than reported this as a job. Even in Sleman, where agriculture is much more commonly identified as a primary or secondary occupation, participation in agricultural tasks exceeded the figures for other types of work.

AGRICULTURAL ACTIVITIES: WIFE-HUSBAND DIVISION OF LABOR

Respondents were asked about their performance of a series of tasks in agricultural production, looking at rice and other crops separately. Only households that reported participating in these tasks are included in the analysis. For both rice and nonrice cul-tivation, we asked who primarily performs eleven main tasks: (1) field preparation; (2) field cultivation; (3) planting; (4) replanting damaged plants; (5) weeding; (6) harvesting; (7) maintaining and observing irrigation; (8) repelling pests and scaring away unwanted animals; (9) applying fertilizer; (10) applying pesticides; and (11) marketing the crop. Responses are grouped into four categories: (1) husband; (2) wife; (3) paid labor; and (4) other family members. In the survey, it was also possible to indicate son(s) or daughter(s). However, very few respondents selected these categories, and we combined the few cases into the category "other family members," with the numbers of sons or daughters indicated in parentheses. The results provide information on who is engaged in both rice and nonrice farming processes and allows comparisons of the wife-husband division of responsibility for each task across the two villages.

Table 4.3 displays the division of labor for rice cultivation tasks in each village. We find a gender division of labor that is similar to the traditional pattern identified in previous studies: No wife is involved in field preparation or cultivation and tilling. Included in these activities are plowing, hoeing, preparing the seedbeds, and harrowing the field. There is less husband involvement in these activities in the more urbanized village of Bantul than in Sleman, partly because of lower overall involvement of the people from this village in the agricultural sector. Other activities that are considered more appropriate for men are managing irrigation and applying pesticides and fertilizer. Our data show that for both villages, these tasks are conducted mainly by the husbands. Few women perform these tasks in either village.

The use of paid labor for farmwork is almost uniformly higher in Bantul, with the exception of field cultivation. The involvement of other family members is also higher, especially in the three male tasks of irrigation, pesticide application, and fertilizer application in this more urbanized village. Farmers generally avoid using paid laborers for these tasks since they are perceived to be less physically demanding. Yet those who are in the more urbanized village are under pressure to perform these three activities in a timely manner. The agreements made in the farmers' group require specific

Table 4.3: Rice Cultivation Tasks by Who Is Responsible and Village

Tasks:		Sleman (N = 58)				Bantul (N = 51)			
		Husband	Wife	Paid Labor	Other Family	Husband	Wife	Paid Labor	Other Family
Field prep	*	38	C	18	2 (1)+	22	C	25	4 (1)+
	%	65.5		31.0	3.4	43.1		49.0	7.8
Field cultivation		22		34	2 (1)+	16		31	4 (2)+
	%	37.9	C	58.6	3.4	31.4	C	60.8	7.8
Irrigation	**	49	1	5	3	31	1	7	12
	%	84.5	1.7	8.6	5.2	60.8	2.0	13.7	23.5
Pesticides	***	47	1	5	5 (2)+	28	2	8	13
	%	81.0	1.7	8.6	8.6	54.9	3.9	15.7	25.5
Fertilizer	*	44	3	5	6	29	3	6	13
	%	75.9	5.2	8.6	10.3	56.9	5.9	11.8	25.5
Pest control	***	19	22	4	13 (1)+	20	4	8	19
	%	32.8	37.9	6.9	22.4	39.2	7.8	15.7	37.3
Planting	*	3	10	39	6	6	2	39	4 (1)+
	%	5.2	17.2	67.2	10.3	11.8	3.9	76.5	7.8
Replanting	***	17	20	7	14	21	3	12	15
	%	29.3	34.5	12.1	24.1	41.2	5.9	3.5	29.4
Weeding	***	18	22	6	12	18	5	11	17
	%	31.0	37.9	10.3	20.7	35.3	9.8	21.6	33.3
Harvesting	**	1	13	42	2	1	2	45	3
	%	1.7	22.4	72.4	3.4	2.0	3.9	88.2	5.9
Marketing	***(++)	12	34	3	2	4	19	12	1
	%	20.7	58.6	5.2	3.4	7.8	37.3	23.5	2.0

Differences between villages are significant at: * p # .1; ** p # .05; *** p # .01

+ Indicates cases where sons perform this task, with number of cases in parentheses.

++ Discrepancy in total number for marketing is because some households do not sell what they grow

timing. To meet these obligations and to save production costs, family members are recruited to assist in these activities.

Planting and harvesting are considered to be female jobs, and few husbands are involved in these tasks in either village. The husbands generally prepare the seedling for planting but delegate the actual planting process to paid labor. These activities are very labor-intensive and time-consuming, so most farmers need to use paid labor. There is relatively little difference between the two villages in the use of paid labor for these two activities. The wives' involvement in these presumed women's jobs, however, is minimal in the more urbanized village. Only two persons (3.9 percent) in Bantul indicated that wives perform these tasks, while in Sleman ten (17.2 percent) and thirteen persons (22.4 percent) state that the wives perform these two tasks (planting and harvesting). In the more rural village, replanting damaged plants, weeding, and repelling pests are mostly tasks for wives, even though husbands also participate in these activities. However, for the more urbanized village of Bantul, only a few wives are involved in these activities. The situation is quite different for their husbands, however. There is little difference in husbands' involvement in these activities between the two villages. The involvement of paid laborers and other family members is higher for all three activities in the more urbanized village. Therefore, it seems that the minimal involvement of the wives in these activities in the more urbanized village is compensated by the higher involvement of paid labor and other family members. For marketing the rice, the involvement of both husbands and wives is higher in Sleman, the rural village. In Bantul, more farmers sell their rice in the field (mostly using the tebasan system) or consume the rice in their own families.

Table 4.4 compares the division of labor across the two villages for nonrice cultivation. Similar to rice cultivation, there is no wife involved in field preparation, cultivation, or tilling. In general, husbands' involvement in the urban village of Bantul is less than in the rural village of Sleman. The use of paid labor and other family members does not differ in the two villages. For managing irrigation and applying fertilizers and pesticides, as predicted, the husbands' involvement is the highest for both villages compared to other actors. In the rural village of Sleman, no wife is involved in managing irrigation and applying pesticides, and only five respondents (8.3 percent) report that wives are involved in the application of fertilizer. In the more urbanized village, there are wives involved in these three activities, but the numbers are small. The use of paid labor differs little across the two villages for these three activities. The involvement of other family members

Table 4.4: Nonrice Cultivation Tasks by Who Is Responsible and Village

Tasks:		Sleman (N = 60)				Bantul (N = 44)			
		Husband	Wife	Paid Labor	Other Family	Husband	Wife	Paid Labor	Other Family
Field prep	***	34	C	22	4	19	C	23	2
	%	56.7		36.7	6.7	43.2		52.3	4.5
Field cultivation	***	22		32	5	15		26	3 (1)+
	%	38.3	C	53.3	8.3	34.1	C	59.1	6.8
Irrigation	***	42	C	9	9	24	1	7	12
	%	70.0		15.0	15.0	54.5	2.3	15.9	27.3
Pesticides	***	46	C	7	7 (1)+	23	1	8	12
	%	76.7		11.7	11.7	52.3	2.3	18.2	27.3
Fertilizer	***	38	5	7	10	22	2	8	12
	%	63.3	8.3	11.7	16.7	50.0	4.5	18.2	27.3
Pest control	***	17	17	7	19	14	2	9	19
	%	28.3	28.3	11.7	31.7	31.8	4.5	20.5	43.2
Planting	***	8	6	23	23	9		33	2
	%	13.3	10.0	38.3	38.3	20.5	C	75.0	4.5
Replant	***	12	20	8	20	15	2	13	14
	%	20.0	33.3	13.3	33.3	34.1	4.5	29.5	31.8
Weed	***	10	20	7	23	12	2	13	17
	%	16.7	33.3	11.7	38.3	27.3	4.5	29.5	38.6
Harvest	***	3	12	29	16 (1)+	4	1	34	5
	%	5.0	20.0	48.3	26.7	9.1	2.3	77.3	11.4
Market	***(++)	10	30	7	4 (1)+	4	23	13	1
	%	16.7	50.0	11.7	6.7	9.1	52.3	29.5	2.3

Differences between villages are significant at: * p < .1; ** p < .05; *** p # .01
+ Indicates cases where sons perform this task, with number of cases in parentheses.
++ Discrepancy in total number for marketing is because some households do not sell what they grow.

is slightly higher in the more urbanized village of Bantul. We conclude that these three activities are performed mainly by the husbands, with help from paid labor and other family members for both villages.

Unlike rice cultivation, wives' involvement in planting and harvesting of other crops is minimal, especially in the more urbanized village. In Bantul these two activities are primarily performed by paid laborers, while in Sleman, a combination of paid labor and other family members do most of the work. For replanting damaged plants, weeding, and repelling pests, wives have substantially higher involvement in the more rural village. Husbands and paid laborers do more of this work in the more urbanized village. The degree of involvement of other family members in replanting and weeding does not differ much across the two villages. The only activity with similarly high involvement of wives in both villages is marketing (50 percent in Sleman and 52.3 percent in Bantul). The husbands do much less marketing (16.7 percent in Sleman and 9.1 percent in Bantul). In Bantul, more respondents report that they sell their agricultural product directly from the field; traders commonly come to the fields just before the plants ripen and buy the crop prior to harvest.

These results indicate that the wives' involvement in agricultural tasks other than marketing for both rice and nonrice cultivation is much lower in the urbanized village. This is especially pronounced in nonrice cultivation. Husbands' involvement in these activities is also lower in Bantul, but the village difference is not as great as for their wives. Wives' participation in traditional women's agricultural tasks is more prominent in the more rural village of Sleman. In this village, the wives report substantial participation in weeding, replanting damaged plants, and repelling animal pests, for both rice and nonrice crops. In the more urbanized village, however, the wives' involvement in these three activities is minimal, but husbands have higher involvement in both rice and nonrice cultivation. In general, the use of paid labor is higher in the more urbanized village in both types of cultivation. The participation of other family members is also slightly higher for some activities in the more urbanized village.

All Agricultural Tasks. A more comprehensive picture of the household division of labor in agriculture is obtained by looking at participation in all agricultural tasks combined. To compare involvement of each category of actor (husband, wife, paid labor, and other family members) in all agricultural tasks for the two villages, we have created summary measures of agricultural activity. We sum all agricultural tasks in both rice and nonrice cultivation to create a measure of total agricultural activity for households in each village and for each category of labor. The total number of tasks performed by each category of labor in each village is divided by the total number of agricultural tasks to determine proportionate wife-husband and other types of labor participation in agriculture in each village. Table 4.5 shows results of t-tests used to compare village and gender/household differences in total activity.

Table 4.5: Mean Number and Percentage of Agricultural Tasks by Who Is Responsible and Village

	Sleman			*Bantul*			*Total*	
	$\bar{X}$ # of Tasks	Maximum #	$\bar{X}$ % of Tasks	$\bar{X}$ # of Tasks	Maximum #	$\bar{X}$ % of Tasks	$\bar{X}$ # of Tasks	$\bar{X}$ % of Tasks
Husband	6.9**	20	38.4	4.4	26	36.8	5.5	37.7
Standard Deviation	5.4			5.5			6.1	
Wife	4.1***	14	21.7***	1.0	14	8.6	2.5	15.7
Standard Deviation	4.7			2.4			4.0	
Hired Labor	4.1	20	24.6*	4.2	20	35.0	4.1	29.4
Standard Deviation	4.6			5.7			5.2	
Other Family	2.6	16	15.3	2.3	20	19.6	2.5	17.2
Standard Deviation	3.8			4.4			4.1	

Differences between villags significant at: * p < .05; ** p < .01; *** p < .001

The t-test results show that there is no significant difference between the two villages in the percentage of husbands' involvement in agricultural tasks. In both villages the husbands are involved in almost the same proportion of activities in the agricultural sector. The percentage of all agricultural activities performed by husbands in the rural village of Sleman is 38.4 percent compared to 36.8 percent in Bantul. There is a very significant difference, however, between the two villages in the degree of the wives' involvement in agricultural tasks. The percentage of all agricultural activities done by wives in the rural village is 21.7 percent, while in the urban village of Bantul the wives perform only 8.6 percent of agricultural tasks. There are also significant differences in the use of hired labor in the two villages. The proportion of agricultural tasks conducted by hired labor for these households is higher (35.0 percent) in the more urban village than in the rural village (24.6 percent). Yet there is no significant village difference in the degree of the involvement of other family members in agricultural tasks. In the rural village of Sleman, other family members are involved in 15.3 percent of the overall agricultural tasks, while in Bantul the number is 19.6 percent.

Agricultural Decision Making. The previous results show that wives' actual participation in agricultural tasks is very limited in the more urban village of Bantul. In this section we examine whether this also means that the wives have a smaller role in agricultural decision making. In table 4.6 we compare wives' and husbands' roles in decision making in four areas: who should be hired as paid labor; how many paid laborers should be used; how to market the agricultural product; and how to spend the money for buying agricultural means of production (e.g., spending for fertilizers, pesticides, seeds, equipment). Respondents were given the choices of wife alone, wife dominant, both together, husband dominant, husband alone, and others. We compare results for the two villages to determine whether they differ in the amount of influence wives and husbands report in the decision-making process.

Table 4.6: Wives' and Husbands Roles in Agricultural Decision Making in Two Villages*

Decision: Who decides:	Sleman (N = 62)				Bantul (N = 51)			
	Who To Hire	Number To Hire	Market	Spend	Who to Hire	Number To Hire	Market	Spend
Wife Alone	4	4	15	1	8	9	21	8
%	6.5	6.4	24.2	1.6	15.7	17.6	41.2	15.7
Wife Dominant	1	2	5	1	4	2	8	2
%	1.6	3.2	8.1	1.6	7.8	3.9	15.7	3.9
Husband-Wife Together	9	9	16	9	11	9	9	9
%	14.5	14.5	25.8	14.5	21.6	17.6	17.6	17.6
Husband Dominant	19	21	16	22	3	2	2	3
%	30.6	33.9	25.8	35.5	5.9	3.5	3.9	5.9
Husband Alone	29	26	9	29	20	24	7	23
%	46.8	41.9	14.5	46.8	39.2	47.1	13.7	45.1
Other	0	0	0	0	5	5	4	6
%	0	0	0	0	9.8	9.8	7.8	11.8

*All village differences significant at p ≤ .001

Our results show that in agricultural decision-making, wives are more active in Bantul, and husbands are more active in Sleman. Larger percentages of wives either decide alone or dominate the decision making when it is done together in the more urban village. The reverse is generally true in Sleman, the more rural village, where respondents attribute greater influence to men. Rates of combined husband-wife involvement are also higher in Bantul, except in marketing. This is because this area is more definitively identified as the wives' province in this village, whereas in Sleman, although wives appear to have greater influence on these decisions than any of the other decision areas, they still are less likely to be as influential as their husbands.

It should also be noted that there may be discrepancies between husbands and wives in the accounts of agricultural involvement as demonstrated by the full text of Pak Mul's and Bu Arti's description of her labor. Pak Mul from Bantul states: "My wife has never helped in the farm, she just helps in selling the harvest. It is she who determines the price and negotiates with the trader; it is all up to her. I don't want to interfere with this matter."

His wife, Bu Arti, on the other hand, paints a more complicated picture: "In the dry season we usually plant beans; I sometimes help in the field when we plant the beans. I helped in drying the beans in the field. We usually ask our neighbors to help us in doing the bean cultivation. We have never planted any other plant. I decide how many people should be hired and how much we should pay for the labor. Because my husband doesn't know how much we should pay for the workers."

She then goes on to confirm her husband's assertion: "My husband doesn't allow me to work in the rice field."

Our data suggest that although women are not the major decision makers in either village, they are more likely to participate in decisions in the urban village and to be the dominant influence. In other words, the minimal involvement of wives in the physical labor of the agricultural sector in Bantul is not matched with an equally minimal influence in agricultural decision making. Even though the women in this village have much lower levels of actual labor in agricultural tasks, they exert more influence on the process of agricultural production. This also means that the introduction of new technology or production processes, such as Insus (which was partly implemented in the urban village in Bantul), is not necessarily associated with lower levels of decision making concerning agricultural tasks.

Post Krismon. In 1997, the Asian financial crisis threatened the Indonesian economy, reversing decades of economic growth that had reduced poverty rates and improved living standards for many segments of the population. For the next two years, there was a real decrease in GDP, sharp fluctuations and declines in the value of the rupiah, and massive increases in prices and the cost of living, especially the price of food. With food making up 57 percent of rural household budgets on average, the increase in prices and decline in incomes created serious hardship (Strauss et al. 2004, 1–5). However, effects of the crisis were highly uneven across the country and for different population groups. Many rural areas escaped relatively lightly and some food producers and regions profited as prices for their commodities rose. Although the official poverty rate in rural Yogyakarta increased by two points between 1997 and 2000, from 12.6 percent to 14.6 percent, this rate was initially lower than other rural areas and regions and remained so while the recovery gained ground (Strauss et al. 2004, 30–34).

Households in rural areas served as refuges for urban migrants who lost their jobs or who no longer could afford the soaring costs of urban living. Informants in Sleman and Bantul interviewed in the years following the crisis allude to this phenomenon, and there were many discussions of the effectiveness (or its lack) of government programs to alleviate hardship for the poorest. Distribution of government-subsidized rice, or *raskin*, targeted for the poorest was frequently political, subject to charges of corruption, and often openly distributed broadly to include more-affluent families "to preserve social harmony." By 2004, however, when we conducted extensive follow-up interviews with participants from the initial study, there was a general air of prosperity in both villages, major improvements in infrastructure, and clear evidence of material comfort in many participant households.

Nevertheless, informants in both villages complained about high prices, rising costs of agricultural inputs, the vagaries of the market for different crops, and the need to work harder to maintain the same standard of living. As one Bantul resident stated: "People work harder for the same income; they have more money, but the cost of living rises, too." Another claimed that in the past, daily labor could cover family needs, but now a week's wages cover only three days of living expenses. The owner of a catfish pond in Bantul complained that he could no longer afford to hire labor and had to do all the work himself. In Sleman, one informant was nostalgic for the New Order era, saying the economic situation was better then because Suharto paid more attention to farmers and provided agricultural subsidies; now it's necessary "to become more creative to earn money."

In spite of these problems and complaints, most respondents appeared to be doing reasonably well, and some had clearly prospered. In both villages, children had grown and had advanced their educations, found jobs, and started families. In a few cases they had returned to work on family land and enterprises. Older members shifted jobs, retired, and in some cases passed away. Dry-season crops changed, depending on prices, markets, and crop diseases. Households still used diverse strategies to piece together livelihoods. One informant from Sleman went so far as to assert that krismon had little impact because people have diversified income strategies and agriculture was not affected adversely.

Although some differences between the two villages had diminished, the basic distinction between a primarily agricultural economy and a much more urbanized mixed rural economy was unchanged. Agricultural pursuits continued to be the focus for residents of Sleman; in Bantul it was peripheral. As a sign of the times, a new housing development had appeared in former farm fields of Bantul, and a number of large, upscale houses dotted the landscape in fields near the main road, further signifying the encroachment of urban development. In Sleman, the big changes were paved roads, electrification, and the near universal adoption of tractors for land preparation, the latter having little impact on the gender division of labor but significantly impacting how men's work got done.

In Sleman, informants were very focused on the changes in the agricultural economy. They discussed the advantages and problems of "agribusiness" crops—watermelon, chili, eggplant, tobacco, and some animal husbandry— more profitable but also more expensive and risky, increasing the gap between wealthier and poorer farmers in an increasingly globalized sector of the economy. The gender division of labor remained much the same, although informants stressed the need for flexibility as family circumstances changed. Anecdotally, it appeared that more women also were involved in nonfarm labor, such as working in a local Japanese-owned eggplant-processing factory as the need for income increased. The children of original study respondents, especially those who had acquired more education and training, often worked outside the agricultural sector. In this regard the Yitno family is instructive. While some of the children, especially older sons, were active farmers, younger children found jobs in the manufacturing and service sectors, sometimes spending periods of time as labor migrants, sometimes at significant cost to the older generation to give their children these opportunities.

In Bantul, far fewer people worked in the agriculture sector initially, and their children have even less interest in this sector. Finding farm labor also increases in difficulty, with recruitment extending far outside the village to seek workers from poor mountainous regions. The traditional markets where local farmers bring their crops to traders such as Bu Muji are declining, causing great concern among local officials. Among some households such as the Mujis, farming is subsidized by other livelihoods rather than vice versa, a reversal of a pattern identified by earlier research in Java (Wolf 1992).

Conclusion

Variations in the structure and opportunities of the rural economy have an impact on the intrahousehold division of labor. Wives and husbands play different roles in agriculture in the two villages. In the more urban village, the involvement of wives in the farming sector is very limited, while more of their husbands continue to be active in this sector for both financial and cultural reasons. Women in the more rural village maintain high levels of participation, as do men. Similarly, the two villages differ in how agricultural tasks are allocated. The "traditional" wife-husband division of labor in agricultural tasks is much more closely adhered to in the rural village. There is an indication that husbands in the urban village are involved in the tasks previously assumed to be women's, such as weeding, repelling pests, and replanting damaged plants. In the more urban village, most wives do not identify agricultural work as either their primary or secondary job, nor do they report much involvement in any agricultural task.

However, the picture is also more complex, since other sources of labor beyond wives and husbands are employed in agricultural production, and village differences are evident in these practices. In general, the participation of paid labor is higher in the more urbanized village, for both rice and nonrice cultivation. More households use paid labor to perform agricultural tasks in the urban village, and they are usually employed in planting and harvesting, tasks that are traditionally conducted by wives. The participation of other family members is also slightly higher in some activities in the more urbanized village. What is not known definitively is the gender division for these other categories of labor. These data do not permit us to examine the gender of paid labor and other family members directly to determine whether a shift to male labor is part of the shift to paid and other family labor. However, our field observations suggest that family and hired labor tend to follow the traditional gender roles for specific tasks when a husband or a wife is directly involved. On the other hand, when tasks have shifted to husbands, if hired labor or other family labor is also employed, these also will follow the new gender lines, so that men work with men.

Further research is required to determine whether the decline of the wives' involvement in the farming sector is also accompanied by a general decrease in women's paid labor in this sector. The use of the tebasan system for harvesting suggests the involvement of more male labor, and, in fact, mixed groups of men and women harvesters can be observed in the fields, where previously they would be segregated by sex and primarily women. Similarly, women can be observed yielding sickles just like the men. The increasing short-age of agricultural labor described by our respondents may lead to a breakdown of the rigid gender division of labor, but the exact composition of the penebas groups remains speculative in the absence of additional data.

Of special interest, our research suggests that lack of involvement in the actual practice of agricultural does not necessarily mean lack of involvement in agricultural decision making. Women may not physically work in farming, but they still have considerable influence over the agricultural production process. This occurs in the urban village, where women are more likely to be identified as dominant or influential in decisions about farm production, and follows the Javanese tradition of women's vigorous participation in economic activities.

In general, there is decreasing involvement in the farm sector in the more urban village compared to the active participation of women in Sleman. These contrasting results are clearly expressed again and again in statements made during interviews in each village. In Sleman, one woman describes how work in the fields blends seamlessly with other social relations:

> Nobody stays idle at home here. I am a new person here, have just moved here to follow my husband; sometimes I am bored at home and would like to see and talk with others. When I come to my neighbors' home nobody is there, then I come to the field, there I find many people working so that I join them in the field to talk and work. . . . So the social environment encourages me to go to the field and work as well as to be able to socialize with the people here.

In Bantul, however, a very different picture emerges. Many women stated some variant of "I am too busy to work on the farm," or that "women's main responsibilities are taking care of the chores inside the home." Similarly, a male farmer stated, "It is okay for women to work in the farm, but it is not really appropriate because the work is physically demanding." Perhaps the most forceful expression of the growing attitude that farmwork is demeaning for women was stated by one woman: "Young women are ashamed to work in the agricultural sector now. Only old women want to work [there]."

Our observations and interviews indicate that the trend in the urban village is for both women and men to leave the agricultural sector when they are able to find other jobs. The younger generation, especially those with junior and senior high school educations, expresses its unwillingness to work in the farm sector. This could lead to a shortage of farm labor, a concern expressed by a number of people during the interviews both pre- and postcrisis. On the other hand, during the economic crisis it was extremely difficult to find jobs, especially for those with limited education. The farm sector provided a safety net during times of hardship, whether the result of individual hard luck or the more widely experienced outcome of economic crisis.

The patterns revealed in this chapter go to the heart of the original contradiction experienced by Javanese women. They are expected to be major players in the household economy, traditionally in the agricultural sector, increasingly in other occupations. Even when the women don't identify a job, they still have substantial responsibility in this realm; yet they rarely receive full acknowledgment for the work they do. They, along with other members of their households, often minimize the importance of their roles, or in extreme cases, such as that of Bu Ani and Pak Muji, acknowledge the discrepancy in earnings and effort, but still maintain the appearance of male authority. The trends that result in fewer women in agriculture do little to lessen the contradiction, perhaps exacerbating it by making it more difficult to reconcile the difference.

Chapter 5

INVOLUNTARY VOLUNTARY SERVICE

Gender and Social Welfare in Crisis and Reform

It is good if a woman is active in the society. However, she should not neglect her tasks in her family.

—Pak Roto, Bantul

INDONESIA'S NEW ORDER government initiated community-based social welfare programs that were designed to mobilize support for the government's domestic policies and agenda while minimizing the cost to the state. Women were the primary targets of these programs, and although their participation was formally voluntary, in fact, their time, labor, energy, and other resources were conscripted for these programs. After the Asian economic crisis and subsequent political reform, the association of these programs with the repressive New Order initially led to their decline amid implementation of other forms of welfare provision. Ten years after the crisis, however, New Order programs experienced a revival, but with modified emphases and gender politics. This chapter analyzes gendered social welfare activities and programs before and after the demise of the New Order government, illustrating with examples from the two rural Javanese villages.

We explore how official gender ideology serves the state and determines the parameters of women's power and authority in the family and in the larger community.

Crisis and Its Aftermath

In 1997, more than thirty years of economic growth were abruptly reversed when *krismon*, or Indonesia's version of the Asian economic crisis, hit the country. Although the underlying causes stemmed from a combination of factors that started long before Indonesia fell victim to the Asian economic crisis, the immediate financial crisis was coupled with severe El Niño–induced drought and the lowest international oil prices in decades. The ensuing sharp reduction in the production of food staples, particularly rice, and a major decline of export revenue, led to rapidly declining living standards and political and social unrest (Bappenas 1999; Feridhanusetyawan 1998; World Bank 1999). There were major increases in poverty, unemployment, hunger, and malnutrition. Before the crisis in 1996, the official figure for the population under poverty was 11 percent, or 22.5 million people (Oey-Gardiner 1998, 80). An estimate shows that in 1997–1998, the crisis led to an additional 60 to 70 million (30 percent of the population) living under the poverty line in Indonesia.

The crisis led to labor displacement and a sharp increase in the unemployment rate. Those who were employed had to work longer hours to compensate for their rapidly declining purchasing power, and many households had to mobilize all their resources of labor and capital to survive (World Bank 1999, 9). The gap between the rich and the poor became more pronounced, social jealousy was rampant, ethnic and religious conflicts multiplied, and the control of the central government was weakened, so that by the spring of 1998, the New Order government of Suharto, which had held power for more than three decades, was toppled.

Pushed by international agencies, an emergency social safety-net program was launched to help the poor and to reduce social and political unrest. The main elements of the program were to provide staple food at affordable prices for the poor, create employment and income maintenance for needy families, and ensure provision of basic social services such as health care and education. The enhanced new social safety-net programs were designed to incorporate the involvement of civil society and local communities into their implementation and monitoring stages.

This form of state welfare provision was a new undertaking in Indonesia. Like most other developing countries, the Indonesian state under the New Order government did not directly provide state welfare payment programs for the unemployed, retired, elderly, children, or other groups targeted by safety-net programs. Retirement benefits, unemployment, or disability compensation was not available for the majority of people. There were limited social welfare assistance programs, but these were accessible to only a tiny minority of disadvantaged groups. Social welfare provision relied on the services of extended families, neighborhood associations, and community networks.

Nevertheless, it would be a mistake to interpret the lack of a formal welfare state to mean that the state had no involvement in its provision. Despite the minimal availability of state-directed welfare provision programs, the New Order government intervened to create and reinforce forms of community-based social welfare activities and networks that appeared on the surface to mobilize voluntary labor and services but, in fact, were rigidly and centrally implemented and enforced (Ministry of Social Affairs 1984, 1986; Roestam 1993). These programs and networks were initiated and controlled by the government, hierarchically using bureaucratic lines of authority that emanated from the central government bureaucracy down to village-level officials. They were designed to stimulate people's participation in creating and maintaining their own familial and social welfare services and networks within local communities, but under the state's supervision. Most social services took this form.

Women were particular targets of these programs, and the combination of a centralized state bureaucracy; a widely promulgated national system of symbols, norms, and values; and a well-articulated gender ideology were used to create an "involuntary voluntary" social welfare provision system situated in local communities and dependent on women's labor. We focus on the operation in the two villages of the most prominent of welfare programs, the PKK, or Family Welfare Program, to illustrate how these elements were combined to mobilize women's labor in creating social services and how they varied in their impacts and effectiveness. We use this account of precrisis welfare provision to provide a foundation for considering post–New Order developments. Finally, we consider the theoretical implications of these results as they apply to conventional distinctions between public and private spheres and gender roles and relations.

The New Order State

To support the primary goal of creating economic development, the Indonesian New Order regime under past president General Suharto built a strong, centralized bureaucracy. The regime created powerful bureaucratic channels leading from the central government down through the village level, controlling popular initiatives and the flow of resources to implement its policies and enforce its power (Bulkin 1983; Santoso 1993). In this system, power and participation in national decision making were concentrated in the highest echelons of the state bureaucracy, especially among trained specialists or technocrats and high-ranking military officers (Jackson 1978, 3). These elite bureaucrats were not responsive to the general population. Their promotion and fortune depended on their close associations with central power, especially the president and his cronies. In this system, most "public servants" did not serve the public but served their superiors.

This highly bureaucratized authoritarian regime was created in response to political instability under the previous Sukarno regime (1945–1965), in which numerous political parties and popular movements existed. To launch its new economic development programs and promote growth, the New Order demanded political stability. It established stability by minimizing the roles of the political parties and mass organizations, on the one hand, and creating a strong state bureaucracy, on the other, through a coalition of the military, the state bureaucracy, and capitalist elites. The coalition took root both in the central government and in the regional and local bureaucracies and administrative jurisdictions. Most national policies were designed by these elite groups to reflect their values and interests. Regional officials and elites implemented central policies.

Social welfare policies were designed in this political environment. Using its bureaucratic channels and apparatus, the state had concentrated power and control over the design and the implementation of the programs that directly affected local people. The Department of Social Affairs took the lead in designing and implementing national welfare policies, and it was responsible for establishing, supervising, and maintaining the welfare programs to implement policy. Its work was reinforced by other departments, especially the Department of Internal Affairs, acting in its capacity to oversee and administer all governmental activities and agencies both at the central and at the regional levels. In practice, this department had the greatest power and resources for administering policies that directly affected local populations.

The state used its authority to encourage existing local and traditional communal groups to organize and conduct a variety of social welfare activities. Local communities were responsible only for implementing and following the instructions of government officials. Real grassroots-level involvement was minimal, often absent entirely. Administering its policies through the existing communal institutions and relations not only gave the state more legitimacy and support for its policies, but also created the appearance of welfare services and functions with minimal state investment (J.

Sullivan 1992, 1). The state built its bureaucratic lines along existing Javanese communal institutions and relations and then used these channels to institutionalize and reinforce its policies. Thus the state reshaped and re-created communal institutions to its own purposes.

Indigenous Values and Social Welfare Activities

The seond component of New Order welfare policy involved the appropriation of deeply entrenched cultural norms and values[1] to create a form of gendered social capital (O'Neill and Gidengil 2006) that could be harnessed by the state for political and economic purposes. From its inception, the New Order Government co-opted traditional values such as mutual cooperation (*gotong royong*), discussion leading to consensus (*musyawarah*), sense of family togetherness (*kekeluargaan*), and harmony (*rukun*) to encourage popular support for government programs (Ministry of Social Affairs 1986, 5). Although these values appear to be indigenous and traditional, past studies suggest that, in fact, they were given new political meaning and legitimation by the New Order regime to create support for government programs (J. Sullivan 1992, 1). The state became the major interpreter and hegemonic agent for socializing values, while other interpretations were discounted. The government avoided being seen as a coercive agent while enhancing its power and interests through externally imposed programs by positioning itself as the defender of basic family and community values.

Using the ideology of *gotong royong*, or mutual cooperation between the members of the society, coupled with the familialism described in previous chapters, the state created a milieu in which every adult member of the society was responsible for supporting various state social welfare activities. The state pressured every citizen to support these programs by institutionalizing the idea that a nation-state is a family headed by the president, the symbolic father of the nation. The father/head of state has the most power over the nation and its citizens and, not coincidentally, all the rights and privileges that a patriarchal system confers.

The New Order regime mobilized not only "indigenous" values but also existing communal networks and organizations. Traditionally, communities had their own practices for providing social services for their members. For example, many communities had long-standing organized saving-and-loan groups and rotating credit associations to provide their members with easy access to cash and credit, especially for those with financial problems, and to provide alternative financial institutions. Other communal efforts are mutual self-help groups, or *gotong royong*, to provide service exchanges for those who are in need. These types of communal organizations are commonly found in many other societies that lack a formal safety net. The New Order state of Indonesia appropriated and in some cases revitalized these types of existing local communal organizations as the foundation for its policies in administering state social welfare activities.

Mobilization of indigenous values and existing local communal groups created popular support for social welfare programs, but one additional element was necessary to create a viable system. In particular, women were viewed as an underutilized resource for development efforts and thus became a major target of state interest (Ministry of Social Affairs 1984, 59). The New Order government's policies on women were based on a set of assumptions about women's natural and desirable roles and status that became the basis of a gender ideology that lay at the heart of its social welfare policies and its policies for women.

Gender Ideology, Bureaucratic Power, and Women's Social Welfare Activities

Social welfare activities for women were designed and administered centrally through government bureaucratic resources to incorporate the state's gender ideology. The New Order policies concerning women assumed that women's primary roles were those of mother and wife, and all government policies reinforced this view (Suryakusuma 1991, 73). As described in chapter 1, the state was organized on the patriarchal principle that the state is one big family headed by the father figure of the president; women were perceived to be the mother of the state (Suryakusuma 1991, 71). The promulgation of a gender ideology of state ibuism drafted women's participation in national economic development programs (Suryakusuma 1996). State ibuism teaches that being a mother and a wife is the ultimate destiny (*kodrat*) for women, and other roles are secondary. Women were exhorted to follow their *Panca Dharma Wanita* (a woman's five responsibilities). This ideology discourages women from full involvement in civic affairs, but is advantageous for power holders, by mobilizing women within a highly circumscribed and repressive range of activity.

The implications of this ideology are seen in the development of social welfare policy. The underlying assumption of these programs was that social welfare is the responsibility of each family and community. Women became the main targets for the state's social welfare efforts based on the widespread belief that they are the principal actors responsible for creating and sustaining the welfare of families and communities. Family welfare is perceived to be part of women's domestic roles and their social and cultural obligation is perceived to be to maintain social harmony. By endorsing and elaborating a gender ideology that allocates these roles to women, the state legitimized its efforts to recruit and mobilize women's labor and resources for its social welfare programs.

Thus women became both the recipients and the agents for community-based social welfare services in organizations such as the PKK (Pembinaan Kesejahteraan Keluarga, or Family Welfare Program); the UPGK (Usaha Peningkatan Gizi Keluarga, or Family Nutrition Improvement Program); BKB (Bina Keluarga Balita, a program for families with children under five years of age); P2WKSS (Program to Improve Women's Roles in Healthy and

Prosperous Families); family planning; saving-and-loan groups; and *arisans*, or rotating credit associations. The gendered characteristics of these activities put most of the responsibility for service provision into women's hands without significant compensation for their time or labor. Building on the assumption that women are mostly responsible for the welfare of their families and community, the state utilized its power to mobilize women's resources, making them responsible for providing social services for the family as well as the community under the state's direction and supervision. As a consequence, women were blamed when the system failed to enhance the lives of their families and communities.

THE PKK EXAMPLE

In different guises, PKK (the Family Welfare Program) was the single most important institution in Indonesian rural areas for implementing state social welfare programs by and for women. It provides the prime example of how the New Order regime designed social welfare activities that incorporated gender ideology to reinforce its power and redefine the roles of women to promote the regime's interests. By institutionalizing PKK, the state used women and their resources to provide welfare services.[2]

PKK actually predates the New Order. The first version originated in 1957 during a seminar on home economics in Bogor and then was institutionalized in the national educational curriculum as Pendidikan Kesejahteraan Keluarga (Family Welfare Education) during the 1960s. The emphasis was on institutionalizing goals to be achieved by families through educational institutions, including community educational programs (PENMAS). In 1967, the wife of Central Java governor Isriati Moenadi adapted PKK programs to address economic and social problems, especially widespread poverty found in Central Java. She organized the PKK from the provincial level down to lower levels of government administrations using the provincial budget to finance them.[3]

PKK, with the new name of Pembinaan Kesejahteraan Keluarga, or Family Welfare Guidance, became an important part of national development programs under the New Order government in December 1972, when President Suharto instructed the Minister of Internal Affairs to issue a decree to make it a national program. The name change represented a significant reorientation of the program. *Pembinaan*, meaning "guidance," signified guidance from the central government in implementing its programs despite the assertion that PKK was a grassroots movement. PKK was embedded in village governance, serving as part of LKMD (Lembaga Ketahanan Masyarakat Desa, or Village Resilience Organization). The original ten goals[4] of PKK were modified to include comprehension and implementation of *Pancasila*, or Pedoman Pengahayatan Pengamalan Pancasila or P4, representing guidance, internalization, and the implementation of the five principles. The P4 was one of the New Order's programs to institutionalize the teaching of its national ideology of Pancasila (the five principles of Pancasila are: [1] belief in the one and only God; [2] a just and civilized humanity; [3] the unity of Indonesia; [4] democracy guided by the inner wisdom in the unanimity arising out of deliberations among representatives; and [5] social justice for the whole of the people of Indonesia).

The PKK was defined as a voluntary and democratic social organization, but scrutiny of its organizational structure and operations shows that it was neither. PKK programs were formulated centrally, organized to be integrated with government bureaucracies and operated largely through the government structure. The officers of PKK boards were all appointed hierarchically on a functional basis to correspond to particular bureaucratic levels or branches of government. They consisted of the wives of the government functionaries at the respective levels. The administration and heads of various levels of local government supervised these boards. Thus, at the highest or national level, the PKK board was chaired by the wife of the minister of Internal Affairs, who in turn was supervised by her husband, the minister of Internal Affairs (Roestam 1990, 16).

At the local rural-village or equivalent urban-district level, the PKK formed one section of the LKMD (Village Resilience Organization). The LKMD provided the means for the government to execute its developmental policies by recruiting local formal and informal leaders as the members of this organization. Local PKK branches receive detailed instructions for program implementation (Petunjuk Pelaksanaan, or JUKLAK) and how to organize branches and meetings. Central control did not extend to funding programs. Local PKK branches often had to be creative to figure out how to finance implementation of the programs they were instructed to adopt.

As in other social welfare programs, PKK programs were designed to promote the values of cooperation, harmony, and family/community togetherness. Women were seen as the most appropriate agents for socializing and guarding these values as the realization of their kodrat. The PKK programs clearly represented the implementation of a state-sponsored gender ideology that circumscribed women in their domestic roles as wives and mothers, while men were assumed to be the primary income earners and household heads. These assumptions were further embodied in an organizational structure that assumed all government functionaries were men whose wives automatically were available to be appointed as the chairs of the corresponding PKK organizations.

PKK not only furnished the government with an effective channel for ideological socialization, but also provided it with a means for controlling or curbing women's political participation and activism. These governmental policies limited women's actions and roles by setting boundaries on the agenda of women in social welfare activities. By prescribing that women should emphasize their domestic roles, the government limited women's involvement in public and political arenas and enhanced patriarchal power through surveillance and supervision of women's activities.

This was further accomplished through co-opting preexisting communal activities and organizations to implement PKK's agenda (Roestam 1990, 5). For example, many Indonesian communities have a long tradition of organizing their own saving-and-loan groups and rotating credit associations to avoid complex regulations in formal institutions and to escape the high interest rates charged by moneylenders. PKK used these activities to attract women's involvement in its other programs. The existing communal organizations were co-opted and reshaped to conform to government policies and were incorporated into the larger national agenda. As a consequence, community groups lost their autonomy and had to follow the government's guidelines for how these activities were conducted.

In summary, social welfare provision was a function of centralized bureaucratic authority using existing communal social structures and relations, patriarchal gender ideology, and appeals to Indonesian norms and values to solicit local support for state programs. These strategies provided firm, centralized control over social welfare activities and both their agents and their participants, while creating the impression that the activities represented grassroots efforts that were fully supported by local populations or even originated in communal efforts and local value systems.

Social Welfare Activities in Sleman and Bantul During the New Order

The two villages in Sleman and Bantul illustrate how social welfare provision was organized at the local level. Overall, the same pattern was found in both villages: Social activities were highly segregated by gender, tasks and topics mirrored "traditional" ideas about the gendered division of labor, and women reported many more activities than men. Only rarely were both men and women present at the same occasions, and then they were assigned to separate seating locations. This corresponds to a gender ideology that states that men and women have separate (but equal) roles and that men's concerns entail larger political issues. Discussions at men's meetings centered on public matters such as village repair, building projects, and how to implement direct governmental instructions. Women's meetings concerned family, health, education, and welfare. Because women were so much more active in programs directly relevant to welfare provision, we concentrate on their activities, examining patterns that apply to both villages and comparing patterns across the two villages.

When asked to explain the greater activism of women in social welfare groups, respondents (both women and men) stated that women are easier to organize and have fewer other obligations, resulting in their having more time for these activities. Regardless of whether this is accurate, the amount of time available depends on class and stage in the life course. Most of the organizers were middle-class women with no formal employment. Programs were often unsuitable for women from other socioeconomic backgrounds, and time and money constraints were major obstacles to participation mentioned by respondents. Working women and women with very young children faced the biggest time constraint. They stated that they faced the dilemma of having to choose between household and community obligations. Many women became active only after their children were grown or when they had help with household chores.

In principle, conflicts between private family and social activities were not seen as problematic. Popular opinion strongly asserted that women should give priority to their private familial obligations over social activities, but that it should be possible to accomplish both. Almost all respondents (both women and men) stated that women could wisely manage their time to perform all productive, domestic, and social activities. In practice, it was not so simple: Women found it difficult to manage their time or to escape from involvement in these activities, especially in the village where local government actively supported numerous social welfare activities. Without engagement in these social activities, they were at risk of losing support networks in times of crisis. Those who were inactive in these programs were socially alienated and stigmatized by the belief that they were trying to evade their social responsibilities. In general, a strong feeling of social obligation to higher authority and to the community prevailed, as expressed by Bu Ari: "I often say that when we die we will not bring anything; it is important now to help each other. As a member of the society, when the subvillage head asks something, I have to do it. I will need his favor sometime, so I need to take his command. It is a sin not to obey the command of the subvillage head, because I am a member of the society."

One institution played a pivotal role in mobilizing and maintaining support for social welfare programs. Almost all social activities were combined with a rotating credit association (*arisan*) or saving-and-loan activities. The basic arisan is an activity in which each member of a group makes a contribution of a fixed amount of money or goods (usually rice, sometimes furniture or household utensils), the sum of which is then distributed in its entirety at set time intervals to each member or several members in turn (C. Geertz 1956, 5). No interest is given in the basic arisan, but most arisans in Bantul and Sleman were combined with saving-and-loan activities. Interest for the loans varied from 1 percent to 5 percent per month, a rate considered much lower than the interest charged by individual moneylenders. Originally, most of the arisans were organized voluntarily by the villagers.

Government policies strongly encouraged these activities, using the arisan as a major motivator to participate in social welfare activities. Informants pointed out that there are people who really don't care about other government programs or activities but attend the arisan meetings to gain easy access to cash and credit. Although now linked to government goals, this use of the arisan follows a long tradition in which it assumed different forms. Historically, the arisan functioned more as a social institution to strengthen community solidarity and cooperation (*gotong royong*) than as an economic institution (C. Geertz 1956, 6).

Although both villages share many features, there were major differences in the villages and how their welfare programs operated and how they were perceived. Bantul is the site of the more urbanized village that has been the target of more government-intervention programs. All local women's social organizations were extremely active in this village, and every subvillage had its own active branch of PKK. At the time of the initial field research, a very active woman, the wife of the previous village head, led the local village PKK. PKK was the most important organization in this village, coordinating almost all formal women's social activities. It had numerous routine meetings and designated a series of working programs to be implemented by PKK branches in the subvillages. The village PKK board also actively advised and monitored program implementation. Programs included immunizations, infant weighing and health checks, supplemental nutrition for children under five years of age, and contraceptive distribution.

Because of its active history of strong participation in PKK programs, this village was selected by the provincial governor and the district head (*bupati*) to administer the P2WKSS program (Peningkatan Peranan Wanita Menuju Keluarga Sehat dan Sejahtera, or Program to Improve Women's Roles in Healthy and Prosperous Families) from 1993 through 1996. The village PKK branch was responsible for implementing and coordinating this integrated program. The objective was to improve women's position and income in the poorer and less-developed subvillages. Two less-developed subvillages were appointed as the program sites (both subvillages were included in the research).

The consensus among study informants was that the P2WKSS program produced some positive effects for women. It enhanced women's knowledge and skills, provided loans for their businesses, and raised gender consciousness. This was evident not only from direct testimony, but from the comparison of women's knowledge of basic legal rights such as marriage and property law with the other village that did not have similar programs. The program enabled the relatively backward subvillages to develop at a pace similar to that of other subvillages. At the same time, the extent of overlap between PKK and other programs created extra burdens for women. Many of the women were already pressed to the limit with subsistence activities and had very little free time. Furthermore, the use of arisans to lure women to participate in these programs may have created financial hardships for women who already had limited resources and numerous other obligations.

The P2WKSS was centrally organized and granted government funds for four years, two years for actual implementation and two years for follow-up programs. A general evaluation and competition were conducted at the end of the second year. The field research took place two months after the evaluation/competition. According to respondents, activities gained momentum only during the competition, and some programs ceased to be active after the formal evaluation ended. Programs were heavily dependent on support from state agencies without much input from the grassroots participants. Women indicated that they were pressured by the village government and the PKK leaders to join the activities. In many cases local authorities appointed the organizers and cadres (lower-ranking officers and members), seemingly arbitrarily and in a heavy-handed manner. An interview with Bu Fat clearly describes this process:

> We did not have the initiative to found the women's cooperative. We [with two other women] were invited to come to the office of the subdistrict's head. It turned out that the village authorities proposed us to be appointed as the organizers of the women's cooperative. I was appointed as the treasurer and the other two women were the chair and the secretary. They showed us the letter of appointment and advised us to set up the cooperative immediately. Therefore, we have to execute the instruction.

In fact, the appointment of the cadres (organizers) was based mainly on social and economic status. High-status and middle-class village women were appointed to supervise and monitor rank-and-file participants who were drawn from mostly lower social classes. The outcome produced patronizing social relations that maintained or even widened social distance between women from different classes and reinforced feelings of subordination to the higher-status women and men who supervised the participants' performance. Ironically, despite their positions of authority, many of the cadres whose tasks included assisting women in their economic enterprises were themselves housewives who had little direct experience in managing businesses or other economic activities.

These differences between the cadres and the participants created different perceptions of the programs. Bu Mar describes this situation as follows:

> The cadres came here and told me to keep my house tidy. It is difficult for me; I have to work constantly at home and while working we are always cluttering. I could keep my house clean and neat if I stop working. It's impossible. During the championship they especially urge me to make my house orderly since the evaluation team will come here. I said to the cadres, give me Rp 10,000 to replace my daily income and I will not work for that day so that I can make my house nice. They refused to do so and decided that my house would be eliminated from the evaluation.

The minimal input from the participants on programs planned and conceptualized by higher-status officials resulted in programs that did not always match the lives or meet the needs of the poor women participants who were the objects of the programs. They were largely passive recipients who were required to accept the programs as they were presented.

The final problem identified with this program was its limited scope. While programs were often viewed as intrusive for participants, at the same time, many women who could have benefited were not eligible to participate. The P2WKSS targeted women already involved in income earning, neglecting those without direct experience in productive activities. Many such women desired to start small businesses or other remunerative activities. Yet, under this P2WKSS program, these women were not eligible for loans.

The example of the P2WKSS in this village illustrates the power and the problems inherent in the kind of centralized control exercised over women's social activities. First, it significantly reduced local autonomy and initiative, hampering efforts for women to mobilize on the basis of their own perceptions of their needs. Second, it reduced women's opportunities to create their own "free space"—opportunities for social interaction in which they might express grievances and mobilize for change. Third, it reinforced existing patterns of inequality. Finally, since few people became actively engaged in the program, support diminished as soon as government funds and sponsorship decreased.

WOMEN'S SOCIAL WELFARE ACTIVITIES IN SLEMAN

The second village, Sleman, is more rural and isolated than Bantul and received less attention from the central government. The village PKK branch had fewer activities than in Bantul, and it did not intensively evaluate and supervise subvillage activities. This created more room for the PKK subvillage branches to design and control their own programs. The subvillages decided their own times for meetings, and they tended to be informal. Only rarely did representatives from the village PKK organizers attend or monitor meetings of the lower levels. Unlike Bantul, only a very limited number of specific programs were imposed on the subvillage branches by the village PKK.

Formally, each subvillage had its own PKK branch, but in practice only a few held routine meetings and activities. Only one of the three subvillages in which the research was conducted had relatively large numbers of PKK meetings. Unlike the situation in Bantul, despite the fact that most women in this village were heavily involved in income-earning activities, there were few complaints about numbers and frequency of PKK programs. Local PKK branches were flexible in scheduling and developing their programs. Political and social pressures for joining these activities were not intense, so that participation was more voluntary, and many women participated enthusiastically. "Joining the social activities added to my experiences and knowledge as well as [my] friends," according to Bu Mahmud.

The informal atmosphere was evident at the meetings. Women appeared to be more relaxed and treated the meetings as opportunities to socialize. Casual conversation filled the time before and after meetings. Common topics covered included financial problems, bad harvests, extramarital relations, family conflicts, and problems related to reproductive activities such as side effects of contraceptives—typical issues of daily life shared among friends and neighbors. Activities were not programmed and evaluated directly by higher authorities, so that the women felt much less direct pressure, but the activities were seen as both socially desirable and personally fulfilling. Husbands such as Pak Ari generally supported their wives' participation:

> The existence of various women's social activities here is good. By participating in the social organizations, women could help our local society. For example, we could help the poor by giving them loans through the organizations. I agree for women to join the arisans because they can help each other; besides, women have a need to gather and to share their personal problems with others. For example, [if] they are bored or have problems at home, they can release some of their problems by attending the arisans or social meetings.

Despite the fact that these activities were organized hierarchically by the PKK, many of the meetings were combined with local initiatives such as *kerja bakti*. These public works included the activities of environmental cleanup and the collection of money for funerals or to assist victims of other misfortunes.

As in Bantul, arisans were the driving force behind the meetings. Most arisans in this village involved less money than in Bantul, so that the members did not find them as burdensome. Additionally, saving-and-loan activities also served as a motivating factor. Many of the saving-and-loan activities in this village charged interest rates between 2.5 percent and 5 percent per month. Yet these interest rates did not discourage participation and support. The village is located quite far from a bank, and most people did not feel comfortable dealing with formal financial institutions. Even though the arisan had high interest rates, they also offered informality and direct social support for participants. At the end of the year most of the money earned from interest was divided by the members and organizers for the benefit of all.

In conclusion, PKK was seen as much less intrusive in this village, despite the fact that it, too, organized a number of women's activities. This made the social activities less burdensome for the women and created more room for women to have their own space to voice their problems and exchange concerns. Yet, as was typical of other PKK branches, most of the organizers were from the upper and middle classes and were hierarchically organized under the supervision of government officials, reinforcing centralized power and inequalities.

Comparison

The New Order government used local values and activities to mobilize and integrate communities into its social welfare activities and programs. It co-opted old practices and used its centralized power to promote programs that served its political, social, and economic needs. The rigidity of bureaucratic control over local institutions and social welfare programs left little room for local people to take the initiative in pursuing their own interests. The result was a system of social welfare provision that often had little connection to people's real needs and interests.

The contrast between the two villages illustrates the contradictions in this system. Where pressure was intense and externally controlled, as in Bantul, people perceived the programs as burdens. They participated, but under pressure and with little enthusiasm or real allegiance. They remained involved as long as there were external pressures but withdrew support as soon as these diminished. When there was room for participants to take a more active role in the design and implementation of programs, as in Sleman, there was greater genuine support and enthusiasm.

The major difference between the two villages was found in the sources, forms, extents, and effectiveness of coercion applied to produce this "voluntary" effort. In both cases, however, the assumption was that women's voluntary labor was expected to provide the major source of welfare provision. In the process women received mixed messages: Their work was crucial for the welfare of their families, communities, and nation; and yet the importance of their work was undermined because it and the women themselves were defined as secondary. Government policies limited women's actions and roles by setting boundaries on women's agenda in social welfare activities. Moreover, elements of the preexisting gender ideology were exploited and reinforced to support the programs. Thus the government institutionalized a gender ideology that underscored women's subordinate position. As in development discourse, women faced a contradiction in that state promotion of values of progress and modernity was undergirded by a gender ideology that required women's subordination (Smyth 1993, 127). They faced an additional contradiction in that the voluntary provision of service was involuntarily conscripted, producing an "involuntary voluntary" system.

Social Welfare Activities in the Aftermath of the New Order

The political and economic system that had fostered PKK programs was subjected to severe shock. Economic and environmental crises were accompanied by growing political unrest. By the mid-1990s, pressures for more democratic politics escalated. Public awareness and dissatisfaction with rampant oppression, injustice, violations of human rights, corruption, and unlawful conduct triggered movements for democratic reform from student and grassroots organizations. Efforts toward political reform successfully forced Suharto to step down in May 1998 and created support for building a more democratic society with a bigger role for civil society. In the wake of strong political pressure to decentralize and dwindling financial resources, the grip of central government on local governments receded. Similarly, insurgent movements in rural communities successfully protested and removed corrupt village heads and local government officials (Aspinall and Fealy 2003).

During this time of political transition, the need for welfare provision greatly increased. Faced with falling real wages, scarce employment opportunities, rising prices for food, health care, and education, and with very limited savings and public sector safety-net programs, many Indonesians faced severe hardship. In this atmosphere of economic crisis and political upheaval, new social welfare policies were created as a response to growing pressures for economic assistance and the involvement of civil society. A number of income, health, food security, and educational programs were formulated with pressure and support from international agencies. At least in theory, these programs provided the poor with a safety net that represented a major break with past forms of social welfare provision. Subsidies, loans, and direct assistance programs provided households with resources beyond those supplied by the social networks both formal and informal that characterized previous forms of welfare provision.

At the beginning of Reformasi, the PKK became the target of criticism from local governmental organizations for its close affiliation with the New Order regime. Even in areas such as Bantul with a formerly very active PKK, local branches almost disappeared. PKK was perceived as an authoritarian, undemocratic institution that no longer had legitimacy in the reformation era. During the administrations of Abdurranhman Wahid and Megawati Sukarnoputri, PKK suffered a major decline as these two presidents distanced themselves from the organization. Many PKK activities fell dormant, and there was pressure to disband the program entirely. Even programs with strong support such as *posyandu*, the local health-care clinics and family planning services, were neglected or abandoned.

In response, PKK launched a *munaslub* (a special session of a national meeting) in 2000. After much debate over its continued existence, they decided to keep PKK, but with important modifications designed to demonstrate its democratization. PKK once again changed its name to Pemberdayaan dan Kesejahteraan Keluarga, or the Family Welfare and Empowerment Program. Another significant change was a statement that the head of the village PKK does not have to be the wife of the village head, although all other PKK heads, from the central government to the subdistrict level, continued to be the wives of the respective government officials. Finally, support for human rights and gender equality were added to PKK goals. To implement these goals, even though the organization acknowledged that women were the movement's primary actors, men were permitted to participate as members and organizers.

The future of PKK continued to be uncertain until the election of Susilo Bambang Yudhoyono as president coincided with the reemergence of support for the view that PKK had positive impacts on local development. In late 2004 and early 2005, PKK launched its sixth national meeting (Rakernas VI). Originally the meeting was going to be opened by the president's wife, but eventually the president himself opened the meeting, signifying a revival of government support for PKK amid growing evidence of deteriorating social conditions, including declining health status and family planning programs and a rise in poverty, especially among women. At the same time, the euphoria of Reformasi and efforts to disband New Order programs subsided.

New social welfare programs developed after the crisis were plagued with severe problems in delivery, distribution, information, targeting, and effectiveness (Booth 2000; Hull 2000; Pritchett, Sumarto, and Suryahadi 2002). Although the adoption of decentralization policies were supposed to give local communities and civil society a larger voice in defining interests, needs, and implementation of the welfare programs (Bappenas 1998, 11–13), the means and institutions for channeling and disbursing aid were absent or ineffective. Efforts to curb the excesses of corruption, collusion, and nepotism characteristic of the New Order were often ineffective, and they remained rampant in both the local and the central government agencies that were responsible for the programs, leading to mismanagement and poor implementation. Early in their development during 1998–1999, Bappenas, or the National Development Planning Agency, claimed that 8 billion rupiahs were misused from a total of 17.9 billion rupiahs allocated for the social safety network program.[5]

These events provided an opening for a revival of the PKK with its strong and institutionalized infrastructure at various administrative levels and a track record of successful implementation of health, education, and economic programs. The sixth national meeting marked PKK's rejuvenation and its acknowledgment as a government partner in welfare activities. The nature of this partnership has been modified and is not as blatantly hierarchical or authoritarian as during the New Order, but even here there has been reversion to its former structure with the decision to once again automatically appoint the wife of the village head as the chair of the village-branch PKK.

PKK now concentrates more on programs that support gender equality and address problems associated with globalization such as domestic violence, trafficking of women and children, and curbing the spread of HIV/AIDS. PKK also has revived its traditional role in health promotion for women, children, and the elderly; education for young children (PAUD, or Pendidikan Anak Usia Dini), strengthening community health services, and improving women's economic status.

PKK has been struggling to demonstrate that it is not a movement created and supported from above that has only "womanly" activities. Its guidelines state that the organizers do not represent any specific groups or interests; they must become organizers as individuals. They also permit men to be organizers except for certain positions. There is now recognition that women may themselves hold high posts in the government, with a provision to relieve them from PKK leadership on top of their other responsibilities. A woman Minister of Internal Affairs, governor, district head, or subdistrict head may pass her duties on to the wives of those who are second in command. In general, however, the wives of government officials still supply the leadership for PKK.

Despite the fact that PKK has deep roots and strong infrastructure in many localities, it now faces challenges from both nongovernmental organizations and new government programs. Decentralization presents a particularly strong challenge for PKK, since funding for PKK programs now comes from local governments rather than from the central government. Depending on the local government's budget, its perceptions of PKK, and the initiative of both local officials and their wives, PKK may or may not thrive and will adopt different programs and emphases. There are now numerous variations of PKK abilities and activities, depending on local context and policies.

POST-REFORMASI PKK IN BANTUL AND SLEMAN

Immediately following krismon and Reformasi, both villages saw marked declines in PKK participation with much more local variation in program emphases. Under growing pressure for democratization, the hierarchical organization of the PKK came under scrutiny and was severely criticized. Although changes in the PKK meant that leaders should be democratically elected, in practice, the old structure of leadership by officials' wives remained intact in both Bantul and Sleman. Informants from both villages indicated that the lack of central pressure and financial support led to a decline in activities and even resistance to participation.

During the New Order, Bantul had a very active PKK that declined significantly in the immediate aftermath of the economic and political turmoil. However, routine local groups such as the *arisan* (rotating credit association) and *pengajian* (religious gathering) continued to meet, usually in combination. These activities were perceived as useful and have been in existence for generations regardless of changing governmental structure. However, there is also evidence of tension between these traditional activities as religious leaders criticize the consumerism and gossip they attribute to the popular arisan PKK meetings.

The PKK was dormant for approximately two years (2000–2002) and then was reactivated in January 2002 as part of the restructuring of local government with a monthly meeting and associated activities. However, local PKK leaders had much less authority to instruct its members than in the past, when authority had bordered on the coercive. By 2004, the village in Bantul struggled to maintain PKK activities and participation. Even more popular social activities had declining attendance because women were too busy with income-earning activities to attend and were freer to make that choice. All PKK leaders and organizers recounted stories of declining numbers of meetings, members, activities, and funds, although typically some fragment of previous activity was still in place. For example, PKK still conducted national competitions based on themes chosen centrally. Despite some initial effort to avoid involvement, this village was competing in the yearly "sustainable food" contest that entailed growing, preparing, and serving healthy meals and menus. Organizers grumbled about the time and record keeping required as well as the difficulty in recruiting participants. Nevertheless, they were still participating, even if reluctantly. Routine community welfare activities were also still in place, such as contraception and well-baby clinics organized through the posyandu, although in reduced form. One of the big changes appears to be the breakdown in the official reporting system in the absence of pressure from central authorities.

There was considerable difference among subvillages (*pedukuhan*) in the extent of PKK and other welfare activities. In one prosperous subvillage, a new meeting place to house PKK and other community activities had been built and was now being expanded. The men of this same pedukuhan were active in charitable efforts to support scholarships for indigent schoolchildren and a local orphanage that now serves a wider area. Yet another subvillage focused on improving women's livelihood strategies with a variety of schemes to boost their income, including raising organic chickens (*ayam kampung*) for restaurants, producing herbal medicines, and handcraft production. It is probably no accident that this subvillage has a woman head. In one subvillage, only the most minimal RT (*rukun tetangga*—neighborhood association) work occurs, and communal efforts are directed toward a cultural celebration.

Sleman also had a decline in PKK activity, although this village was much less active and had fewer formal PKK programs in the past. The wife of a subvillage head indicated that at the village level, there were now even fewer PKK meetings than previously. Furthermore, village PKK meetings were combined with Dharma Wanita (an organization for the wives of government officials), because for a while the only members of PKK at the village level were the wives of village and subvillage officials. There was also increased political tension between many of these active members attributed to the loosening of restrictions on political affiliation. Village formal leaders are now able to freely choose their political parties, unlike during the New Order, when all were required to belong to the ruling Golkar Party (Golongan Karya). One positive development reported by village informants is that most PKK programs are now focused on poverty alleviation and other local issues. Popular activities such as arisan and religious gatherings (*pengajian*) have persisted because they cater to local needs. As one of the women said, "Arisan grows in popularity because it provides help when people need financial support." Some of the pedukuhan arisan activity involvedcollecting products such as rice and kitchen utensils for distribution rather than money.

The latest developments in both villages are a resurgence of PKK activities. The most frequently reported programs center on health, human capital, and economic development although still maintaining local variation. The bupati in both districts fund village-level programs and encourage participation. And in 2010, as described in the introduction, the former head of the Bantul PKK, the wife of the outgoing bupati, was herself elected bupati of the kabupaten of Bantul as a stand-in for her husband, who was not eligible for another term. She and her husband had been instrumental in promoting and maintaining PKK activities, and continuation of his social welfare programs was among the reasons she was recruited to run for this office. It can be argued that her high visibility in the PKK enhanced her credibility as a candidate for bupati and also provided her a primary source of administrative experience.

Conclusion

The organization of social welfare activities in Indonesia uncovers the darker side of the relationship between gender ideology and state power while at the same time, and somewhat paradoxically, demonstrating new sources for women's mobilization and mobility. In particular, the history of the PKK demonstrates how women's social capital can be artificially assembled, co-opted, and manipulated to substitute for political action. The New Order's use of traditional values to create support for a welfare organization that relied on women's invisibly coerced "voluntary" labor—the "involuntary voluntary" organization we describe—provides a textbook example of patriarchal authority hiding behind maternalistic ideals (Arneil 2006). The result is to gain benefits for the state and the society and to define appropriate gender roles and norms, maintaining women's subordination and the fiction of their confinement to a domestic sphere.

The irony of women's public responsibilities being defined as the outcome of domestic roles demonstrates the flaws in a dualistic conceptualization of public and private spheres to explain the domain in which they are implemented. Social welfare activities are related to private lives, but the activities do not take place only within the private, familial domain. These activities also intersect with the public domain: first, because they are supported by government agencies and administered by bureaucratic lines of authority; and second, because the scope of these activities is at least communitywide or wider. The state rather cleverly conflated the two spheres in its appeals to women's obligations in both domains to accomplish its goals of sponsoring welfare provision and limiting women's political mobilization. Popular perceptions of women's private-sphere responsibilities are combined with public pressures to draft women to serve wider social purposes, resulting in the creation of a social sphere in which women operate in a limited public domain still defined as private.

A substantial body of research shows that a dichotomous concept of public and private spheres cannot be applied in any society, especially in developing countries such as Indonesia (Brenner 1998; Rogers 1980; Rosaldo and Lamphere 1974; Stivens 1990; N. Sullivan 1994). The existence of social welfare activities and other social or community activities, as well as their crucial and widespread influences in the lives of Indonesians, gives further evidence that the dualistic division of public and private domains does not well depict the reality in Indonesia. Social welfare activities are an important part of the daily interaction and lives of the people that cannot be subsumed to either public or private domains. Instead, they are interrelated and intersect with both spheres. Women's central role in welfare provision bridges public and private distinctions, although the public function remains unacknowledged, maintaining the fiction that they are operating in the private sphere of family and local community.

These types of social welfare activities persist, however, as long as other types of institutional resources do not exist to replace them. In a society in which poverty is widespread and financial resources are limited, family- and community-based social welfare activities play substantial roles in people's survival. These activities serve as the only social safety net available for the majority of the population, operating as an example of an informal security regime predicated on the permeability of family, community, market, and state (Gough 2004). What our research makes clear is that this type of welfare function cannot be understood in the absence of a gender analysis.

Finally, as a mass organization of women with a highly developed infrastructure that reaches into almost every village and long experience in mobilizing support, PKK provides one of the strongest foundations for training women in leadership skills and providing an organization run by and to some extent for women. The loosening of political restrictions after the demise of the New Order provides new possibilities for women's greater participation in all realms, including the political.

The revival of the PKK suggests recognition not only by the state that women's labor cannot be so lightly dismissed or disbanded, but also by women themselves that this organization provides opportunity for entering the political arena. The new name of the PKK denoting a change in action from guidance to empowerment may be empty rhetoric, but it may also symbolize the growing mobilization of women. The verdict is still out on how this will unfold. Information from the field shows that the PKK's old organizational structure is largely unchanged. There is a formal commitment to more flexible and democratic appointment of its leaders and to a less strict hierarchical organizational structure, but there is little evidence of actual significant change in either leadership structure or activities in the field. What has changed is the degree to which members participate and acquiesce to its programs. Whether the PKK can be a force for women's empowerment is now an open question.

Chapter 6

MEN'S RIB

Women's Power and Empowerment

> *In general, women and men are different in their*
> *kodrat. No matter how high women's position in*
> *society or career, at home it is the husbands who*
> *take the lead. They should submit to their husbands'*
> *leadership. They will always have the second*
> *position in the household. It is because women are*
> *created out of men's rib.*
>
> —Bu Miniwati, Bantul[1]

BU MINIWATI is the only woman head (*dukuh*) of a subvillage in
Bantul. She applied and was appointed by the *bupati* (at that time
also an appointed position) during the New Order in 1988 after
gaining the approval of her husband and father to take such a
bold step. For more than twenty years she has worked tirelessly
to create and run programs to improve the social and economic
lives of Tanah Kaya villagers in Pedukuhan Tengah. She has been
especially diligent in finding ways to assist women in developing
new income sources, and she has also worked to provide activities
for the youth of the area to keep them out of trouble. As a woman
dukuh, she has no wife to take care of the substantial burdens created by the traditional responsibilities of a government official's

wife, tasks that include running the local chapters of PKK and Dharma Wanita and providing support and labor for social activities required by this position. Nevertheless, she identifies herself as a housewife and reaffirms a very traditional view of women's place in society. In the village, Bu Miniwati is both a pioneer for women's empowerment and a standard-bearer for traditional values. She embodies the same contradictions in the village that Megawati represents for the nation and Midiwati represents for the district.

Accurate statistics on women's representation in leadership roles are hard to come by, especially at the lower levels of local government. In our study, Desa Danau in Sleman also has one pedukuhan with a woman dukuh, whom we interviewed, even though her subvillage was not formally part of our study. Women in these positions were rare under the New Order and remain exceptional after Reformasi, despite efforts by and for women to increase their political power and participation. In this final chapter, we examine the extent and limits to women's power and empowerment before and after the new political era ushered in by Suharto's resignation and the end of the New Order. Despite great change in the political order and new efforts to empower women in national politics, they remain marginalized in the political sphere. The same contradictions found in the household and the community are reproduced in the political arena, whether at the village level or the national level. We examine these contradictions to show how they are yet another manifestation of the inconsistencies embedded in women's status in Indonesian society and mark the limits of their power, whether in the household or in the nation. At the same time, these contradictions provide the key to understanding opportunities as well as barriers for women's empowerment in Indonesia's future.

Political Reformation and Decentralization

In 1999, after the fall of the New Order government, Indonesia passed legislation to decentralize its highly centralized political system. The hallmark of the New Order system of governance was hierarchically organized, autocratic, centralized authority. Despite, or perhaps because of, the diversity and dispersion of Indonesian territory, population, and culture, the thirty-two years of Suharto's rule were marked by extreme top-down rule from Jakarta, regardless of local practice or tradition. During this period the imposition of a secularized state ideology of national unity (*Pancasila*) was matched by a tightly controlled administrative structure that extended the absolute authority of the central state bureaucracy down to the smallest local level in virtually every corner of the archipelago. A facade of nominally democratic procedures at the national level that gave only very limited electoral choice to citizens had even fewer counterparts in the periphery, where administrative units were appointed and supervised from the center. Although much of the democracy movement was directed toward the center with demands for an end to repression and corruption and increased representation in the national government, there were also strong pressures to reexamine the relationship between the center and the periphery, particularly the amount of autonomy given to regional and local governments. Thus the demands to democratize and decentralize the Indonesian polity became political priorities after Suharto's fall.

In 1999, after "Indonesia's first relatively free and fair general elections in 44 years," the national legislature passed laws to radically decentralize the government (Aspinall and Fealy 2003, 3). Laws No. 22 and 25[2] gave unprecedented power and resources to regional districts (*kabupaten*) as a means of making government more representative, more accountable, and more accessible to local interests and constituencies. The advent of constitutional amendments that provided for direct election of the president, vice president, and national legislature (MPR) by 2004, as well as the various arrangements to phase in elections of subnational officials, have resulted in a greatly enlarged democratic process with increased representation at all levels of political life and at least the potential for a political process that can be responsive to democratic pressures.

Decentralization was a primary component of the effort to democratize Indonesian politics. Regional autonomy legislation was a response to calls to reverse the long-standing practice of transferring resources from outlying regions to the core, while simultaneously avoiding empowering the provincial governments with their greater claims to territorial, political, or sociocultural identity. The result was a compromise between demands for increased federalism centered on the provinces and a desire to maintain a strong central state by the delegation of substantial power to the districts (*kabupaten*), a level of government not historically associated with political activism.

The purpose and outcomes of decentralization can be interpreted in different ways: as a response to emerging separatist tendencies in rich provinces in the outer islands; as an effort to democratize the Indonesian polity after decades of authoritarian rule by making government more accountable and representative of regional and local interests; as a response to international pressures to create a more stable investment climate through implementation of a neoliberal agenda of "good governance" measures; or as a gambit in the contest between different elite factions to capture or (recapture) power and resources. Under any interpretation, Indonesia's experiment in decentralization reflects a larger global movement to devolve power and resources from nation-states, partly because of and partly in opposition to globalization.[3] A dozen years into the process, decentralization has become firmly institutionalized into Indonesian governance and politics.

Women's Political Participation

As an important constituency and active participants in the democracy movement, women also have had much at stake in the new political system. However, both before and after Reformasi, women have had a very limited place in the public arena. As in many liberation movements, women were active in the struggle for independence,[4] but under both Sukarno's Guided Democracy and Suharto's New Order, few women were actively involved in government. During Sukarno's rule, with his encouragement, women organized to further goals of both women's advancement and Indonesian nationalism, most infamously in the women's branch of the Communist Party, GERWANI (Gerakan Wanita Indonesia) (Wieringa 2002). This and other women's organizations were suppressed or discouraged after Suharto's accession to power.[5] During the New Order, women's political organizations were limited to state-sponsored auxiliary types of programs such as the PKK and Dharma Wanita, always tightly controlled by central government authority and harnessed to national development goals using a highly patriarchal gender ideology (as described in previous chapters).[6] Although women's political activism and organizations expanded dramatically in the run-up to the fall of the New Order and its aftermath, their representation in the formal political arena remains circumscribed.

The first parliamentary election in 1955 resulted in 17 women and 272 men, giving women just over 6 percent of the representatives in the DPR (Dewan Perwakilan Rakyat). The larger constituent assembly, charged with developing a new constitution, included 25 women but only 5 percent of this legislative body and was dissolved several years later by Sukarno for failing to reach consensus. Women's representation reached a high point in the 1987 elections at 13 percent, declining steadily until reaching a new low at 9 percent (45 women) in 1999 in the first DPR elections under Reformasi. It rose slightly in the next election to 62 women, or 11 percent of the representatives, in 2004 (Parawansa 2006). Finally, in 2009 it exceeded the 1987 figures with 18 percent women.

In 2004, the formation of a second chamber, the DPD (Dewan Perwakilan Daerah), to provide regional representation to the legislature, provided an additional opportunity for women's participation. Unlike the other chamber, in which elections remain mediated by political party, members were directly elected. Women were more successful, with 27 out of 128 women representatives (22 percent) elected to this body and then 26 percent in 2009 (UNDP 2010, 17). Khofifah Indar Parawansa (2006), the Minister for Women's Empowerment under the Abdurrahman Wahid administration and subsequently Megawati,[7] has speculated that in some regions, women candidates are able to mobilize sufficient numbers of women voters to have a better chance of electoral success than when their access to the ballot is controlled by political parties.

Women remain underrepresented at other levels of government. Decentralization brought greater autonomy to elections in the provincial and district legislative bodies, but this did not greatly improve women's representation. Writing in 2006, Parawansa states: "In 1999, approximately 6 percent of the members of provincial DPRDs and fewer than 5 percent of the members of district DPRDs were women. Accurate figures for the number of women members of DPRDs are still not available after the 2004 elections—which speaks for itself" (85).

She goes on to say that women's underrerpresentation is not believed to have changed significantly. Furthermore, there were no women governors and only five women heads of districts or regencies (1.5 percent). Statistics from other government offices suggest that women do somewhat better in appointed office, but nowhere do they reach as much as a quarter of the incumbents and typically, the figure is much lower (Parawansa 2006, 85). By the summer of 2008, these figures showed only slight improvement. Out of 33 provinces, 375 kabupaten, and 90 *kota* (cities headed by mayors),[8] women were represented as follows: governor: 1; vice-governor: 1; bupati: 8; vice-bupati: 11; mayor: 1; vice-mayor: 6.

The low numbers come in spite of substantial pressure to increase women's representation from a variety of sources, including expanding numbers of women's movements and organizations to support women's rights in law and in society. Nevertheless, efforts to increase women's formal representation have been highly uneven. An important manifestation of this trend was an attempt to require 30 percent of candidates for the legislature to be women. Although the effort to make the 30 percent rule binding by law was unsuccessful, the 2004 election law did include a "new provision requiring parties to 'bear in their hearts' the desirability of 30 percent of nominated candidates being women, which can be described as a 'maybe quota'" (Parawansa 2006, 84). The political parties paid lip service to this goal, and many even made formal efforts to comply. However, both structural constraints and the political parties' unwillingness to provide the resources necessary to women candidates to make electoral success a likely outcome undermined efforts to successfully reach this goal. Then, in late 2008, the whole effort was dismantled when the constitutional court issued a ruling that negated the quota and required the election to be completely determined by popular vote. Thus, during the 2009 election, the 30 percent stipulation was not in effect. However, pressure to increase women's representation remained strong, and despite the absence of formal rules, many political parties increased the number of women candidates.

An interview conducted by Siti in 2008 with a woman member from the Golkar Party of the Yogyakarta provincial legislature (DPRD) outlines the obstacles women face, including new barriers from the reforms introduced by Reformasi. The most qualified women by virtue of their education and experience are likely to be found in the ranks of the civil service. Under Suharto it was possible to run for office while maintaining a government career, but this has changed and now candidates must first resign. Few women are willing to risk their careers to run for office, especially since the odds of winning are stacked against them. Therefore, only retired women civil servants are easily recruited to run for office, but then they are criticized for being too old and out of touch.

Other problems are familiar, beginning with the expense of running a campaign. This woman estimated that a provincial-level campaign costs approximately 200,000,000 rupiah (approximately US$20,000), an amount well out of reach of most "qualified" women. Even if a woman has this kind of cash, she must get permission from her husband or father to spend it this way, and then after the election, she is expected to expend additional resources to pay the party and other supporters who ask for assistance. Finally, the need for party backing eliminates many potential candidates who lack the long involvement with party affairs necessary to generate support. Even when support is forthcoming, it tends to be low-level, placing women at the bottom of candidate lists where they are unlikely to secure votes.

One of a very few successful women serving as bupati was elected in the Central Java kabupaten of Kebumen in 2002.[9] In an interview published in the popular press, she expresses both the aspirations and the challenges that women who seek office face:

> The fact that Javanese culture positions women as "the friend behind" does not make women lose their hope to play important roles in public lives in this region. This is supported by the fact that Central Java has more women as district heads compared to other provinces. However, this value also serves as a challenge and barrier for women to be in leadership positions.[10]

The same article goes on to describe the numerous challenges faced by another Central Java woman bupati before finally gaining office. She points out that in addition to political opposition, she has to deal with her "kodrat as a woman who has husband and family. [A woman] cannot avoid this ethical value even when she has high position. I am the leader in the governmental structure of the district of Karanganyar, but in my family I am the wife who has to respect my husband's position as the head of the household."[11]

More recently, the 2010 election of a female bupati in the kabupaten of Bantul, where one of the study villages is located, reinforces the difficulties and contradictions faced by the women who manage to reach high office. The account of the election of Bu Midiwati that opened this volume shows that her political career is primarily an extension of her husband's, not planned or sought by her directly. In an interview with Siti shortly after the election, she recounts how her husband's supporters entreated her to run as his stand-in to ensure the continuation of his "signature programs." Notably, these were primarily social welfare–related programs involving maternal and child health, early childhood education, and other family-oriented programs, areas that are popularly viewed as consistent with women's roles.

Before running, Bu Midiwati consulted with the sultan's wife and Megawati. Both counseled her to be careful and to be strong. They pointed out the risks for women in entering the political arena. She seemed well aware that she faced all sorts of pitfalls, ranging from those that would be encountered by any officeholder, regardless of gender, to the potential resentment of male rivals who believed she represented usurpation of their prerogatives, and the condemnation of conservative religious leaders who still believe women are unfit for office.

The election itself was highly engineered. Although her husband was a member of one political party, PDIP, or Partai Demokrasi Indonesia Perjuangan (Indonesian Democratic Party of Struggle), her primary support came from PAN, or Partai Amanat Nasional (National Mandate Party); the Golkar Party, or Golongan Karya (the party of functional groups); PKPB, or Partai Karya Peduli Bangsa (Party for the National Concern); and GERINDRA, or Gerakan Indonesia Raya (Great Indonesian Movement Party). The reason for this was that PDIP nominated a *jago belehan* (Javanese for slaughtered cock in a cockfight), in other words, a stooge, to provide the appearance of a contested election to pave the way for her win. Once it appeared that there was a contest, two other parties, PKS, or Partai Keadilan Sejahtera (Prosperous Justice Party), and the Democrat Party, jumped in with a real candidate; however, he was unable to command much support. Midiwati won with 67 percent of the vote.

Now in office, Midiwati did not hide that her husband was the real power behind her position. She appointed him *staf ahli khusus*, or special expert adviser, and made it clear that his duties encompassed virtually all tasks associated with her office, including spending time in Jakarta to lobby the central government for money for the district. She tapped his *tim sukses* (success team), to be her organizational support in each subdistrict and the district legislature. She saw herself as an instrument and continuation of her husband's administration, saying:

> I have to be very careful. If I have to make decision and I am not sure about it, my husband said, bring it home so that I can help you in making the decision. This is especially connected to decision on funding; it's very difficult. My husband will not leave me alone; he will support me. Many journalists criticize me and say why I only want to continue my husband's program, I tell them that this is what people want; they want the people-centered programs to continue.

It remains to be seen how Midiwati's administration will develop. At this time, however, it is clear that her access to office was as a proxy for her husband.

Khofifah Indar Parawansa (2006), the former Minister of Women's Empowerment, summarizes obstacles to women's election. These include:

- The prevailing patriarchal culture that relegates women to the family and private sphere;
- the disproportionate control of party politics by small groups of elite men who are unaware of women's interests and issues;
- the failure of the media to recognize and publicize women's issues and campaigns;
- conflict and lack of coalition building between women's organizations and interest groups;
- opposition from women's husbands and families;
- lack of education and qualifications, reducing the pool of available candidates;
- lack of time and money required to run a successful campaign; and
- lack of party facilitation and support, leaving women low on party candidate lists.

For all these reasons, women remain marginal to the political process and positions of power and authority at both the national and the local levels.[12]

Gender and Local Politics

Under the New Order, rural government was placed at the bottom of the pecking order, without autonomy or independent authority. This position was further reinforced through the 1979 law No. 5 regulating rural government using a Javanese prototype of village structure. The only democratic process involved was the direct election of village heads in rural areas. Once elected, however, they were subordinate to both Golkar, the government party, and to higher levels of the government bureaucracy, with little accountability to their constituents. The appointment had to be approved by the district head and the governor. Direct election was used to create legitimacy and support from rural people, while in practice the rural government acted as an agent for the ruling party and central government. Selection of subvillage heads (called *dukuh* now, *kadus* then), who actually handle most of the daily tasks of village administration and who directly deal with rural populations, was tightly controlled by district and subdistrict governments; they were not directly elected by the people until very recently. They remained appointed positions long after direct elections were established in most other levels of government.

Once appointed, dukuh had virtually unlimited terms; as long as they remained willing and able to serve, they kept their office. As "street-level" officials, the dukuh are the link between villagers and higher authority and wield a great deal of authority that rests in a gray area between formal power and informal leadership and persuasion. They are not paid directly but receive land use rights—*bengkok*—usually a hectare of village communal land that they can farm. The amount of land is significantly larger than what most villagers own or have access to, and its use forms an important economic strategy for the dukuh's household or family. Often a spouse, a parent, or another relative actually works the land, although the dukuh himself (or herself) also may spend time working in the fields.

During our research, each of the two study villages in Sleman and Bantul had a subvillage with a woman dukuh. There have been women elected as village heads in both Bantul and Sleman, but none in the study villages, although Siti witnessed an election campaign for village head in Bantul that included a woman candidate. The situation involving the two successful local officials, the unsuccessful candidate for village office, and the wife of a village head is instructive for understanding the barriers to women's access to political power at the local level.

Women as Subvillage Heads

We have already heard from the long-standing dukuh of Tanah Kaya in Bantul, a woman who simultaneously breaks tradition while affirming women's subordinate position in the family. In the course of a single interview she asserts the importance of male leadership in the family, yet maintains that her family has a gender-blind division of household labor. She acknowledges criticism of her leadership and position as a woman in high office, but goes on to state that "in my opinion people can accept woman leaders."

Despite her contradictory views, she clearly has been an effective leader. She describes herself as leading by example and consensus, using *musyawarah*, or traditional discussion and deliberation, to resolve problems and disagreement. It is undoubtedly her ability to create consensus and unite different factions that has enabled her to work successfully in this position and in a community that previously was factionalized by class differences. This particular subvillage includes both affluent and very poor residents, physically segregated in different parts of the community. Her main rival for the dukuh position was another woman,[13] but one unambiguously associated with the wealthier faction.

Bu Miniwati, from a middle-class background, had good relations with the poorer parts of the hamlet and actually lived in this part of the community. The combination of these connections, a compromise with her rival promising control over PKK activities to her and her supporters (thereby also eliminating the burden and dilemma of her responsibility for its activities), and possibly the exchange of money or favors, resulted in her appointment. Her longevity and the many successful livelihood activities she has initiated and coordinated in her community for low-income residents, ranging from raising organic chickens to handcraft production, speak to her energy and effectiveness as a local leader. Her husband, now retired, has been supportive of her work and seems content to let her do her job even when it takes her away from family responsibilities. Despite being designated by his wife, Ibu Miniwati, as the family leader, he is clearly the less dynamic of the two.

If Bu Miniwati embodies the contradictions that persist for women who do make it to positions of power and authority at the local level, her counterpart in Desa Danau in Sleman demonstrates a more disturbing picture of women's leadership, one that suggests the existence of barriers and limits to women's exercise of power even when they are nominally successful. Although we attempted to interview this woman several times, regardless of whether she was physically present or absent, her husband did most of the talking.[14] Pak Tosa, a schoolteacher, described in some detail how he was the natural choice and the popular choice for the position of dukuh when the previous incumbent was promoted. However, as a schoolteacher, he was not eligible to hold two civil service jobs at the same time. Resignation from his teaching job would have significant negative financial consequences the family could not afford, even with the compensation provided by the bengkok accompanying the dukuh position. At the same time, his wife had been unsuccessful in her numerous attempts to apply for a teaching job of her own. In Pak Tosa's words: "Since I could not run for the position, they suggested that my wife run for it. At first I argued that it was not appropriate for a woman to run for the position; it is better for a woman to be a treasurer but not a *kadus* [subvillage head]."

He changed his mind and then took the highly unusual step of engineering an informal election won by his wife to demonstrate to village and district officials the acceptability and viability of his wife in this role. At that time and until very recently, the dukuh remained an appointed position requiring a stringent application procedure that included taking an exam, but was not subject to an electoral process. His wife eventually was appointed to the job, and Pak Tosa assumed the role of shadow dukuh while retaining his teaching position.

> Basically, I have the concepts and theory, and my wife applies them. I stand behind her and give her suggestions and ideas/concepts so that she can apply them in her government. If my wife has problems, I help solve the problems. . . . For example, before making a public speech, she usually asks me what should be said. I give her inputs, and she is the one who actually gives the speech.

This parallels the standard Javanese notion that women can be entrusted to be managers and implementers, the active members of a partnership, but not the center of power or source of ideas.

On top of her official responsibilities, his wife sells chilies in the market. Pak Tosa is magnanimous about concessions necessary to support her heavy time commitments:

> Since my wife is busy, she cannot do all of the household chores, yet I have to accept this because I know that she does not have enough time. It also means that I have to participate more in doing the household chores. We have to finish up the chores together and accept the imperfect conditions. For example, my wife sometimes forgets to make a drink for me. Normally a husband will get furious if his wife does not make him a drink [tea or coffee], but I understand this.

Pak Tosa's views of women are consistently paternalistic, whether concerned with their roles in the household or in society, essentially defining their interests as domestic:

> Women usually do not express their ideas in KKLKMD (Kelompok Kerja Lembaga Ketahanan Masyarakat Desa, or Working Group for the Village Resiliency Board) meetings, in which we discuss government programs. The women usually give input on how we should provide snacks and meals (*konsumsi*) when we discuss building a mosque, for example. Physical development is usually supported by men rather than women. Many men are capable of making decisions about the government programs, so the women trust these men. It does not mean that the women are passive, but they do not say anything because they agree with what we do.

Although he maintains that educational opportunities for women and men are equal, he is unable to resist asserting his authority on the basis of superior education:

> Differences in education between husband and wife might create some frictions and misunderstanding. For example, I have higher education than my wife, so I am trying to educate her so that the gap between us is minimized. Sometimes I give her opportunities to make important decisions while I am backing her [from] behind. But sometimes there are things that I have to decide because my wife does not yet know the potential risks of the decisions.

When decisions have to be made, even if they are understood to be in her domain, he has delegated them. Big issues require his authority: "Since women tend to use their feelings, it is important for men [husbands] to decide important matters in the household."

There is no way of knowing how typical the views and practices described in this example are for other women in similar positions. Yet they are suspiciously like a somewhat more sinister version of newly elected Bupati Midiwati's story. The point is that they are not considered extraordinary. Most likely, they are unusual because few women find themselves thrust into the situation that Bu Tosa finds herself in, not because they are outside the mainstream.

Certainly, Pak Tosa's beliefs are well within the norm of Javanese gender ideology, and he acts in accordance with these views. Whether his wife resents them can only be a matter of speculation; she does not rebel.

There are two other examples of women's experience in local politics that are instructive for understanding women's political opportunities. During the first part of the field research before Reformasi, Siti witnessed an election for village head (*lurah*) that included a woman candidate. Many years later, we spent time with the wife of this village's head and her husband the lurah (but not the same one described in the election below), and this also provided insight into gender politics.

Village Head Election in Tanah Kaya, Bantul, During the New Order. In 1996, this village held an election, creating significant political and social tensions in the village.[15] There were nine candidates—eight males and one female—in the election. The woman in this campaign had to resort to special strategies to run a credible campaign. For example, each candidate ran as an individual without having to represent any political party or organization. The only female candidate used this to repeatedly stress that she was running as an individual, not representing any group, and especially not depending or directly including her husband. She was trying to subtly dissociate herself from her husband, whose reputation was tainted by a conviction for corruption that previously had forced him to resign as village head. At the same time she was trying to demonstrate her gender inclusiveness, reinforcing the message that she would represent both men and women and did not care only about women's interests. Unlike the male candidates, her spouse did not accompany her to public events; instead, the woman who served as secretary of the local PKK branch accompanied her. This also signaled that if elected, there was a woman readily available to assume the local PKK's chair, since as a man, her husband was not eligible.

Despite the candidates' assertions of independence, scrutinizing their backgrounds and listening to their speeches, it was apparent that candidates represented different social factions. For example, religious affiliation was obvious from the opening of their speeches—one candidate came from a non-Muslim group (probably Catholic), while all Muslim candidates used the Arabic greeting that is standard Islamic practice. At least two candidates cited verses from the Qur'an in their speeches, and one candidate was affiliated with a local Islamic school (*pondok pesantren*) that is connected with the NU, Nahdlatul Ulama, the biggest Islamic organization in Indonesia. Class and subvillage interests also were apparent.

The campaign, which lasted for nine days, was centrally organized by the office of the village head and took place in several rounds located in different subvillages. Afterward the candidates were not allowed to directly campaign publicly, although they were permitted to conduct private gatherings and post their symbols in strategic locations. Candidates gave required speeches in each round, describing their programs and publicizing the symbols they used to enable illiterate voters to recognize them. In this election, each candidate was represented by a different type of fruit (e.g., mango, papaya, pineapple, starfruit, durian, and so on).

In each round, candidates were given ten to fifteen minutes to deliver a speech with no debate or direct interaction with the audience, which was composed of leaders and respected members of the community. Candidates were not supposed to attack or even address one another directly. All candidates participated in the preliminary stage with only the top three candidates proceeding to the final step. The campaign proceeded routinely until the morning of the public announcement regarding which candidates qualified as finalists, when confusion, leaks, and gossip almost led to an open conflict. As the guest of one of the candidates, Siti was able to witness these events.

After an anxious night filled with special preparations to ensure good luck, very early in the morning, several hours before the scheduled 10:00 a.m. public announcement, several of the keen supporters of this candidate came to claim that they had received reliable information that he was one of the finalists. The source of this information was not obvious, yet they seemed very certain that it was accurate. Some mentioned that they learned it from "insiders" (officials from subdistrict and district levels who were involved in the selection process). His family was jubilant.

That morning, all the candidates were invited to attend the meeting in the office of the subdistrict head to learn about the decision on the finalists. Wearing their best clothes, often riding in borrowed vehicles, and accompanied by their spouses and a few close friends or advisers, they arrived at this very important meeting that would determine their future. The situation was very tense; many supporters of each candidate anxiously awaited the outcome of the "cockfight" for the fate of their "cock," as they literally called their candidates.

The decision turned out to be contrary to the expectations fueled by the rumor. As a consequence anger, disappointment, and a desire for retaliation dominated the atmosphere and attitudes of this man's supporters. There were hysterical cries and emotional reactions almost everywhere in his house. One of his first reactions after learning of his defeat evoked the cockfight imagery when he stated, "I feel like a cock being slaughtered after a fight because somebody treated me unfairly." This contrasted with the joyous celebrations that marked the supporters of the three finalists, the woman candidate and two men.

The disappointed host's losing supporters turned their anger and resentment against the woman candidate. They believed that she did not deserve to be a finalist and that she used money and connections to secure her place in the final round, displacing their candidate as a finalist. This was in stark contrast to their views about the two male finalists, who they felt deserved this outcome. This perception positioned the woman candidate as the main target for their resentment and resulted in extreme reactions. Attacks on her house and supporters were contemplated, but the impulse was tempered by cooler, older heads who suggested going to the district office of the people's representative board (DPRD, or Dewan

Perwakilan Rakyat Daerah). Some younger supporters ended up marching around the village holding posters and yelling protests expressing the unfairness of the election. Older supporters then went to the DPRD to express their concerns. In the end, these efforts did not change the decision. Grievances and disappointment remained, but the tensions gradually receded, and the election continued. In the end, the female candidate was defeated, and a male candidate who worked as a staff member in a local state university won the election.

One of the problems tainting the election was that the criteria for selecting the finalists were not very clear. Formally, numbers of votes the candidates received in the preliminary stage and the results of the written examinations taken by the candidates were among the most important deciding factors. Yet a tally of the voting was not conducted publicly, and evaluation of the written examination was also unclear. Candidates did not actually see the results or their scores on the exams, which were organized and tallied in the subdistricts (*kecamatan*). These practices created serious possibilities for manipulation and money politics. The power of the government officials directly involved in organizing the process may also have affected the outcome. Candidates spent a considerable amount of money (several million rupiahs, or several thousand dollars) to bribe voters, hold meetings, feed supporters, and bribe government officials. Prospective voters who came to meetings held in candidates' homes commonly received money and meals for their attendance. Recommendations from higher government officials also helped candidates' chances, and money usually was required to get these recommendations.

The entire election process demonstrated the gendered nature of elections and a distinct gender division of labor. In the meetings held at the candidates' homes, women and men were usually in different rooms, with women in the back (mostly in the dining and kitchen area) cooking and men in the front room discussing the strategies and other political issues to help the candidates win. Women relatives, neighbors, and friends of the candidates usually spent a lot of time preparing the meals continuously served in all of the meetings. This was also an indirect way to show their support for the candidates. On the other hand, men dominated public space. They led the meetings, served as advisers for the candidate, designed strategies, and organized the campaigns.

Meetings organized by the woman candidate followed a similar pattern, except that there were a few women (her closest confidantes) who accompanied her "in front" in the men's domain. She solicited women's support in local women's meetings and gave gifts to prominent women and PKK leaders. Most of her advisers were men, foremost among them her husband behind the scenes, despite the scandal that forced him to avoid direct public appearance.[16] Opportunity in this case appears to reflect thwarted male ambition as much as female aspiration.

Gender Politics in the Tanah Kaya, Bantul, Village Head's Household. The last example of the contradictions inherent in women's political roles is illustrated by examining the experience of the wife of a more recent village head and her husband, the lurah elected in 2004. Bu Rani was a college graduate with a law degree who did not practice; rather, she devoted her time to village and domestic duties. Her family was wealthy and their money and business enabled her husband, who did not have a higher education, to earn a living and to run for office. Energetic and enthusiastic about using her position as the lurah's wife to pursue women's welfare, she was instrumental in rejuvenating PKK in the village, with explicit goals of empowering women amid the usual mix of cultural and domestic programs. These ranged from domestic and cultural pursuits such as the revival of a gamelan orchestra and cooking and eating lessons (including field trips to fancy restaurants to learn "European" eating style), to traditional health and welfare activities and livelihood enhancements.

She was quite outspoken about the importance of women's empowerment and the need to enhance women's status in society, citing a variety of forms of direct discrimination that women still experience in school and the workplace as well as indirect outcomes of socialization and assumptions about women's inferiority and secondary status. She displayed a sophisticated feminist consciousness that encompassed recognition that these are gender issues, not just women's problems, and that men need to be sensitized to gender equity as well.

At the same time, the nature of her relationship with her husband clearly demonstrates the power of traditional gender roles and the contradictions experienced by even an ardent feminist. She described how once Javanese women are married, their husbands have power over them. She must ask permission of her husband in order to leave the house, especially at night. She calls meetings of the PKK that she then must cancel if her husband doesn't give her permission to attend. During our interview she startled Ann by asking if she, too, must get her husband's permission for her social activities (leading to a discussion of the complexities of schedule negotiations) and indicated somewhat ruefully that this is a situation that is deeply embedded in Javanese culture, going back hundreds of years, "going on since Kartini," and that village women who faced the same situation understood her predicament. Although she completed a law degree during her marriage, her husband did not let her practice, saying it would be inappropriate for the wife of someone in his position and that her job is to take care of the house and the children.[17]

The More Things Change . . .

In each of these examples, spanning a decade of social change, the views expressed by women leaders are at odds with their practice. Where they are relatively politically powerful, they work hard to assert their husbands' dominance and the importance of traditional family roles, as in the case of Bu Miniwati. On the other hand, even a strong proponent of gender equity such as Bu Rani, bolstered by education, wealth, and social position, is undermined by the strength of convention and traditional gender expectations practiced by her macho husband. While not every woman experiences such extreme gender contradictions, these examples illustrate how pervasive they are in women's political experience as well as in the household economy.

These views are widely shared among villagers in this study. Although we did not systematically ask all respondents whether they would support women political leaders and under what circumstances, the issue came up in many of the interviews. More than two-thirds of villagers who expressed an opinion indicated that all else being equal, they would prefer and support a male candidate over a woman. Men had especially strong feelings about this subject, with more than three-quarters asserting a male preference. The majority of women—approximately 60 percent—also preferred a male candidate, although 20 percent indicated a female preference. Reasons for the male preference ranged from belief in their superior leadership qualities to concern for the propriety and safety of women working in circumstances that would take them out at night and into a variety of public functions. Pak Mul from Bantul states: "But if I have to choose between a woman and a man, I will choose a man as the leader or to occupy certain government positions. It is because men are more mobile and able to make decisions."

Pak Sudi elaborates:

The man is the leader/caretaker (*pamomong*). If the leader is a woman, when members of the society [presumably men] face a problem, they cannot express their problem freely [*kurang bebas*]. But if the leader is a man, if a woman asks for help, it is okay/appropriate. For example, it will be embarrassing for me if I as a man ask help from a woman [who is the leader]. For example, [if] I ask to get help to obtain a *hak warisan* [inheritance] or to divorce, and consequently I have to spend a lot of time with her [the woman village head], it won't be appropriate.

Women echo the reasons cited by men but also frequently describe their perceived weaknesses. Bu Arif's reason for preferring a man as leader is that "a woman is usually carried out by her emotion. She tends to be more complicated." Bu Wati feels that "men are more wise, respectful. The female one may be wise and respectful, too, but she still prefers the male candidate. It is the destiny of men to be more respected."

A few men and slightly more women indicate that they would unconditionally back a woman leader in preference to a man to show support for women and the notion that men and women are equal with equal rights. However, most supporters of women qualify their support by reference to who is the more qualified or the nature of the specific position. Interestingly, a number of villagers indicate that they would be more likely to support women for higher office than for subvillage head, on the grounds that the duties are less likely to involve night work or other inappropriate encounters. Pak Jono from Sleman states: "It is more appropriate for men to be the head of [a] subvillage because they have more abilities and mobility to do the job. But for the village head or secretary of the village, it is okay for either men or women, because the job is more administrative and less involved in the society."

Bu Yono from Bantul echoes this sentiment: "The reason is that most people still think that a man is more mobile because the position needs the leader to be available night and day, and to mingle with men and women. However, if it is a ministerial level, there will be no problem because she will have bodyguards and deputies."

The views of Bu Mahmud from Sleman underscore the contradictions that lurk just under the surface for most villagers: "It is okay for a woman to have a governmental position such as be a subvillage head as long as her husband grants her permission. We live in an era of women's emancipation, so it should be okay for women to have such a position. As a subvillage head, most of her work is done at home so that her husband could help her."

Gender and Political Power Since Reformasi

The political reforms introduced by Reformasi opened more space for political participation by all Indonesians, including women, and many have demonstrated a desire to occupy this space. Women have many more channels and opportunities for activism in both formal and informal spheres. During the New Order, political activity was tightly controlled, and there were few outlets for civil society. The most promising opportunities for women with political ambitions were through official channels either in a relatively narrow range of jobs in the civil service or in official organizations such as the PKK or Dharma Wanita, organizations whose basic design was to create a nominally parallel structure for women that remained subordinate to male centers of power and that reinforced traditional roles while simultaneously deploying their labor for state objectives.

Reformasi opened many new possibilities for activism in new political parties, in NGOs, and in civil society more generally, and women were well-represented in the social movements that initially led to political reform (Blackburn 2004; Collins 2007; Nyman 2006). Women's efforts to play a more visible political role were reinforced by a growing (although fragmented) women's movement and by international support for women's empowerment as a strategy for development, along with gender mainstreaming as a requirement for aid. Even the growing prominence of religious parties and an increasingly political Islamic movement explicitly incorporated women's interests into their platforms (Rinaldo 2008, 2010). Thus a reform-oriented religious party such as the PKS (Partai Keadilan Sejahtera, or Prosperous Justice Party) that advocated strict implementation of syari'ah regarding gender roles strongly supported women's political participation and activity at the same time that it promoted traditional domestic pursuits and even gender segregation.[18]

However, the basic contradictions that militate against women's participation remain in force. Like women everywhere, Indonesian women struggle to juggle competing and often contradictory roles and expectations. While they have made gains in the political sphere, these are almost always tempered by expectations that their primary role, their *kodrat*, remains in the domestic sphere and that it is their job to make sure these obligations are met. The false dichotomy between public and private becomes a means to control women's activism. Although their work in social welfare clearly demonstrates a public role, it is defined as private and therefore not really a violation of traditional gender roles. In political work, since this is formally defined as public, their domestic roles are used as justification to limit access to more significant roles in the public sector, again reinforcing traditional roles conducted in appropriate realms.

Women's political activities and responsibilities are relegated to domestic categories considered appropriate for women, such as health and welfare.[19] Finally, the expectation is that however far women advance politically, they will advocate the primacy of home and family. The majority of women we interviewed who had political ambitions or who had attained political office worked hard to maintain a facade of a traditional gender division of labor, even when the evidence clearly indicated that this was not strictly the case. Other women in leadership roles clearly were subordinate and acted as proxies for their husbands who were unable to attain office directly in their own right. In either case, one of their obligations was to protect and promote their husbands' prerogatives as men and family heads, thereby maintaining the gender order.

Of course, the extent to which these patterns prevail and the vigor with which norms about gender relations are enforced will vary by individual and by factors such as class, region, and religious orientation. Nevertheless, as case studies of the structure of gender relations in rural Java, the two villages surveyed have been remarkably stable in both beliefs and practices over the fifteen years of observation. Furthermore, they exhibit relatively few meaningful differences despite changes in both the villages and the larger society. This is not surprising given the power of a hegemonic gender ideology that was heavily enforced with state power and institutions and reinforced by cultural tradition, religious teaching, and the practices of daily life. Even if state efforts have let up in the formal inculcation of these beliefs, they remain compatible with dominant cultural themes and social arrangements and, therefore, are not likely to exhibit swift and dramatic reversal.

Power and Empowerment

Does this mean that Indonesian women are stuck in relatively subordinate and powerless roles? Or are they increasingly empowered in a society that needs their contributions? Is the glass half empty or half full? Women's participation is encouraged and even mandated. Gender mainstreaming is widely promoted, yet it lacks the full force of law to make it happen. The failure of the attempt to ensure the presence of women candidates through modification of the election laws exemplifies the uncertainty surrounding empowerment efforts. Nevertheless, its existence speaks to an enlargement of women's opportunities to access political power beyond the narrow parallel channels previously permitted or the occasional exception that proved the rule. Whether these represent real advances beyond the constraints experienced by the Miniwatis at the local level, the Midiwatis at the regional level, and the Megawatis in the national arena remains to be seen.

We began this study with questions about the seemingly contradictory assertions of women's status and power in Indonesia, whether at the macrosocietal level or within the household. This research has demonstrated that these contradictions are real and persistent; they are rooted in history and culture, and they pervade virtually every aspect of daily life. In their pervasiveness they are accommodated and assimilated as normal by both women and men. Unlike Western views of contradiction, they are not perceived as necessarily incompatible or unfair or creating undue hardship, but rather they are part of ordinary existence, and it is the individual's task to live with them, to reconcile them, and, ideally, to create a harmonious existence out of them. Cultural competence demands and is displayed by the facility with which this is accomplished. The conundrum we identified as the subject of this research is not an illusion to be explained away but rather the reality of everyday life.

As we have scrutinized this reality, our own views of contradiction have changed. We realize that in evaluating the gender roles and practices of villagers, even as we abjured the imposition of false binary oppositions, we had imposed an "either/or" logic on their thinking that they did not share and had little relevance for how they lived their lives. Accommodation to contradiction is not an obstacle that is knowingly tackled by Javanese villagers, but rather part of normal complexity. We have learned to heed our own words (in chapter 1):

> Rather than trying to explain the contradiction away, it is important to face it head-on. Each account represents different facets or dimensions of women's status that have to be pieced together and scrutinized both separately and as a larger package. Without a multidimensional approach that can embrace even contradictory assessments of women's position, it is not possible to fully understand the fluid, contested, and negotiated aspects of gender roles and relations in which different factors and values are constantly in contention.

Our efforts to "face it [contradiction] head-on" have resulted in a deeper understanding of the complexities and fluidity of women's roles as both women and men themselves understand them.

This is not to dismiss the problems that women face as they contend with obstacles barring their access to power and empowerment. Indonesian and Javanese gender ideology is permeated with forms of paternalistic and patriarchal ideology and practices, as we have demonstrated. These have been adopted and adapted in successive political regimes and eras to reinforce those who are in power, whether at the level of the state or the family. Javanese gender ideology and practice are conducive to giving women a fair amount of control and influence as "managers" but relatively little opportunity to be masters (N. Sullivan 1994). This may be changing, but it has not yet changed. Because of the changes in state and society, however, the contradictions may be more apparent and appear more extreme, stretching the accommodations that have served in the past and creating yet new tensions and challenges.

In this manner, the contradictions form a dialectical process that may create new opportunities or limitations. Indonesia is in transition as it emerges from the repressive and corrupt regime of the New Order with its future very much contested. The roles that women play are similarly in transition, with no clear outcome in sight. The new election law perfectly reflected this ambiguity. It demanded that 30 percent of the candidates be women, and then went one step further, requiring that for every two men there must be a woman, but there were no teeth in this law, no means to enforce it or ensure its implementation, and ultimately it was nullified by the constitutional court. Under the New Order, there were only a few opportunities for women to gain political experience or play leadership roles, and the few that existed were tightly controlled and regulated. Nevertheless, organizations such as the PKK provided some of the few "free spaces" (Evans and Boyte 1986) in which women could organize and mobilize, and these, in fact, served this purpose. Now there are many new organizations and places where women can gather, network, organize, and build social and political capital. Whether these can be used by women to empower women either on their own behalf or for larger political purposes remains to be determined.

The persistence of the influence of the Javanese concept of power remains a barrier to women's empowerment, despite the new opportunities and spaces for women in all arenas. If a woman asserts her authority, she is in direct opposition to the traditional display of power (as deemed appropriate for men), which is witnessed by the opposite, the ability to command respect and obedience without appearance of effort. Thus, she is likely to be dismissed as a typical if overly noisy and pushy woman. Yet the fact that a woman is not privy to the traditional source of power means that if she doesn't make this effort, she is likely to go unheard and ignored. Megawati became the poster child for this dilemma. Whether unintentionally or by design, once in office, she opted to follow traditional expectations of women's demeanor and performance and was widely criticized and perceived as ineffective as a direct result.

Over the dozen and more years of this study, we witnessed great change in Indonesia as a nation, in the two villages, and in the families and individuals who were its focus. Initially this study began as a comparison between the residents of two villages that varied in degree of rurality, development, and state intervention. Although we found obvious and real differences in women's roles and statuses between the two villages, even at the beginning the commonalities outweighed the differences, at least as they affected women's access to power and position. Over time these have diminished to the point where it makes more sense to view these villages as two nodes in a rapidly modernizing society, reflective of the urbanized, commercial culture of Yogyakarta and other large cities, increasingly penetrated by global enterprise, even in the heart of traditional Javanese society. Convergence between the two villages and the increasing evidence of participation in a global economy do not diminish the importance of Javanese tradition and culture in the practice of gender roles. If anything, the contradictions of women's position have become more intense and their roles more contested.

Notes

1. Bahasa Java, or Javanese, has different levels or forms that depend on age, sex, and status of speaker and addressee. Witnessing and understanding who spoke what to whom (for example, which form wives and husbands use with each other) provide important additional cues to power and status. See chapter 1 for more detail.

2. One complication created by the ongoing changes and upheavals is that almost as fast as we write about new developments, they again change. For example, the process of democratizing and decentralizing the political system at both national and local levels, with its consequences for women's status and gender roles, has seen almost continuous change in the years following Reformasi. A corollary problem is the choice of tense. When reporting the results of past fieldwork or of conditions that typify times past, we often use the past tense; otherwise, we normally use the present tense of scientific and literary narrative.

1. This is questionable, however, since by United Nations Development Program (UNDP) measures, Indonesia compares poorly to other East and Southeast Asian nations on the gender related development index (GDI) and the gender empowerment measure (GEM). Others argue that these rankings are artifacts of the particular indicators used (such as number of women in the legislature) and don't really fully capture relative situation (Blackburn 2001; Hancock 2001).

2. Anderson's influential perspective on the Javanese conception of power has historical roots in the origins of the Javanese kingdom of Mataram and the history of Javanese colonialism. It was initially the outcome of the insecurity of the Mataram dynasty (ca. 1550–1945 CE) and its need for legitimation. The Mataram dynasty originally came from a peasant family that rose to the throne. Their lower-class origins created an urgent need for a view of power that supported and legitimated their reign (Moedjanto 1986, 26). Institutionalization of a concept of power that arises from divine energy and sources made it difficult for the opposition to question their legitimacy as long as they were able to successfully maintain that they were the people chosen to have the spiritual, divine power. The long influence of the Mataram Kingdom in Java resulted in an ingrained concept of power based on the dynasty's interests. Suharto's background is similar to that of the Mataram dynasty—'he came from a lower-class agrarian family and was not highly educated. He also found it useful to build his legitimacy based upon the Javanese concept of power.

3. The current president of Indonesia, Susilo Bambang Yudhoyono (SBY), and his media advisers play to this perspective as well, promoting the image of the strong, quietly confident leader rather than the active initiator of programs and policies.

4. Oxford English Dictionary, 2nd ed., s.v. "syncretic."

5. Even now this tradition permeates Yogya political debate. The present sultan of Yogyakarta has five daughters and no son. Traditionally, only a son could inherit the throne in Yogyakarta's kingdom. There have been suggestions that changing cultural values mean that a woman should be able to become sultan. This idea, however, is highly contentious and has generated much debate.

6. In order, the five basic principles of Pancasila are (Frederick and Worden 1993): (1) belief in one God; (2) a just and civilized humanity; (3) the unity of Indonesia; (4) democracy guided by the wisdom of representative deliberation; and (5) social justice for all Indonesians. The use of this ideology and the meanings attributed to the principles changed over time with changing political purposes (Bourchier 2001, 117; Cribb 2001, 307).

7. One of the original objectives of this research was to locate hidden forms of resistance to patriarchal gender roles among village women (James Scott 1990). As will be described in subsequent chapters, we were unable to find meaningful examples.

8. *Kompas*, May 18, 2004, accessed July 4, 2009, http://www2.kompas. com/kompas-cetak/0405/18/utama/1030000.htm.

Chapter 2. Two Villages in Yogyakarta

1. Both the special status of the province and the role of the hereditary ruler have been debated in the new political climate, especially as direct elections have become the norm for local offices. However, at the time this was written nothing had changed.

2. Exact estimates vary by source.

3. As of the summer of 2010, this was the most recent census available.

4. Although the village in Sleman is poorer and more rural and remote than the Bantul village, the two districts overall are just the opposite: The kabupaten of Sleman adjoins an affluent part of urban Yogya where Gadjah Madah University is located and urban property values are high, whereas the kabupaten of Bantul is more agricultural and less developed.

5. Muhammediyah and NU are two umbrella grassroots Islamic organizations in Indonesia (*ormas* or *oganisasi masa*), dating from the early part of the twentieth century, that provide a combination of social and political affiliation, religious guidance, and social services. They are not the same as religious denominations or sects but tend to loosely organize participants' beliefs and practices. They differ in their interpretations of religious texts and sources and their openness to local culture. Both also have women's auxiliaries that have been an important source of guidance and interpretation of Islamic law for women (Van Doorn-Harder 2006, 3).

6. After the administrative reorganization that accompanied Reformasi, the subvillages then known as *dusun* are now called *pedukuhan*, the original term for such settlements, and titles for village officials also have changed. We will use the current terminology to avoid confusion, but it should be noted that at the time of the initial fieldwork, the old terms prevailed.

7. Under current law (Regional Government Law No. 32 of 2004), villages also have an elected board of representatives that shares power with the head. The lurah has a six-year term, with a limit of twelve years or two terms.

8. Formerly, all subvillage heads (*dukuh*) were appointed positions. As part of democratization and decentralization, districts have made this an elected position in recent years, with varied implementation dates. Some regions waited for the retirement of subvillage heads to implement the new law. Sleman made the change in 2000, Bantul in 2007.

9. After Reformasi, in theory, these positions were opened to anyone; in practice, they are still held by the wives of village officials.

10. This is a pseudonym, as are the names of all subvillages and village

residents who are identified by name. Only district (*kabupaten*) and higher-level places and public officials are identified by their real names.

11. A woman is counted as the head of a household only if there is no adult male present, regardless of the actual situation (Jones 2002).

12. Village statistics available at the time of initial fieldwork state that 929 people, or 49 percent of the economically active population, work in the agricultural sector, but this counts only the primary job of individuals reporting occupations. Similarly, officially, 608 persons (32 percent) worked in trade and services, and 345 (18 percent) worked in the handicraft sector. Village statistics should be interpreted cautiously, since they are notoriously unreliable, and there are a number of inconsistencies in the data as well as large numbers of persons who have multiple jobs that are not reported in these records.

13. By 2002, this subvillage head had become one of the division chairs in the village government. The subvillage head of the first subvillage also became the interim subvillage head for the second subvillage.

14. By 2007, this subvillage head was retired and the subvillage head of the first subvillage also became the interim subvillage head for the second subvillage.

15. The appointment was made by the district-level government.

16. According to the Indonesian marriage law, it is legal for a Muslim man to have up to four wives if he meets certain requirements, including the formal agreement of the previous wife and her inability to bear a child. However, the practice was not common in these villages. In an interview with the first wife, she acknowledged that she gave her husband permission to have a second wife because she cannot bear a child. She said that after many years of marriage without a child she felt that it was better to let her husband have a formal second marriage rather than see him have illicit affairs. Before she consented to this arrangement, her husband had been seeing another woman and had a child outside marriage, increasing pressure for her to give formal consent. Yet it is not completely clear why she opted to stay in the marriage rather than to file for divorce. Social status and economic reason may affect this decision. Divorced women tend to have lower social and economic status and have difficulties in maintaining their previous prestige and status; social stigma accompanies divorce.

17. At the time of the initial fieldwork, the subvillage head was not directly elected by the people; instead, any individual could register to compete for the position. The candidates have to take written exams. Local formal and informal leaders may give their recommendations, but final decisions were in the hands of district, subdistrict, and village officials. It

was quite common that good political connections and money influenced the decision. After Reformasi, districts began to replace appointment of subvillage heads with an electoral process. This happened relatively early in Bantul, much later in Sleman.

18. In 2007 the house was totally renovated again after suffering damage in the Bantul earthquake and now has a somewhat different arrangement.

CHAPTER 3. GOATS AND DOVES:
CONTRADICTIONS IN GENDER IDEOLOGY AND
THE GENDER DIVISION OF LABOR

1. There is a vast literature on the meaning of gender and gender roles rooted in different disciplines and geography. While it is beyond the scope of this account to provide a comprehensive review of gender roles in either context, this study builds on and is indebted to the many feminist theorists and researchers engaged in this enterprise, including Connell (2002); Epstein (1988); Lorber (1994); Mitchell (1971); Walby (1990); and West and Zimmerman (1987) for conceptual treatment of gender; and Brenner (1998); Errington (1990); H. Geertz (1961); Hatley (1990); Keeler (1987, 1990); Locher-Scholten (1992); N. Sullivan (1994); and Tiwon (2000) for applications in Indonesia and Java, as well as many others cited throughout the text for specific ideas and formulations.

2. Janaka is a character in the *wayang*, or shadow puppet theater, who symbolizes male virility and invincibility, qualities derived not from his physical prowess but from self-control and spiritual power.

3. See Connell (2009) for an extensive review and discussion of the literature on views about biological difference.

4. These are the areas that are often viewed as in the public domain and men's sphere of influence. However, it is often pointed out that this is an artificial distinction, especially in societies other than late twentieth-century industrialized societies. Research on Indonesia has been quick to observe the lack of separation between household and commercial enterprises or sites of production and reproduction (Brenner 1998; N. Sullivan 1994).

5. The explicit articulation of women's role as mother of the state predates the New Order. Martyn (2005, 206) quotes the language used by the Women's International Club in 1955 celebrating *Hari Ibu* (Mother's Day): "The celebration of this day stresses the tasks and duties of the

Indonesian woman as a mother, not only as a mother of the family, but also as a mother of the whole community and nation!"

6. The New Order was not alone in this practice in Indonesian history. Blackburn (2004) provides a comprehensive overview of the incorporation of gender ideology into state policies throughout Indonesian history from precolonial days through the fall of the New Order, and Martyn (2005) elaborates on the period following independence through the 1950s. However, it was during the New Order that gender was most explicitly and deliberately deployed as a tool of national development.

7. This is another obvious, albeit minor, contradiction. Wide-scale participation in public life for women was predicated on promoting an ideology of domesticity.

8. This is not to assert that Islamic views of women's roles and gender ideology are uniform and without profound disagreements and controversy. Quite the contrary, there is much debate on these issues, and Islam is used to find support for widely divergent views of women's rights, especially their place in the public sphere (Rinaldo 2010). There would be little disagreement, however, about the importance of upholding traditional wife and mother responsibilities.

Chapter 4. Gender and Agricultural Production

1. Portions of this chapter were published in Kusujiarti and Tickamyer (2000).

2. Village administrators keep records on residents and their activities, but at least at the time of the initial research, these were not always accurate or current and were difficult to reconcile with other sources of information. They are reported as an indicator of the official account.

3. Unlike Bu and Pak Yitno, in this family, the wife is known by her own name, as is more typically the case in Javanese families. Occasionally we refer to them collectively as the Mujis. Bu Ani and Pak Yitno were noted in the previous chapter as an example of a couple in which the wife earns the money and the husband has the power.

4. Many respondents report sudden die-offs of their chickens, and the countryside, once teaming with chickens running loose, is now remarkable for their absence. Presumably they have been victims of the avian flu.

5. Between 1999 and 2004–2005 the agriculture sector, previously a focus of the New Order central government, was neglected in favor of

industrial development and finding cash crops that could compete in the global marketplace. Rice production declined, forcing importation of rice where, formerly, self-sufficiency had been a point of pride. Under decentralization, the *kabupaten* (districts) assumed responsibility for creating and funding agricultural programs. In many places, funding for extension workers (PPL, or *petugas, penyuluh lapangan*), whose jobs had been to assist and enforce central agriculture polices, was eliminated or greatly reduced.

CHAPTER 5. INVOLUNTARY VOLUNTARY
SERVICE: GENDER AND SOCIAL WELFARE IN
CRISIS AND REFORM

1. Many elements of official New Order ideology were derived from Javanese cultural norms and values, adopted and imposed as part of a deliberate effort to create a unifying national ideology for a geographically, ethnically, religiously, and linguistically diverse and disparate nation.

2. Newberry (2006) points out that the PKK's promotion of domestic roles also was an important component of dealing with Indonesia's surplus labor, keeping women out of the labor market by promoting informal sector work that was compatible with reproductive responsibilities. She documents PKK activities in a working-class urban neighborhood (*kampung*) in Yogyakarta in the early 1990s.

3. See http://pkk.malangkota.go.id/ltb.php.

4. The ten programs of the PKK in abbreviated form are: (1) Pancasila; (2) mutual self-help; (3) food; (4) clothing; (5) housing; (6) education; (7) health; (8) cooperatives; (9) environment; (10) health and family planning (Newberry 2006, 24).

5. *Kompas*, April 22, 1999.

CHAPTER 6. MEN'S RIB:
POWER AND EMPOWERMENT

1. Although not referenced in the Qu'ran, the Old Testament account of the creation of the first woman from Adam's rib is a commonly held belief.

2. Laws No. 32 and 33, of 2004, have been issued to replace previous decentralization laws.

3. *Decentralization*, defined as "the transfer of authority and responsibility for public functions from the central government to subordinate or quasi-independent government organizations and/or the private sector," is widely recognized as "a complex multifaceted concept" (World Bank Decentralization Thematic Team, n.d.). Although the process always entails restructuring political arrangements to shift from larger to smaller political entities, there are many different forms and overlapping uses of the term in the literature. For example, different forms are identified, including political, administrative, and financial decentralization. Similarly, the term is sometimes used interchangeably, other times distinguished from related concepts of devolution, deconcentration, delegation, deregulation, and privatization. In this research we follow the work of Donahue (1997) and Rodrigues-Pose and Gill (2003) and define it as part of a multifaceted devolutionary process that encompasses three components: subnational legitimacy, decentralization of power, and decentralization of resources. Subnational legitimacy refers to the particular political or administrative units that are newly empowered. Decentralization of power entails the transfer of power and authority to these lower-level units, which may or may not be accompanied by a corresponding transfer of centrally controlled resources.

The form that decentralization takes in a polity depends on the specific configuration of these factors. Pressure to decentralize comes from both internal and external sources. International organizations have advocated devolution and decentralization as part of the development process, as a reform measure, and as a condition for aid. It is advocated as a means to improve governance, increase participation and representation, and decrease corruption and elite monopoly of state assets (Colongon 2003). There are also often strong sources of internally generated support in countries struggling to realign the distribution of power, especially where internal cleavages along historical regional, ethnic, religious, or cultural identities have been suppressed in favor of centralized authority or a dominant group.

4. An Indonesian women's movement was active from the early years of the twentieth century with goals of both independence from colonial domination and women's equality, including legal parity, education, and opportunity for advancement (Nyman 2006, 128). A confederation of women's organizations committed to principles of equality, human rights, and unity, regardless of religious or ethnic differences, emerged from early organizing efforts and ultimately coalesced in 1946 as KOWANI (*Kongres Wanita Indonesia*) or Indonesian Women's Congress, following independence (Nyman 2006, 129; Suryochondro 2000, 229). Both prior to

the New Order and following it, the Indonesian women's movement and its organizations have been quite diverse, encompassing a wide variety of sources and sometimes conflicting views (Blackburn 2004, 11–12).

5. The brutal suppression of GERWANI is credited by many analysts for the "depoliticization and domestication of women that would last for 30 years" (Nyman 2006, 131), that is, the duration of the New Order.

6. Although Suharto's New Order is credited with imposing this form of organizational structure on Indonesian women, it had a predecessor and model during the Japanese occupation. According to Nyman (2006, 129), Fujinkai was a women's group mandated by the Japanese with a hierarchical organizational structure very similar to Dharma Wanita and with social service objectives.

7. Although Megawati's party won the election and therefore should have made her president, backroom deals between Amien Rais and Wahid created a coalition that put Wahid in office. Megawati became vice president and then president when Wahid was impeached in 2001.

8. The numbers of administrative districts keep changing under decentralization as provinces and especially kabupaten are split to make new ones. As of 2008 there were thirty-three provinces, compared to twenty-seven prior to 2000 (http://id.wikipedia.org/wiki/Provinsi, accessed December 28, 2008). The 2008 number of kabupaten and kota with elected mayors (http://id.wikipedia.org/wiki/Daftar_Kabupaten_dan_Kota_Indonesia, accessed December 26, 2008) reflects ongoing expansion of these administrative units.

9. In 2008 she became the vice-governor of the Central Java province.

10. *Kompas*, January 26, 2004, transl. Siti Kusujiarti, accessed April 7, 2008, http://www.unisosdem.org/article_printfriendly.php?aid=3678&coid=3&caid=10.

11. Ibid.

12. Ironically, in 2008 Khofifah herself ran for governor of East Java and initially narrowly lost in a close election whose heavily contested outcome was overturned by the constitutional court and a new election ordered on the grounds of massive election fraud (http://old.thejakartapost.com/detailweekly.asp?fileid=20081203.@02, accessed December 26, 2008). Nevertheless, in the final outcome, the result remained the same and she lost.

13. This is highly unusual, given that the role of dukuh is generally seen as unsuitable for women because of their active presence in village affairs, such as paying visits in the night to distressed households, leading funerals, and so on.

14. One of the very few statements made by Bu Tosa toward the end

of the first interview was that she was better off before marriage, because she had more freedom then. She was immediately contradicted by her husband, who asserted that she was happier now and then proceeded to again monopolize the conversation.

15. Although this was a great opportunity, it also created complications, since her host was one of the candidates. Siti's description of the dilemma:

That put me in a seemingly non-neutral position. People tended to assume that I supported him in his bid as a village's head. It was quite challenging to explain that I did not really have a political affiliation connected to him and did not necessarily agree with all of his political opinions. On the other hand, my host and his family assumed that I automatically was on their side. They even tried to ask me to help in their campaign.... He asked me to write his campaign speeches, especially those that were related to women's activities and women's status and roles. Even though this opens opportunities for action research and for communicating my ideas, this was not my intention in this research. I did not write his speeches, but I discussed with him some of my thoughts on the issue. Fortunately, by this time I had completed most of my interviews so that the process did not create significant bias in the interviews.

16. To further complicate the gender politics, at the time of this election the woman candidate's husband had a second wife, at the time a relatively unusual occurrence that has subsequently become "fashionable" among government officials.

17. This couple subsequently has divorced, and the lurah was forced to resign on charges of corruption.

18. Tickamyer conducted interviews with PKS women cadres and leaders in Palembang and Jakarta in the summer of 2004 that probed these views.

19. For example, in the 1999 election, most of the women elected to the DPR, the national legislature, were found on Commission No. 7 dealing with health, population, social welfare, and women's empowerment. Commission No. 2, which deals with politics, law, and internal affairs, had the least women. The same results held in 2002 with the highest representation of women on Commission No. 6 Religion, Education and Culture and No. 7, Health and Population. Interviews with women members indicate that the reason is that these are not considered women's issues (Parawansa, 2002).

References

Alisjahbana, Sutan T. 1961. *Indonesia in the Modern World*. Bombay: Congress for Cultural Freedom.

Andaya, Barbara Watson. 2000. "Delineating Female Space: Seclusion and the State in Pre-Modern Island Southeast Asia." In *Other Pasts: Women, Gender and History in Early Modern Southeast Asia*, edited by Barbara Watson Andaya, 231–53. Honolulu: University of Hawaii Press.

Anderson, Benedict R. O'G. 1972. "The Idea of Power in Javanese Culture." In *Culture and Politics in Indonesia*, edited by Claire Holt, 1–70. Ithaca, NY: Cornell University Press.

Aripurnami, Sita. 2000. "Whiny, Finicky, Bitchy, Stupid and 'Revealing': The Image of Women in Indonesian Films." In *Indonesian Women: The Journey Continues*, edited by Mayling Oey-Gardiner and Carla Bianpoen, 50–65. Canberra: RSPAS Publishing / Australian National University.

Arneil, Barbara. 2006. "Just Communities: Social Capital, Gender, and Culture." In *Gender and Social Capital*, edited by Brenda O'Neill and Elisabeth Gidengil, 15–44. New York: Routledge.

Asian Development Bank. 1999. *Fighting Poverty in Asia and the Pacific: The Poverty Reduction Strategy*. Manila: Asian Development Bank.

———. 2006. *Indonesia: Country Gender Assessment*. July. Manila: Southeast Asia Regional Department, Regional and Sustainable Development Department, Asian Development Bank.

Aspinall, Edward, and Greg Fealy, eds. 2003. *Local Power and Politics in Indonesia: Decentralisation & Democratisation*. Singapore: Institute of Southeast Asian Studies.

Bappenas (National Development Planning Agency). 1998. "Proyek Penanggulangan Kemiskinan di Perkotaan" (Urban Poverty Project). Unpublished Report.

————. 1999. "Statement of Development Policy: Social Safety Net Program." http://www.worldbank.org.

Barrett, Michelle. 1980. *Women's Oppression Today*. London: Verso.

Barton, Greg. 2001. "The Prospects for Islam." In *Indonesia Today: Challenges of History,* edited by Grayson J. Lloyd and Shannon L. Smith, 244–55. Singapore: Institute of Southeast Asian Studies.

Beneria, Lourdes, and Gita Sen. 1981. "Accumulation, Reproduction, and Women's Role in Economic Development: Boserup Revisited." *Signs* 7 (2): 279–98.

Berninghausen, Jutta, and Birgit Kerstan. 1992. *Forging New Paths: Feminist Social Methodology and Rural Women in Java*. London: Zed Books.

Bhavnani, Kum-Kum. 2004. "Tracing the Contours: Feminist Research and Feminist Objectivity." In *Feminist Perspectives on Social Research*, edited by Sharlene Nagy Hesse-Biber and Michelle L. Yaiser, 65–77. New York: Oxford University Press.

Blackburn, Susan, ed. 2001. *Love, Sex and Power: Women in Southeast Asia*. Victoria, Australia: Monash Asia Institute.

————. 2004. *Women and the State in Modern Indonesia*. Cambridge: Cambridge University Press.

Booth, Anne. 2000. "The Impact of the Indonesian Crisis on Welfare: What Do We Know Two Years On?" In *Indonesia in Transition: Social Aspects of Reformasi and Crisis*, edited by Chris Manning and Peter van Diermen, 145–62. Singapore: Institute of Southeast Asian Studies.

Boserup, Ester. 1970. *Women's Role in Economic Development*. New York: St. Martin's Press.

Bourchier, David. 2001. "Conservative Political Ideology in Indonesia: A Fourth Wave?" In *Indonesia Today: Challenges of History*, edited by Grayson J. Lloyd and Shannon L. Smith, 112–25. Singapore: Institute of Southeast Asian Studies.

BPS (Biro Pusat Statistik or Indonesian Statistical Bureau). 1995. *Wanita dan Pria di D.I. Yogyakarta*. Statistics Office of the Special Province of Yogyakarta, Yogyakarta, Indonesia.

————. 2004. Country Paper Official Statistics and Its Development in Indonesia. Economic and Social Commission for Asia and the Pacific. Subcommittee on Statistics First Session February 18–20, 2004. Jakarta: BPS.

Brenner, Suzanne A. 1996. "Reconstructing Self and Society: Javanese Muslim Women and 'The Veil.'" *American Ethnologist* 23:673–97.

———. 1998. *The Domestication of Desire: Women, Wealth, and Modernity in Java*. Princeton, NJ: Princeton University Press.

Bulkin, Farchan. 1983. *State and Society: Indonesian Politics Under the New Order (1966–1978)*. PhD diss., Seattle: University of Washington.

Bush, Robin. 2008. "Regional Sharia Regulations in Indonesia: Anomaly or Symptom?" In *Expressing Islam: Religious Life and Politics in Indonesia*, edited by Greg Fealy and Sally White, 174–91. Singapore: Institute of Southeast Asian Studies.

Chandrasekaran, Rajiv. 2001. "Indonesia Turns to an Enigma; Megawati Has Stayed in the Background." *Washington Post*. July 24. Accessed August 18, 2009. http://www.lexisnexis.com/us/lnacademic/results/docview/docview.do?docLinkInd=true&risb=21_T7166222842&format=GNBFI&sort=BOOLEAN&startDocNo=151&resultsUrl Key=29_T7166222845&cisb=22_T7166222844&treeMax=true&tree Width=0&csi=8075&docNo=159.

Collier, William L. 1980. *Declining Labor Absorption (1878 to 1980) in Javanese Rice Production*. Agro Economic Survey. Rural Dynamics Occasional Papers No. 2. Bogor, Indonesia.

Collier, William L., Jusuf M. Colter, Sinarhadi, and Robert D'A Shaw. 1974. "Choice of Technique in Rice Milling on Java." *Bulletin of Indonesian Economic Studies* 10 (1): 106–20.

Collins, Elizabeth Fuller. 2007. *Indonesia Betrayed: How Development Fails*. Honolulu: University of Hawaii Press.

Collins, Elizabeth Fuller, and Ernaldi Bahar. 2000. "To Know Shame: Malu and Its Uses in Malay Societies." *Crossroads: An Interdisciplinary Journal of Southeast Asian Studies* 14 (1): 35–69.

Colongon, Arellano A., Jr. 2003. "What Is Happening on the Ground? The Progress of Decentralisation." In *Local Power and Politics in Indonesia: Decentralisation and Democratization*, edited by Edward Aspinall and Greg Fealy, 87–101. Singapore: Institute of Southeast Asian Studies.

Connell, Robert W. 2002. *Gender*. Cambridge: Polity Press.

Connell, Raewyn. 2009. *Gender in World Perspective*. 2nd ed. Cambridge: Polity Press.

Cribb, Robert. 2001. "Independence for Java? New National Projects for an Old Empire." In *Indonesia Today: Challenges of History,* edited by Grayson J. Lloyd and Shannon L. Smith, 298–307. Singapore: Institute of Southeast Asian Studies.

Djajadiningrat-Nieuwenhuis, Madelon. 1992. "Ibuism and Priyayization: Path to Power?" In *Indonesian Women in Focus: Past and Present*

Notions, edited by Elsbeth Locher-Scholten and Anke Niehof, 43–51. Leiden: KITLV Press.

Donahue, John D. 1997. *Disunited States: What's at Stake as Washington Fades and the States Take the Lead.* New York: HarperCollins.

Eisenstein, Zillah. 2000. "Writing Bodies on the Nation for the Globe." In *Women, States, and Nationalism: At Home in the Nation?*, edited by Sita Ranchod-Nilsson and Mary Ann Tétreault, 35–53. New York: Routledge.

Elmhirst, Becky. 2000. "Negotiating Gender, Kinship and Livelihood Practices in an Indonesian Transmigration Area." In *Women and Households in Indonesia: Cultural Notions and Social Practices*, edited by Juliette Koning, Marleen Nolten, Janet Rodenburg, and Ratna Saptari, 208–34. Richmond, Surrey: Curzon Press.

Epstein, Cynthia Fuchs. 1988. *Deceptive Distinctions: Sex, Gender, and the Social Order.* New Haven, CT: Yale University Press; New York: Russell Sage Foundation.

Errington, Shelly. 1990. "Recasting Sex, Gender, and Power: A Theoretical and Regional Overview." In *Power and Difference: Gender in Island Southeast Asia*, edited by Jane Monnig Atkinson and Shelly Errington, 1–58. Stanford, CA: Stanford University Press.

Evans, Sara M., and Harry C. Boyte. 1986. *Free Spaces: The Sources of Democratic Change in America.* New York: Harper and Row.

Feridhanusetyawan, Tubagus. 1998. "Social Impact of the Indonesian Economic Crisis." *Indonesian Quarterly* 26 (2): 325–64.

Frederick, William H., and Robert L. Worden, eds. 1993. *Indonesia: A Country Study.* Washington, DC: GPO for the Library of Congress. Accessed June 26, 2009. http://countrystudies.us/indonesia/86.htm.

Geertz, Clifford. 1956. *The Development of the Javanese Economy: A Socio-Cultural Approach.* Cambridge, MA: Center for International Studies.

Geertz, Hildred. 1961. *The Javanese Family: A Study of Kinship and Socialization.* Glencoe, NY: Free Press.

Gerke, Solvay. 1992. *Social Change and Life Planning of Rural Javanese Women.* Fort Lauderdale, FL: Verlag Breitenbach.

Gough, Ian. 2004. "Welfare Regimes in Development Contexts: A Global and Regional Analysis." In *Insecurity and Welfare Regimes in Asia, Africa and Latin America*, edited by Ian Gough and Geoffrey D. Wood, 15–48. Cambridge: Cambridge University Press.

Gramsci, Antonio. 1971. *Selections from the Prison Notebooks.* New York: International Publishers.

Hancock, Peter. 2001. "Gender Empowerment Issues from West Java." In *Love, Sex and Power: Women in Southeast Asia*, edited by Susan Blackburn, 75–88. Victoria, Australia: Monash Asia Institute.

Hatley, Barbara. 1990. "Theatrical Imagery and Gender Ideology in Java." In *Power and Difference: Gender in Island Southeast Asia*, edited by Jane Monnig Atkinson and Shelly Errington, 177–208. Stanford, CA: Stanford University Press.

Hefner, Robert W. 2000. *Civil Islam: Muslims and Democratization in Indonesia.* Princeton, NJ: Princeton University Press.

Hesse-Biber, Sharlene Nagy, and Michelle L. Yaiser. 2004. *Feminist Perspectives on Social Research.* New York: Oxford University Press.

Huesken, Frans. 1984. "Capitalism and Agrarian Differentiation in a Javanese Village." ZZOA Working Paper No. 44, University of Amsterdam.

Hugo, Graeme J., Terence H. Hull, Valerie J. Hull, and Gavin W. Jones. 1987. *The Demographic Dimension in Indonesian Development.* Oxford: Oxford University Press.

Hull, Terence H. 2000. "Alleviating Poverty: Conundrums of Planning, Administration, and Governance." Prepared for BAPPENAS seminar on "Renewing Poverty Reduction Strategy in Indonesia," Jakarta, Indonesia, August 1.

Jackson, Karl D. 1978. "Bureaucratic Polity: A Theoretical Framework for the Analysis of Power and Communications in Indonesia." In *Political Power and Communications in Indonesia*, edited by Karl D. Jackson and Lucian W. Pye, 3–22. Berkeley, CA: University of California Press.

Jay, Robert R. 1969. *Javanese Villagers: Social Relations in Rural Modjokuto.* Cambridge, MA: MIT Press.

Jones, Gavin W. 2002. "The Changing Indonesian Household." In *Women in Indonesia: Gender, Equity and Development*, edited by Kathryn M. Robinson and Sharon L. Bessell, 219–34. Singapore: Institute of Southeast Asian Studies.

Keeler, Ward. 1987. *Javanese Shadow Plays, Javanese Selves.* Princeton, NJ: Princeton University Press.

_____. 1990. "Speaking of Gender in Java." In *Power and Difference: Gender in Island Southeast Asia*, edited by Jane Monnig Atkinson and Shelly Errington, 127–52. Stanford, CA: Stanford University Press.

Koentjaraningrat. 1967. "A Survey of Social Studies on Rural Indonesia." In *Villages in Indonesia*, edited by Koentjaraningrat, 1–29. Ithaca, NY: Cornell University Press.

———. 1980. "Javanese Terms for God and Supernatural Beings and the Idea of Power." In *Man, Meaning and History: Essays in Honour of H. G. Schulte Nordholt*, edited by Reimar Schefold, Johan W. Schoorl, and J. Tennekes. The Hague: Martinus Nijhoff.

———. 1985. *Javanese Culture.* Singapore: Oxford University Press.

Komter, Aafke. 1991. "Gender, Power, and Feminist Theory." In *The Gender of Power*, edited by Kathy Davis, Monique Leijenaar, and Jantine Oldersma, 42–65. Newbury Park, CA: Sage.

Kumar, Ann. 2000. "Imagining Women in Javanese Religion: Goddesses, Ascetes, Queens, Consorts, Wives." In *Other Pasts: Women, Gender and History in Early Modern Southeast Asia*, edited by Barbara Watson Andaya, 87–104. Honolulu: University of Hawaii Press.

Kusujiarti, Siti. 1995. "Hidden Power in Gender Relations Among Indonesians: A Case Study in a Javanese Village, Indonesia." PhD diss., University of Kentucky.

Kusujiarti, Siti, and Ann Tickamyer. 2000. "Gender Division of Labor in Two Javanese Villages." *Gender, Technology and Development* 4 (3): 415–39.

Locher-Scholten, Elsbeth. 1992. "Female Labour in Twentieth Century Java: European Notions—Indonesian Practice." In *Indonesian Women in Focus: Past and Present Notions*, edited by Elsbeth Locher-Scholten and Anke Niehof, 77–103. Leiden: KITLV Press.

———. 2000. *Women and the Colonial State: Essays on Gender and Modernity in the Netherlands Indies, 1900–1942.* Amsterdam: Amsterdam University Press.

Lorber, Judith. 1994. *Paradoxes of Gender.* New Haven, CT: Yale University Press.

Manderson, Lenore. 1983. *Women's Work and Women's Roles: Economics and Everyday Life in Indonesia, Malaysia, and Singapore.* Development Monograph No. 32. Canberra: Australian National University.

Martyn, Elizabeth. 2005. *The Women's Movement in Post-Colonial Indonesia: Gender and Nation in a New Democracy.* London: RoutledgeCurzon.

Mather, Celia E. 1982. "Industrialization in the Tangerang Regency of West Java: Women Workers and the Islamic Patriarchy." Working paper no. 17, Center for Sociology and Anthropology, University of Amsterdam.

Mayer, Tamar, ed. 2000. *Gender Ironies of Nationalism: Sexing the Nation.* London: Routledge.

McGirk, Tim. 2001. "Fire Over Indonesia." *Time*, August 6. Accessed

August 19, 2009. http://www.time.com/time/magazine/article/0,9171, 1000459,00.html20.

Mies, Maria, Veronika Bennholdt-Thomsen, and Claudia von Werlhof. 1988. *Women: The Last Colony.* London: Zed Books.

Ministry of Social Affairs. 1984. *Pola Dasar Pembangunan Bidang Kesejahteraan Sosial (Basic Policies for the Development of Social Welfare).* Jakarta, Indonesia.

————. 1986. *Social Welfare Activities in Pictures.* Jakarta, Indonesia.

Mitchell, Juliet. 1971. *Women's Estate.* London: Penguin.

Moedjanto, G. 1986. *The Concept of Power in Javanese Culture.* Yogyakarta: Gadjah Mada University Press.

Mulder, Niels. 1980. *Mysticism and Everyday Life in Contemporary Java: Cultural Persistence and Change.* Singapore: Singapore University Press.

————. 1992. *Individual and Society in Java: A Cultural Analysis.* 2nd ed. Yogyakarta: Gadjah Mada University Press.

Naples, Nancy A. 1999. "Towards a Comparative Analysis of Women's Political Praxis: Explicating Multiple Dimensions of Standpoint Epistemology for Feminist Ethnography." *Women & Politics* 20 (1): 29–57.

Newberry, Janice C. 2006. *Back Door Java: State Formation and the Domestic in Working Class Java.* Peterborough, Ontario: Broadview Press.

Noerdin, Edriana. 2002. "Customary Institutions, *Syariah* Law and the Marginalisation of Indonesian Women." In *Women in Indonesia: Gender, Equity and Development*, edited by Kathryn M. Robinson and Sharon L. Bessell, 179–86. Singapore: Institute of Southeast Asian Studies.

Nyman, Mikaela. 2006. *Democratising Indonesia: The Challenges of Civil Society in the Era of Reformasi.* Copenhagen: Nordic Institute of Asian Studies Press.

Oey, Mayling. 1985. "Changing Work Patterns in Indonesia During the 1970s: Causes and Consequences." *Prisma* 37:18–46.

Oey-Gardiner, Mayling. 1998. "The Impact of the Financial Crisis on Indonesian Women: Some Survival Strategies." *Indonesian Quarterly* 26 (2): 79–90.

O'Neill, Brenda, and Elisabeth Gidengil, eds.. 2006. *Gender and Social Capital.* New York: Routledge.

Parawansa, Khofifah Indar. 2002. "Obstacles to Women's Participation in Indonesia." In International IDEA, *Women in Parliament*. Stockholm: IDEA. (http://www.idea.int), accessed September 2, 20012, www.idea.int/publications/wip/upload/CS_Indonesia_Parawansa.pdf.

———. 2006. "Case Study Indonesia: Enhancing Women's Political Participation in Indonesia." In *Women in Parliament: Beyond Numbers*, rev. ed., edited by Julie Ballington and Azza Karam, 82–90. Accessed March 28, 2008. Stockholm: IDEA. http://www.idea.int/publications/wip2/upload/Indonesia.pdf.

Peluso, Nancy Lee. 1984. *Occupational Mobility and the Economic Role of Rural Women in Yogyakarta*. Yogyakarta, Indonesia: Population Studies Center Monograph, Gadjah Mada University.

PKK Kota Malang. Accessed October 5, 2010. http://www.pkk.malangkota.go.id/ltb.php.

Poovey, Mary. 1988. *Uneven Developments: The Ideological Work of Gender in Mid-Victorian England*. Chicago: University of Chicago Press.

Pritchett, Lant, Sudarno Sumarto, and Asep Suryahadi. 2002. "Targeted Programs in an Economic Crisis: Empirical Findings from Indonesia's Experience." July 31. Paper from SMERU Research Institute, Jakarta.

Pye, Lucian W.. 1985. *Asian Power and Politics: The Cultural Dimensions of Authority*. Cambridge, MA: Belknap Press of Harvard University Press.

Rai, Shirin M. 2008. *The Gender Politics of Development: Essays in Hope and Despair*. New York: Zed Books.

Ranchod-Nilsson, Sita, and Mary Ann Tétreault, eds. 2000. *Women, States, and Nationalism: At Home in the Nation?* New York: Routledge.

Reid, Anthony. 1988. "Female Roles in Pre-Colonial Southeast Asia." *Modern Asia Studies* 22 (3): 629–45.

Rinaldo, Rachel. 2008. "Envisioning the Nation: Women Activists, Religion, and the Public Sphere in Indonesia." *Social Forces* 86 (June): 1781–804.

———. 2010. "The Islamic revival and Women's Political Subjectivity in Indonesia." *Women's Studies International Forum* 33 (4): 422–31.

Robinson, Kathryn. 2001. "Gender, Islam and Culture in Indonesia." In *Love, Sex and Power: Women in Southeast Asia*, edited by Susan Blackburn, 17–30. Victoria, Australia: Monash Asia Institue.

Rodrigues-Pose, Andres, and Nicholas Gill. 2003. "The Global Trend

Towards Devolution and Its Implications." *Environment and Planning C: Government and Policy* 21:333–51.

Roestam, K. S. 1990. *The Family Welfare Movement in Indonesia.* Jakarta, Indonesia: Pembinaan Kesejahteraan Keluarga.

———. 1993. *Pembangunan.* Jakarta, Indonesia: Department of Internal Affairs.

Rogers, Barbara. 1980. *The Domestication of Women: Discrimination in Developing Societies.* London: Kogan Page.

Rosaldo, Michelle Zimbalist, and Louise Lamphere. 1974. *Women, Culture, and Society.* Stanford, CA: Stanford University Press.

Sachs, Carolyn E. 1996. *Gendered Fields: Rural Women, Agriculture, and Environment.* Boulder, CO: Westview Press.

Sajogyo, Pudjiwati. 1979. *Meneliti Peranan Wanita Pedesaan di Jawa Barat: Apakah Faedahnya.* Lembaga Penelitaian Sosiologi Pedesaan. Bogor, Indonesia: Institu Pertanian Bogor.

———. 1983. *Peranan Wanita dalam Perkembangan Masyarakat Desa.* Jakarta, Indonesia: Rajawali Press.

Santoso, Priyo B. 1993. *Birokrasi Pemerintah Orde Baru (Bureaucracy of the New Order Government).* Jakarta, Indonesia: Rajawali Press.

Schiller, B. M. 1978. "Women, Work, and Status in Rural Java." M.A. thesis, Ohio University.

Scott, James C. 1990. *Domination and the Arts of Resistance: Hidden Transcripts.* New Haven, CT: Yale University Press.

Scott, Joan W. 2007. *The Politics of the Veil.* Princeton, NJ: Princeton University Press.

Smyth, Ines. 1993. "A Critical Look at the Indonesian Government's Policies for Women." In *Development and Social Welfare: Indonesia's Experiences Under the New Order*, edited by Jan-Paul Dirkse, Frans Hüsken, and Mario Rutten, 117–30. Leiden: KITLV Press.

Stivens, Maila. 1990. "Thinking About Gender, State and Civil Society in Indonesia." In *State and Civil Society in Indonesia*, edited by Arief Budiman, 99–113. Monash Papers on Southeast Asia No. 22, Clayton. Center of Southeast Asian Studies, Monash University.

Stoler, Ann. 1977. "Rice Harvesting in Kali Loro: A Study of Class and Labor Relations in Rural Java." *American Ethnologist* 4 (4): 678–98.

Strauss, John, Kathleen Beegle, Agus Dwiyanto, Yulia Herawati, Daan Pattinsasarany, Elan Satriawan, Bondan Sikoki, Sukamdi, and

Firman Witoelar. 2004. *Indonesian Living Standards: Before and After the Financial Crisis.* Santa Monica, CA: Rand.

Sullivan, John. 1992. *Local Government and Community in Java: An Urban Case-Study.* New York: Oxford University Press.

Sullivan, Norma. 1994. *Masters and Managers: A Study of Gender Relations in Urban Java.* NSW, Australia: Allen and Unwin.

———. 2000. "Gender and Politics Under the Suharto Regime, 1966–1988." Working paper, Ralph Bunche Institute on the United Nations.

Suratiyah, Ken, Sunarru S. Hariadi, I. Ketut Sudibia, and I. Wayan Sudarta. 1991. *Pembangunan Pertanian dan Peranan Wanita di Pedesaan Yogyakarta dan Bali.* Center for Population Research. Yogyakarta: Gadjah Mada University.

Suryakusuma, Julia I. 1991. "Seksualitas Dalam Pengaturan Negara." (Sexuality in the State's Regulations)*/// Prisma* 7:71–83.

———. 1996. "The State and Sexuality in New Order Indonesia." In *Fantasizing the Feminine in Indonesia*, edited by Laurie J. Sears, 92–119. Durham, NC: Duke University Press.

Suryochandro, Sukanti. 2000. "The Development of the Women's Movement in Indonesia." In *Indonesian Women: The Journey Continues,* edited by Mayling Oey-Gardiner and Carla Bianpoen, 224–43. Canberra: Australian National University Press.

Sutherland. Heather A. 1979. *The Making of a Bureaucratic Elite: The Colonial Transformation of the Javanese Priyayi.* American Studies Association of Australia Southeast Asia Series. Singapore: Heinemann.

Tiwon, Sylvia. 2000. "Reconstructing Boundaries and Beyond." In *Women and Households in Indonesia: Cultural Notions and Social Practices,* edited by Juliette Koning, Marleen Nolten, Janet Rodenburg, and Ratna Saptari, 68–84. Richmond, Surrey: Curzon Press.

UNDP (United Nations Development Programme). 2010. *Partisipasi Perempuan Dalam Politik and Pemerentah (*Women's Participation in Politics and Government)*///* Policy paper no. 90. Jakarta, Indonesia.

Van Doorn-Harder, Pieternella. 2006. *Women Shaping Islam: Reading the Qur'an in Indonesia.* Chicago: University of Illinois Press.

Walby, Sylvia. 1990. *Theorizing Patriarchy.* Oxford: Basil Blackwell.

Wearing, Betsy. 1984. *The Ideology of Motherhood: A Study of Sydney Suburban Mothers.* Sydney: Allen and Unwin.

West, Candace, and Don H. Zimmerman. 1987. "Doing Gender." *Gender and Society* 1 (June): 125–51.

White, Benjamin. 1976a. "Population, Involution and Employment in Rural Java. *Development and Change* 7:267–90.

———. 1976b. "Production and Reproduction in a Javanese Village." PhD diss., Columbia University.

———. 1984. "Measuring Time Allocation, Decision Making and Agrarian Changes Affecting Rural Women: Examples from Recent Research in Indonesia." *IDS Bulletin* 15 (1): 18–32.

Wieringa, Saskia. 1988. "GERWANI and the PKK: Brokers on Behalf of Whom?" Paper presented at Women as Mediators in Indonesia. International Workshop on Indonesian Studies No. 3, Royal Institute of Linguistics and Anthropology, Leiden.

———. 2002. *Sexual Politics in Indonesia*. Basingstoke: Palgrave Macmillan.

Williams, Linda B. 1990. *Development, Demography, and Family Decision-Making: The Status of Women in Rural Java*. Boulder, CO: Westview Press.

Willner, Ann R. 1961. *From Rice Field to Factory: The Industrialization of a Rural Labor Force in Java*. PhD diss., University of Chicago.

Wolf, Diane L. 1992. *Factory Daughters: Gender, Household Dynamics, and Rural Industrialization in Java*. Berkeley: University of California Press.

———, ed. 1996. *Feminist Dilemmas in Fieldwork*. Boulder, CO: Westview Press.

Woodward, Mark R. 1989. *Islam in Java: Normative Piety and Mysticism in the Sultanate of Yogyakarta*. Tucson: University of Arizona Press.

World Bank. 1999. *Report and Recommendations of the President of the International Bank for Reconstruction and Development to the Executive Directors on a Social Safety Net Adjustment Loan in the Amount of US $600 million to the Republic of Indonesia*. http://www.worldbank.org.

———. n.d. Decentralization Thematic Team. Accessed December 25, 2004.http://www.ciesin.org/decentralization/English/General/Different_forms.html.

Wusananingsih, Kodar 1994. *Development Programs for Women in Indonesia: A Review and Recommendation*. M.A. thesis, University of Kentucky.

Yuval-Davis, Nira. 1997. *Gender and Nation*. London: Sage.

Index

activism/agency, women's, 5, 34, 105, 215. *See also* autonomy; empowerment, women's; leaders, women; women's participation in *under* politics

activities, social: village-level, 61, 65, 70, 78, 87, 172, 174; women's, 72–73, 81–82, 108, 173, 175, 178–80, 186, 192

agriculture, activities/processes: decision making, 141, 143, 152–53; Indonesian, 126–60; labor, 77–78, 127, 129, 133–34, 137, 143, 158; production, 25, 62–63, 126, 129–32, 135–42, 145, 154, 158–59; sector of, 76, 129, 138–39, 142–44, 146, 151, 154, 157, 159–60, 224n12; wives' involvement in, 154. *See also* rural *under* culture, Javanese; development, rural; economy, rural; labor, gender division of

arisans, 174, 180, 186–87

autonomy: political, 193–94, 196, 201; women's, 3, 7, 32–33, 94, 124, 172, 177. *See also* activism/agency, women's; empowerment, women's; leaders, women; women's participation in *under* politics

bupatis, 1–2, 91, 175, 187–88, 191, 196, 198, 205

culture, Javanese: beliefs, 36, 41, 53; gender relations, 2–3, 6, 16, 31, 34–35, 37–38, 46, 52, 94–95, 127; language, 38, 75, 221n1; religion, 39, 63–64, 73; rural, 2–3, 10, 66, 106, 215 (*see also* agriculture, activities/processes); social order, 38; society, 2, 24–25, 30–31, 35, 37, 42, 46, 52, 87, 95, 98, 219; worldview, 38–39

decentralization, 7, 22, 44, 46, 61, 91, 141, 183, 185, 193–94, 196, 228–29n3; representation and, 193–95, 228n3. *See also* democracy, process/movement; democratization; elections; leaders, women; politics; Reformasi

decision making, household, 99–101, 106–14. *See also* labor, gender division; agriculture, activities/processes

democracy, process/movement, 22, 193–94. *See also* decentralization; democratization; elections; politics; Reformasi

democratization, 7, 91, 183, 185, 223n8.
See also decentralization; democracy,
process/movement; elections; politics;
Reformasi
development, 3–6, 10, 25, 33, 47–50, 53,
78, 91, 93–94, 102–3, 105, 124–26,
137, 139, 167, 170, 181, 183, 195, 214,
219; economic, 4, 6–7, 10, 47–48, 59,
85, 91, 103, 137, 143, 164–65, 168, 187,
226–27n5; rural, 9, 11; urban, 91, 94,
127, 143, 156; women's involvement
in, 6–7, 33, 47–50, 102–3, 137, 167
Dharma Wanita, 1, 103, 187, 192, 195,
214, 229n6

economy: Asian crisis, 21, 91, 129, 161–
62; rural, 126, 128, 136, 156–57
elections, 22, 45, 66, 193–96, 201, 209,
223n7. *See also* decentralization; democracy, process/movement; democratization; Reformasi
employment, 62–63, 68, 77, 96, 107,
109–11, 113–14, 119–22, 124, 129–30,
134, 140, 143, 163, 173, 182
empowerment, women's, 1, 23, 26, 102,
124, 190, 192, 196, 200, 210, 214, 216–
18, 230n19. *See also* activism/agency,
women's; autonomy; women's participation in *under* politics
equal rights, 31, 48, 213

Family Welfare Program. *See* PKK
feminism/feminists: methods, 33; frame-
work/approach, 9, 15; theories, 13, 33

gender. *See* ideology, gender; *under*
labor; *under* politics; *under* power;
under relations

hegemony, 5, 53
household: decision making, 99–101,
106–14; gender division of labor in,
94–96, 106, 114–22, 124, 133, 157,

202; women's access to resources of,
2, 7, 32

ibuism ("housewifization"), 47, 105, 168,
225–26n5. *See also* ideology, gender;
Panca Dharma Wanita
ideology, gender: differences, 8, 53,
97–98, 100, 129–30, 143–44; order, 8,
46, 215; roles, 3, 5, 7, 9, 11, 22–25, 34,
41, 45, 52, 91, 93–95, 98-99, 105–7,
108, 109, 112–13, 122–25, 127, 129,
158, 164, 188, 211, 214–15, 217, 219,
221n2, 222n7, 225n1; state, 48–49,
226n6. *See also* ibuism; kodrat; Panca
Dharma Wanita; patriarchy; power
independence, political, 33, 43, 55, 195
Islam, 30, 39, 42–46, 50, 55, 63–64, 77;
Idul fitri, 64; pengajian, 64, 77,
186–87; Ramadan, 64, 78; schools, 76.
See also Muslims

kodrat, 7–38, 47–51, 97–99, 104, 108,
121, 168, 171, 191, 198, 214. *See also*
culture, Javanese; ideology, gender;
patriarchy; power

labor, gender division of, 21, 25, 54, 99,
209, 215; in agriculture, 133, 136–52,
157–60; household, 94–96, 106, 114–
22, 124, 133, 157, 202; in production
and reproduction, 96. *See also* decision making; labor *under* agriculture,
activities/processes
leaders, women, 31, 65, 70–71, 84, 211.
See also autonomy; activism/agency;
decentralization; Megawati; Midiwati; Miniwati; women's participation in *under* politics
livelihood, 6, 10, 54, 109, 127–28, 136,
145, 186, 203, 210

Megawati, 2, 22, 24, 26, 29–30, 51, 182,
192, 196, 199, 218, 229n7. *See also*

leaders, women; women's participation in *under* politics

men: characteristics of, 97–98; dominance by, 12, 20, 37, 66, 76, 91, 100–101, 104, 128, 137–39, 141–42, 153, 171, 200, 209–15; gender role perception of, 106–7; kodrat, 37, 99, 121; responsibilities of, 48–49, 66, 77, 99, 114–18, 121, 140, 145–46, 205

Midiwati, 1, 198–99. *See also* leaders, women; women's participation in *under* politics

Miniwati, 191–92, 203, 211. *See also* leaders, women; women's participation in *under* politics

movement, women's, 214, 228–29n4

Muslims, 6, 29, 42–43, 64–65, 70, 77, 85–86, 93, 207. *See also* Islam

nation-building, 6–7; women's role in, 103. *See also* development; women's participation in *under* politics; Reformasi

New Order government/state, 6, 18, 21, 26, 35, 37, 46, 49–53, 61, 80, 91, 101–2, 139, 141, 162–64, 166–67, 170, 180, 193, 227n1, 228–29nn4, 6

organizations, women's, 7, 60, 81, 86, 108, 195, 200. *See also* Dharma Wanita; PKK; social services/welfare

Panca Dharma Wanita, 48, 103, 105, 108–9, 120, 123–24, 168. *See also* ideology, gender; ibuism; kodrat

patriarchy: gender ideology and, 3, 7, 32, 172, 195; "institutionalized inequality," 8, 96. *See also* ideology, gender; kodrat; power

PKK (Pembinaan Kesejahteraan Keluarga; Family Welfare Program), 1, 65, 67, 71, 79, 82, 84, 88, 103, 164, 168–72, 175–76, 178–88, 190, 192,

195, 203, 206, 210–11, 214, 218, 227nn2–4; Pendidikan Kesejahteraan Keluarga, 169; Pemberdayaan dan Kesejahteraan, 65, 183. *See also* social services/welfare; organizations, women's

politics: democratic, 1, 105, 181; gender, 4, 23, 161, 206, 210, 230n16 (*see also* leaders, women); general participation in, 23, 213; women's participation in, 26, 171, 194, 195, 210, 212, 214–15, 230nn16, 18, 19. *See also* decentralization; democracy, process/movement; democratization; elections; Reformasi; public sphere/domain *under* society

power: gendered, 24, 31–37 (*see also* ideology, gender; kodrat; patriarchy); holders of, 36–37, 39, 47, 104–5, 168; in Javanese culture/society, 2, 24, 35–37, 49, 218, 222n2; political, access to, 26, 202, 217, 219; relations, 5, 96; structures, 91; women's, 24, 26, 31–37, 143, 162, 192, 32

Reformasi, 22, 26, 30, 44, 60, 64, 66, 106, 182–83, 185, 192, 195, 197, 206, 213–14, 221n2, 223n6, 224–25n17. *See also* decentralization; democracy, process/movement; democratic *under* politics

relations: gender, 2–6, 8, 12–13, 23–24, 33, 52, 95–96, 102, 105, 215 (*see also* gender relations *under* culture, Javanese); social, 36, 38, 48, 95–97, 140; village-level, 17, 74, 90–91, 159, 177

representation, women's, 192, 195–97. *See also* activism/agency, women's; autonomy; empowerment; leaders, women; Megawati; Midiwati; women's participation in *under* politics

research, field, 13–14, 21, 59, 61, 70, 81–82, 86, 89, 106, 129, 175–76, 206;